A STORY COLLECTION BY
JEREMY HAUN

PRAISE FOR HAUNTHOLOGY

"HAUNTHOLOGY somehow manages to be deeply personal and deeply creepy and cool. Jeremy Haun always delivers and this is no exception. I'm all in!" JEFF LEMIRE • *Sweet Tooth, Gideon Falls*

"Jeremy Haun is an expert craftsman at building short horror stories that dig under your skin and wriggle around there. Fans of great horror comics do not want to miss out on this deeply unsettling collection." JAMES TYNION IV • *Department of Truth, Something Is Killing The Children, Batman*

"The HAUNTHOLOGY is a beautifully presented collection of splintered horrors rendered in intricately considered lines of ink. Peel away the scalp, scratch at the skull, peek inside the mind of Jeremy Haun. I dare you." DECLAN SHALVEY • *Immortal Hulk, Time Before Time*

"The beautiful, surreal, terrifying tales in HAUNTHOLOGY will do more than scare you. They'll stick with you. After reading this book, you'll be pondering the stories, waking from vivid nightmares, and looking over your shoulder for days to come." CULLEN BUNN • *Harrow County, The Sixth Gun, Basilisk*

"I blame Jeremy Haun for my latest bout of insomnia. There are images from HAUNTHOLOGY that have kept me awake at night: with wonder, with fear, with pure cosmic dread. This collection is overflowing with terrifying-slices-of-life that are starkly vivid and wholly unsettling. I devoured every panel and, in turn, it devoured me." MICHAEL D. FULLER • Writer/producer, *Locke & Key, The Mosquito Coast, Quarry*

"HAUNTHOLOGY delivers a sequence of beautifully apocalyptic vignettes. Haun's vision of creeping doom is what I want from cosmic horror: stark, gritty, sensational." LAIRD BARRON • *Swift to Chase*

"Reading HAUNTHOLOGY is like standing in cool sand and watching the tide lap playfully at your feet. Then the tide rises and drowns you, and you realize it's your own damn fault for not putting the book down when you still had a chance to escape. Jeremy Haun has crafted something truly unsettling here, and I can't recommend it enough." ALEX GRECIAN • *The Yard, The Saint of Wolves, Butcher, Proof, Rasputin*

"What Jeremy Haun does in HAUNTHOLOGY is take a collection of horror stories and boil off every morsel of fat until all that's left is hard, gleaming bone, the sweet moment of frisson which is the true reward of the horror story: the spike of fear, the eerie shift, the dreadful revelation. I haven't been this excited and inspired by a horror comic since Emily Carroll's *Through the Woods.*"
NATHAN BALLINGRUD • *North American Lake Monsters, Wounds: Six Stories from the Border of Hell*

"Each of these tales grabs you somewhere uncomfortable and doesn't let go till it has to. Knowing Jeremy, it's easy to see within these pages how personal this project is to him. This is what he sees when he lets the dark grab his brain for that split second. Most of all I'm just glad I made it out of the final page alive." MITCH GERADS • *Strange Adventures, Mister Miracle, Batman*

"Jeremy Haun's HAUNTHOLOGY marries a meticulously detailed artistic style to a series of vignettes gruesome, strange, and disturbing. The world ends, and ends, and ends again. People ready themselves to face the unimaginable. Death looms, and so does what lies on the other side of death. Together, these brief narratives form a dark kaleidoscope. Press your eye to the lens, and see what it has to show you."
JOHN LANGAN • *Children of the Fang and Other Genealogies*

IMAGE COMICS, INC.
Robert Kirkman – Chief Operating Officer
Erik Larsen – Chief Financial Officer
Todd McFarlane – President
Marc Silvestri – Chief Executive Officer
Jim Valentino – Vice President

Eric Stephenson – Publisher / Chief Creative Officer
Nicole Lapalme – Vice President of Finance
Leanna Caunter – Accounting Analyst
Sue Korpela – Accounting & HR Manager
Matt Parkinson – Vice President of Sales & Publishing Planning
Lorelei Bunjes – Vice President of Digital Strategy
Dirk Wood – Vice President of International Sales & Licensing
Ryan Brewer – International Sales & Licensing Manager
Alex Cox – Director of Direct Market Sales
Chloe Ramos – Book Market & Library Sales Manager
Emilio Bautista – Digital Sales Coordinator
Jon Schlaffman – Specialty Sales Coordinator
Kat Salazar – Vice President of PR & Marketing
Deanna Phelps – Marketing Design Manager
Drew Fitzgerald – Marketing Content Associate
Heather Doornink – Vice President of Production
Drew Gill – Art Director
Hilary DiLoreto – Print Manager
Tricia Ramos – Traffic Manager
Melissa Gifford – Content Manager
Erika Schnatz – Senior Production Artist
Wesley Griffith – Production Artist
Rich Fowlks – Production Artist

IMAGECOMICS.COM

Edited by Joel Enos

Book design by Fonografiks

Cover illustration color by Brennan Wagner

HAUNTHOLOGY. First printing. May 2023. Published by Image Comics, Inc.
Office of publication: PO BOX 14457, Portland, OR 97293. Copyright © 2023
Jeremy Haun. All rights reserved. "Haunthology," its logos, and the likenesses
of all characters herein are trademarks of Jeremy Haun, unless otherwise noted.
"Image" and the Image Comics logos are registered trademarks of Image
Comics, Inc. No part of this publication may be reproduced or transmitted, in
any form or by any means (except for short excerpts for journalistic or review
purposes), without the express written permission of Jeremy Haun, or Image
Comics, Inc. All names, characters, events, and locales in this publication are
entirely fictional. Any resemblance to actual persons (living or dead), events, or
places, without satirical intent, is coincidental. Printed in the USA.
ISBN: 978-1-5343-9989-1.

For international rights, contact: foreignlicensing@imagecomics.com.

CONTENTS

Foreword by Nathan Ballingrud   6

Preface by Jeremy Haun   10

Kingdom of Dust and Bone   14

Hastur   16

The Shaft   20

One Summer Night   26

The Monday After Monday   30

The Importance of Making Lists   38

All the Stars   40

The Private   44

The Class of 1894   48

Kit-Cat   54

Sabbatical at The Elms   58

The Package   62

The Old-Fashioned   70

I Will Do Dark Things   76

The Coin   80

The Arsenal   88

Still in Here   92

I'll Sleep   98

A Haunthology Silent Night   102

By the Sea. From the Sea.   106

Shoggoth in an Alley Behind a
Bar in a Small Town   114

The Day the Internet Died   120

Rooms in the Flat House   122

Probable Moments   138

Fever Dream   142

The Love of Old Things   146

To Finish   150

About the Author   152

SOME WORDS ON HAUNTHOLOGY AND THE PALE GREEN PANTS WITH NOBODY INSIDE THEM

FOREWORD BY NATHAN BALLINGRUD

W E KNOW FEAR BEFORE WE KNOW WORDS. We know it in the presence of shadows, and we know it in emptiness. We see and feel fear long before we can harness it in language. Maybe that's why, for me, fear is most potent when it's visual.

The first story I ever fell in love with was about fear: "What Was I Scared Of?" by Dr. Seuss. It's about a young (dog-boy? squirrel-kid?) fellow being chased through a night-enshrouded countryside by a pair of uninhabited pale green pants. This was one of his minor tales, a sort of B-side found at the end of *The Sneetches and Other Stories*. It wasn't the story itself I loved—in fact, I remember thinking the happy resolution where the ghostly pants turned out to be friendly was, for reasons I couldn't articulate then, profoundly disappointing—so much as it was the art. Deep night-blues, dead trees with skeletal, finger-like branches, a cold sickle moon, all worked to inspire a feeling of anxiety and loneliness. That weird yellow guy running in terror from page to page had no one at all to help him. He found no charming Seussian architecture to hide in. There was only the night, the desolation, the terrifying pursuit.

The usual rhymes accompanied the story, but they weren't needed. Everything you needed to know was rendered in the art. I returned to that story again and again. Those pictures lit a brushfire in my mind, and it's been burning ever since.

The other book I remember from my youth—this one came a few years later, when I was able to read for myself—is an underappreciated gem by Ruthanna Long called *Witches, Ghosts, and Goblins*. The story was great, but I'm hazy on the details. A brother and a sister, witches and ghosts of course, pirates and giants and a goblin king… all the good stuff. But what remains as vivid as though I'd read it just last night are the pictures, painted by Paul Durand. They're bursting with an eerie Halloween energy, the sort of creepiness that is as welcoming and cozy as it is unsettling. Witches on broomsticks, mysterious castles in dark woods, a secret passageway into the kingdom of the goblins replete with glittering treasure and cobwebbed skeletons. I adored that story, but the illustrations are why I remember it to this day.

In later years, the illustrated stories I loved got meaner and darker: the lurid morality shriek-shows from EC Comics, characters like John Dee and the Corinthian from *The Sandman*, the grimy working-class horrors of *Hellblazer*; but the pattern remained the same. The stories were heightened, made more awful and more beautiful, by the art.

There's something about seeing. When we see it, we remember what it was like to be a kid, waiting for the melting face to emerge from the closet. Waiting for the lumpy shadows in the corner—surely just a pile of dirty clothes waiting to be put into the hamper?—to lurch across the floor toward our bed. The eye is one of the most potent vectors of fear.

As a writer, I've always leaned heavily on that. It's not even a conscious choice. Nearly all the stories I've written either start with or ultimately hinge upon a visual image planted in the center of the idea, an image that won't dissipate until it's made real. I don't have the skills to draw them, so I write them instead. At least half of my stories are really frustrated comics.

So I was pretty excited when, sometime in the middle of 2020—that grinding murder-engine of a year—Jeremy Haun sent me the first handful of stories that would eventually make up HAUNTHOLOGY. Until that moment, the horror genre and I had been going through one of our occasional chilly spells. It wasn't that I couldn't find anything good to read (there's no shortage of that); it was more that I was already overwhelmed with horror. COVID, the convulsive thrashings of Trump in the fourth year of his presidency, the increasingly dire environmental outlook… I was nearing overdose levels.

HAUNTHOLOGY proved to be just the kind of antidote I needed. A deft combination of seriousness, despair, and tongue-in-cheek fun that provided some much-needed respite from the generalized anxiety of our new normal while channeling it into sharp, potent stories—often nasty, sometimes ghoulishly charming. Reading HAUNTHOLOGY feels like reading the best of the EC Horror comics, watching the best of the old *Twilight Zone* episodes.

But there's something more here, an interesting trick hidden within this bag of treats, one that's made me think about how horror fiction works and how I might approach it in my own writing in the future.

It involves the infamous third act.

The third act is the scariest part of any horror story, but not for the reason it should be. Because if it's all going to turn to shit, that's where it tends to happen. I won't list examples here, but I bet I don't have to; if you're a fan of the genre, you know what I mean. I can't count the number of books I've read or movies I've seen which present exciting, suspenseful set-ups—a terrifying monster, an immersive atmosphere, a plot which functions as an exquisite engine of doom, relentlessly steering the protagonists toward their ghastly ends—only to lose all conviction at the endgame. The monster is handicapped not through the ingenuity of any character but because somebody else—the writer, maybe, or the bean counters looking for a big hit—demanded one of two things, either of which can be fatal to a horror story: victory and an explanation.

This is a particularly Western problem, I think. And we have it really bad here in America. Good must triumph over evil. The human spirit must overcome all adversity. The intrusion of the Other must be successfully repelled by the heroes of the Status Quo.

And so the unstoppable monster is suddenly not so unstoppable after all. The spectral presence can be coaxed into a physical form, so it can be shot or trampled underfoot. The haunted house is set on fire, and all those ghosts are somehow purged from the world as a result. The thing under the bed turns out to be our own soured memories, put to rest with a tearful confession. The priest intones the name of God and the Devil slinks away.

Everything is explained. Atmosphere and fright surrender to the explanation of Why This All Happened: the horror story as a clockwork narrative, the demonic possession as a mathematical formula.

Easy outs. Tedious. Boring. Exactly the wrong kind of dreadful.

Sometimes we're given a little wink at the end, a suggestion that the evil hasn't truly been vanquished, and will certainly return for the sequel. But this is just sleight of hand. We've been served a plate of congealing catharsis. Go out and feel good about your lives, kids, and try not to dwell on that feeling that you've just been cheated.

The exceptions are rare, and exciting enough to tower over these endless hovels of mediocrity.

The stories in Jeremy Haun's HAUNTHOLOGY are exceptions. He's achieved this feat by condensing the horror story down to its most potent element.

He's jettisoned the third act altogether.

Sometimes he even shaves off the first act: we're given instead a scene, sometimes even only a moment, in a longer story. He's boiled off every morsel of fat until all that's left is hard, gleaming bone, the sweet moment of frisson which is the true reward of a horror story: the spike of fear, the eerie shift from one truth into another, the dreadful revelation. There are no disappointments because there are no explanations offered and there is no catharsis to be found.

This is the straight stuff, the pure hit, the high we're looking for when we choose to enter the littered alley and seek out the dealer in the dark.

I love this book. I love the work it does and the way it goes about that work. With HAUNTHOLOGY, Jeremy Haun joins an exclusive pantheon which includes Emily Carroll, Mike Mignola, Junji Ito, and Wally Wood. I hope there are many more like it to come.

Because in these stories, that empty pair of pants chasing you through the dark doesn't want to be friends. In fact, you never learn what it wants. There is no meaning and no reason. There is only the night, the desolation, the terrifying pursuit.

NATHAN BALLINGRUD is an American writer of horror and dark fantasy fiction, and winner of two Shirley Jackson Awards. His novella *The Visible Filth* was adapted into the 2019 feature film *Wounds* from Annapurna Pictures. He lives in Asheville, North Carolina.

FOR THE
LOVE OF FEAR

PREFACE BY
JEREMY HAUN

WHAT SCARES YOU? Like, *really* scares you?

When I was a kid absolutely everything scared me. My parents divorced when I was twelve and we moved from the city to my grandparents' farm. Everything was different. Everything had changed. The ever-present city lights and sounds were replaced with pitch-black nights and the strange noises of the deep woods. I couldn't sleep. I lay there in the heat of the summer, staring at the closet that wouldn't quite close, just… terrified.

Did you know pigs sometimes scream in the night? They do. It's just how they are, but to a twelve-year-old, it was absolutely terrifying.

Somewhere in there, with the sleepless nights, I decided that I couldn't be afraid anymore. I went about it in exactly the way a twelve year old in the late Eighties would—I rented every single horror movie from our local video store and watched them all.

I'm going to admit that may not have been the best approach… but it worked. I saw a lot of stuff I shouldn't. But I also saw the most important thing—that nothing in those films was as scary as the things I imagined slouching their way out of the woods. I got to see the monsters die (mostly) and learned that not all monsters are bad. In fact, I learned that monsters were cool. The second I realized that, there was no turning back. I went from being a kid that was afraid of the dark—afraid of everything—to not only not being scared… but loving it all.

Years passed. I wrote and drew my own stories. I made a career of it. A damned good one. While the majority of my time in comics was spent drawing superheroes, I still looked for any chance to work on horror projects. I still watched and read pretty much any horror-related thing I could get my hands on. Part of me wanted to feel that same fear I felt back on that farm. I kind of missed it.

See, there's something special about fear.

I went from being that kid that was afraid of everything to someone who isn't really afraid of anything at all. Sure, I still have normal, everyday fears. But those are more about the safety of family and friends. I'm talking about the fear of an animal's screams in the night, of that chittering thing that wants in from the woods, of that horror that lives in the closet that just won't quite shut.

One of the things that I truly love is exploring and photographing old abandoned buildings. I think part of it goes back to that thing of wanting to be scared. I walk through those spaces, mostly in the dark. Cautiously, I promise. Don't worry. I'm not going to foolishly fall down an elevator shaft or anything. I'm still careful… just not scared.

But I *want* to be scared. And that's the fun part—the creative part. I can *almost* do it. I imagine things standing down darkened, dripping hallways staring back at me. Part of me even welcomes the idea. I even wrote a story about it for this collection. If there was some ancient, monstrous creature out there in the shadows, I think I'd be okay with it eating me, if I just got to see it first.

Yeah. I'll stand by that. Sure, I'd probably change my mind if it happened, but for now, that's my story.

In 2015 I took the leap from being a full-time artist to focusing on both writing and drawing comic books. It was a big step for me, but I realized the only way I was ever going to be able to tell all of the stories that are bouncing around in my head was to put my own creations first.

Since then I've co-created *The Beauty* and *The Realm* at Image Comics and wrote *The Red Mother* for BOOM! Studios and *40 Seconds* for ComiXology. During that time I realized that, much like with walking through buildings imagining unnamable terrors, I could creep myself out with the things I write. That was the feeling I'd been looking for. And I got hooked on it.

As you well know, March of 2020 changed everything. It was set to be one of my busiest creative years ever. Frighteningly so. I was set to draw two mini-series back to back, write three things, and begin work on a big new project that I'd be writing and drawing. It was a lot. It was also *exactly* what I've been building towards.

Then, yeah… the pandemic.

When the comics industry went "pencils down," everyone tried their best. But everything stopping for an indeterminate amount of time definitely took its toll.

I was incredibly lucky to have *The Red Mother* and *40 Seconds* to work on. Both BOOM! and ComiXology were absolute lifesavers. But other projects, especially things I was drawing, were postponed indefinitely/altogether.

I, we all, were stressed and exhausted beyond belief. We played board games, binge-watched everything, drank a good bit, scavenged for supplies, and got really, really good at baking bread. We just focused on surviving. On being safe. Or... as safe as possible.

The thing is, I was miserable.

I do this thing between projects. I enjoy the time off for a few days. I hang out and do things... but then I absolutely need to get back to work making things—telling stories. It's just how I am.

Sure, I got really good at making sourdough bread and my bartending skills were pretty fantastic, but I needed to tell those stories.

Now here's the tricky part—comics take a long time to make. Putting together a team can take a month or so. Building a pitch packet with the full synopsis and samples of the art can take another month or two. From there, approval from a company takes a while. They get a lot of pitches and have to make sure it fits their lineup and schedule. Once the story has a home and is ready to go, the team has to jump into gear and actually make the book. The industry standard right now is completely finishing three issues of a book before you solicit the first issue. And the first couple issues are hard. They take a long time to make.

That's a lot of inside baseball, but my point is that it's hard to just jump onto a new project when the world changes and a year's worth of plans get put on indefinite hold. But I couldn't be the miserable guy sitting on the couch carb-loading anymore. I needed to create.

I didn't really have a purpose when I started writing that first short story. I had this bit of an idea. And that was enough.

Hastur, the first story, was three pages. I wrote, penciled, inked, and lettered it in a week. It was like a fugue state. It was everything that I'd been needing.

So I did it again.

And again.

Over the past few years I'd been working on a series of stories that kind of connected. It started with the *Bad Karma* project. Things that I established there made their way into *The Realm*. I sharpened that mythos that I was building with *The Red Mother*. Even though *40 Seconds* was more of a sci-fi story, elements of it definitely tied into *The Red Mother*. Friends started joking that I was creating a "Hauniverse." I laughed. I cringed. But... there was truth to it.

I didn't really know what I was building with Haunthology when I started it. I was just telling these short stories. As I went, I realized that I was using these stories to talk about the feelings I, we all, were having during the pandemic. They were stories about isolation, loneliness, longing, anger, and fear. They also kept connecting back to my larger mythos. Sometimes in small ways. Often as hints to longer form stories that I've been wanting to tell.

Working on Haunthology became a lifeline for me in a dark time. In some ways, it saved me. I look at it all now, well over a hundred pages of story, and can't quite believe it exists. I'm grateful for it and for you.

As much as this book exists because of the pandemic and my need to tell stories, it also exists because of you. I hope you get as much enjoyment out of it as I have. I hope, as this weird, dark time goes on, it gives you something good and creepy to enjoy. And if you like this, just know that there is more on its way. After all, I have to tell these stories. I don't really have any other choice.

So now, after all this time—all these years—what scares me? Not telling stories.

What scares you?

KINGDOM OF DUST AND BONE

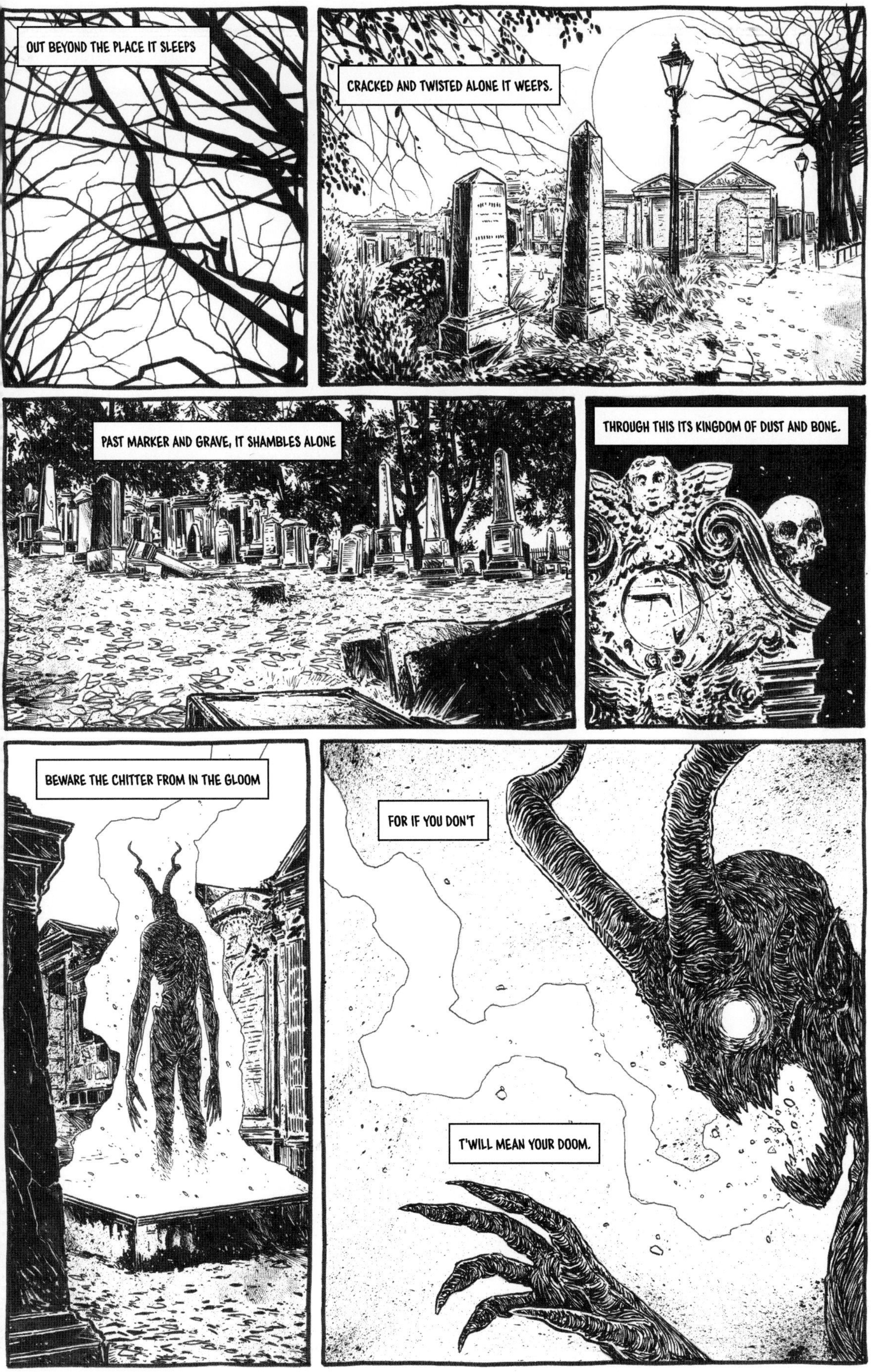
OUT BEYOND THE PLACE IT SLEEPS
CRACKED AND TWISTED ALONE IT WEEPS.
PAST MARKER AND GRAVE, IT SHAMBLES ALONE
THROUGH THIS ITS KINGDOM OF DUST AND BONE.
BEWARE THE CHITTER FROM IN THE GLOOM
FOR IF YOU DON'T
T'WILL MEAN YOUR DOOM.

Hastur

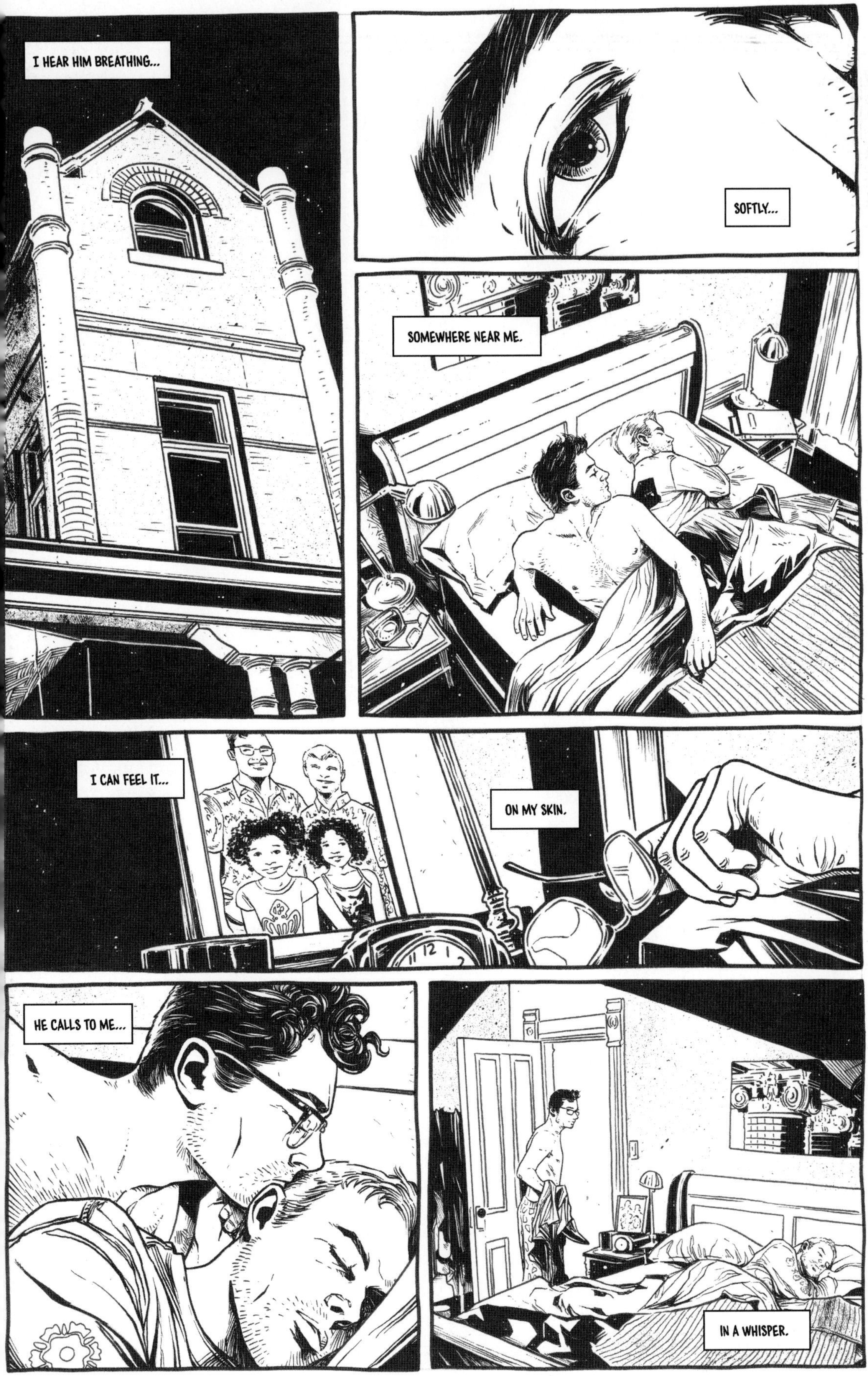
I HEAR HIM BREATHING...
SOFTLY...
SOMEWHERE NEAR ME.
I CAN FEEL IT...
ON MY SKIN.
HE CALLS TO ME...
IN A WHISPER.

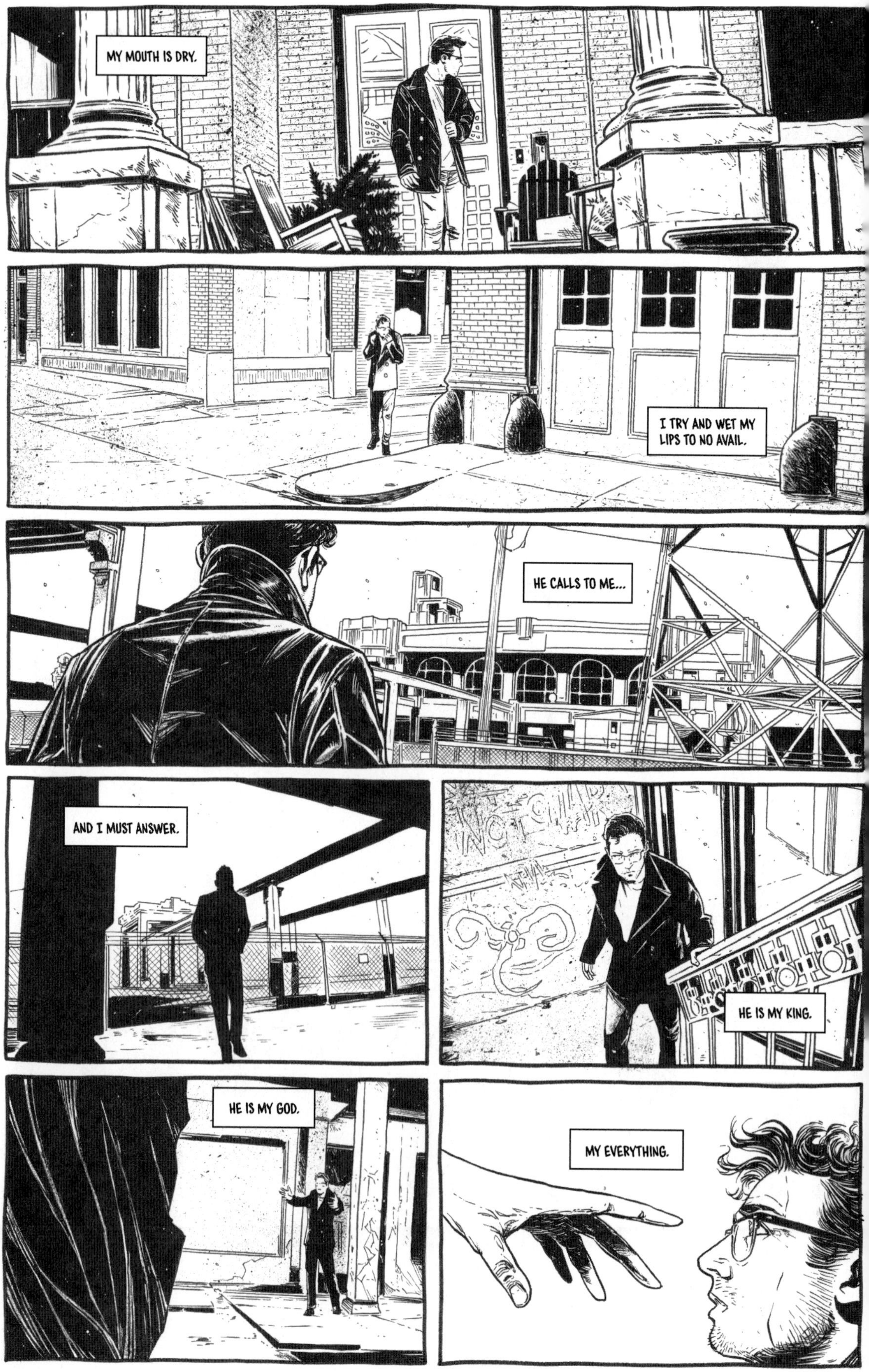
MY MOUTH IS DRY.
I TRY AND WET MY LIPS TO NO AVAIL.
HE CALLS TO ME...
AND I MUST ANSWER.
HE IS MY KING.
HE IS MY GOD.
MY EVERYTHING.

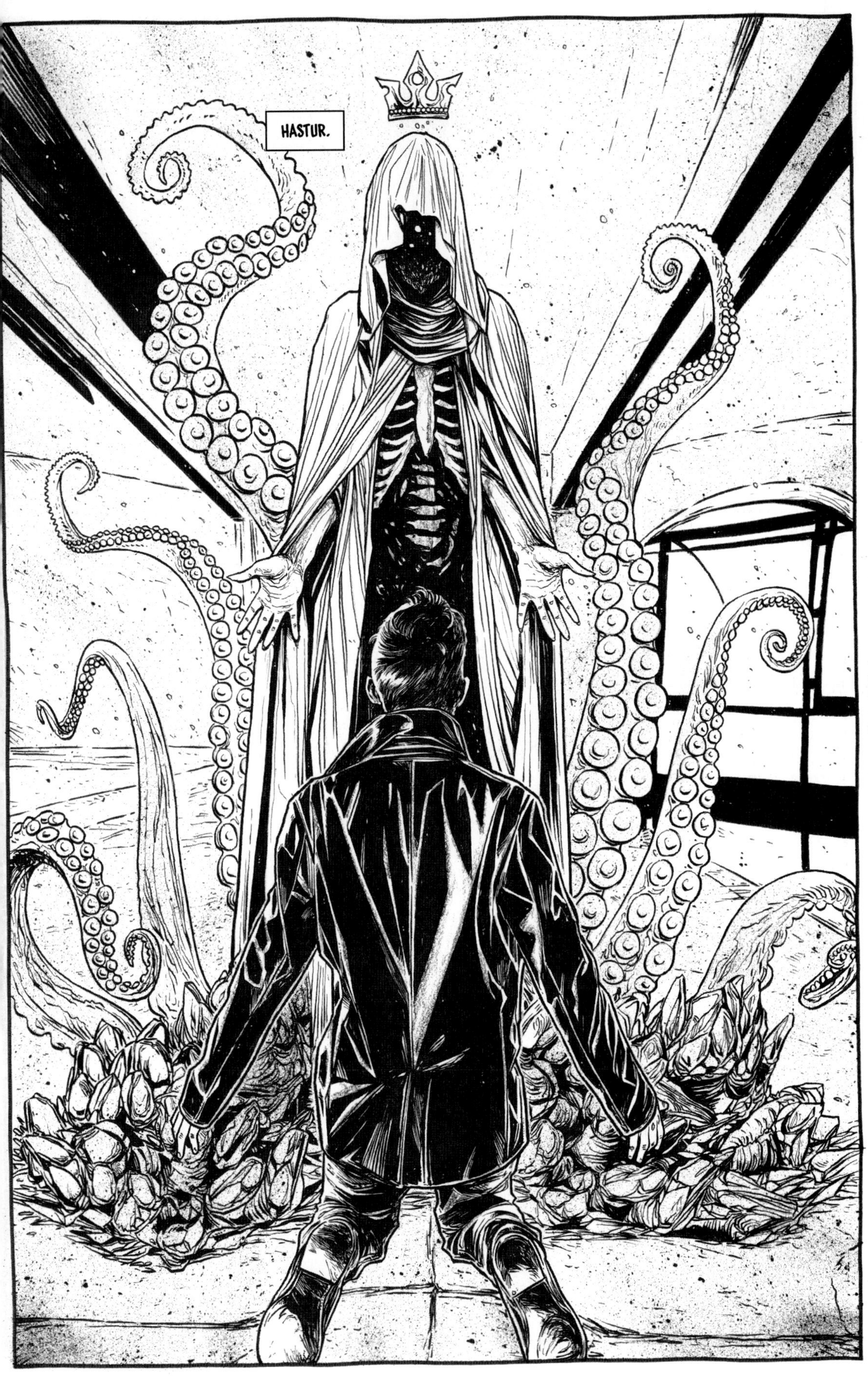
HASTUR.

THE SHAFT

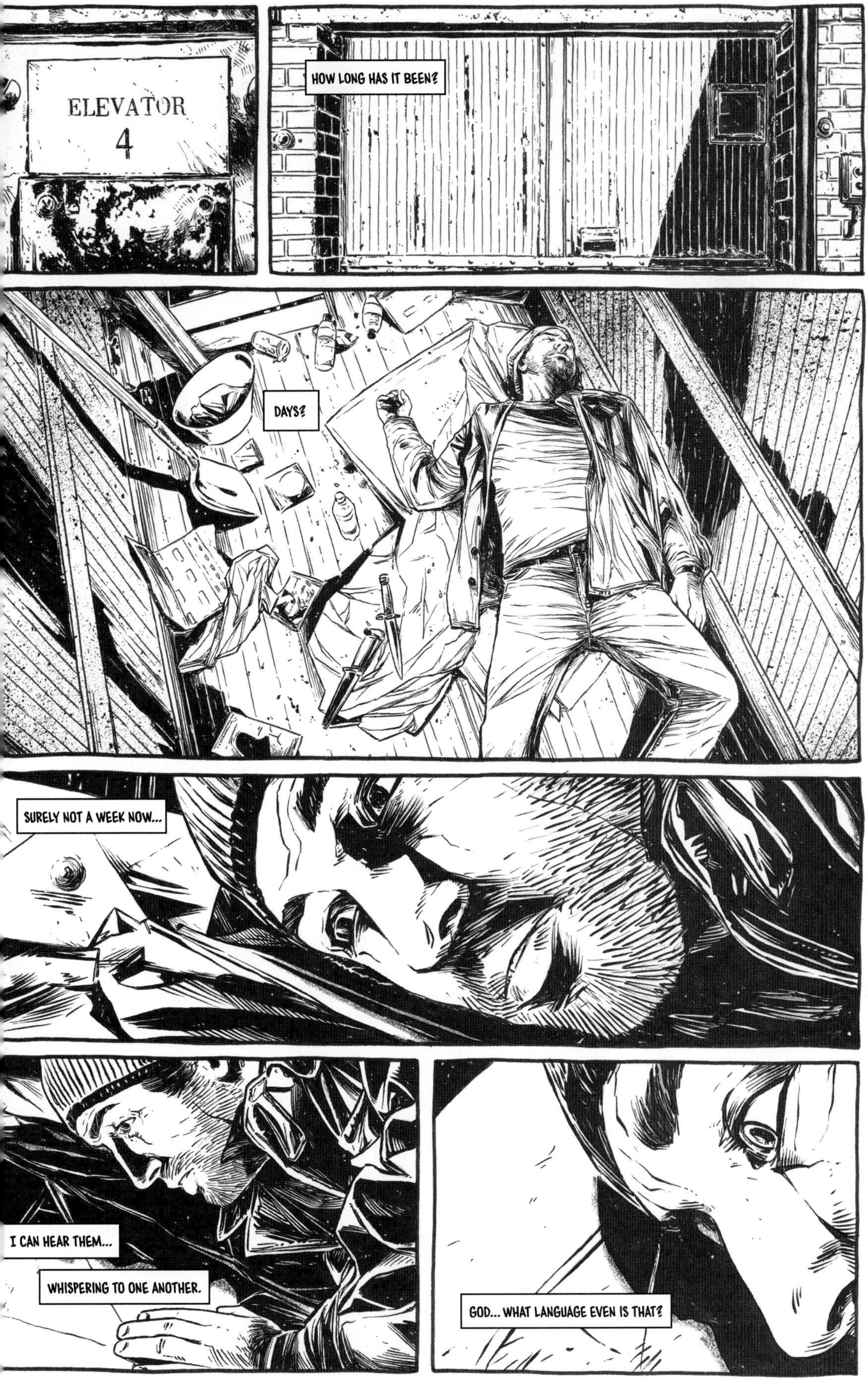
ELEVATOR
4
HOW LONG HAS IT BEEN?
DAYS?
SURELY NOT A WEEK NOW...
I CAN HEAR THEM...
WHISPERING TO ONE ANOTHER.
GOD... WHAT LANGUAGE EVEN IS THAT?

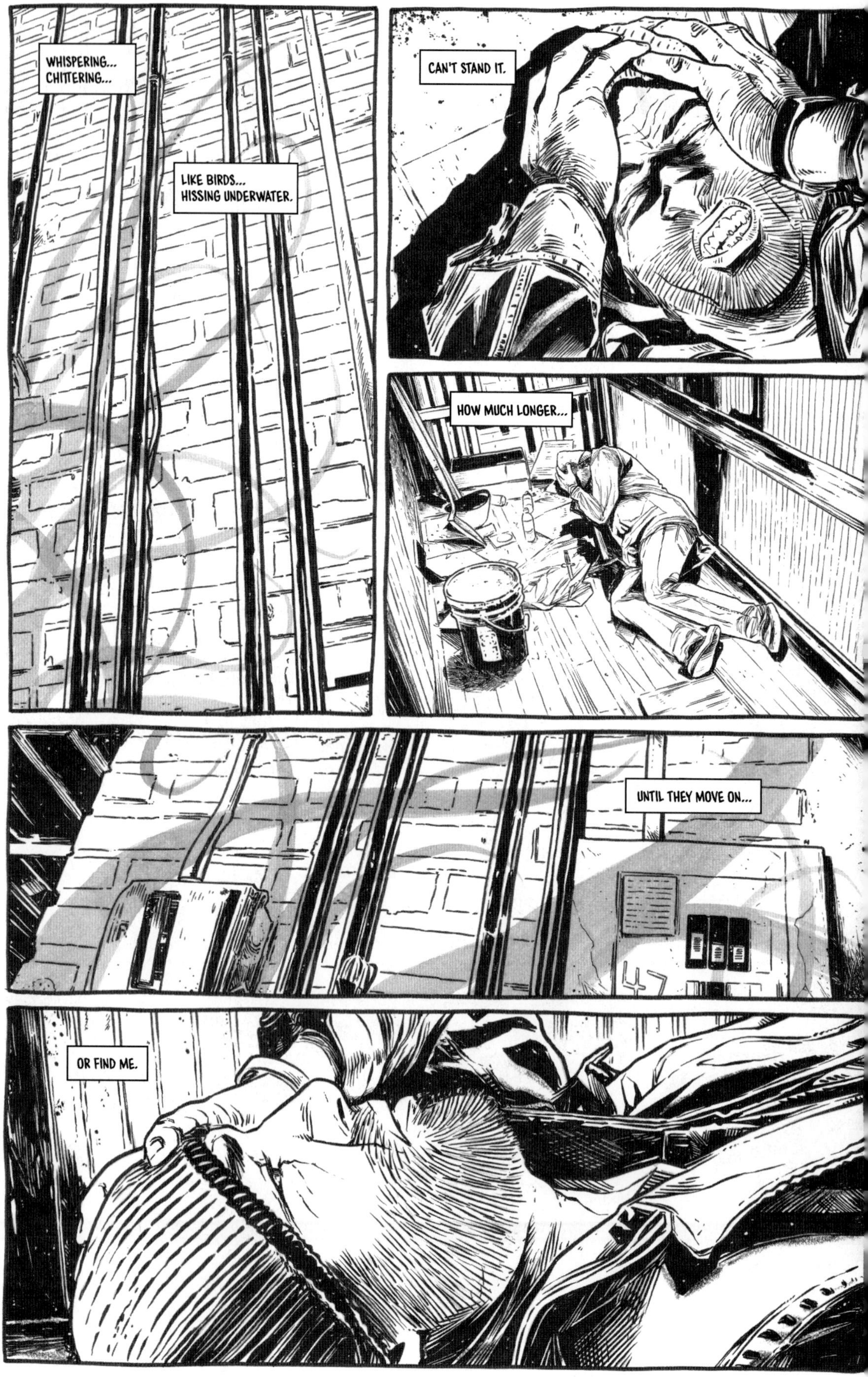
WHISPERING...
CHITTERING...
LIKE BIRDS...
HISSING UNDERWATER.
CAN'T STAND IT.
HOW MUCH LONGER...
UNTIL THEY MOVE ON...
OR FIND ME.

FOOD'S GONE.

WATER....

DAMN.

TWO ROUNDS LEFT.

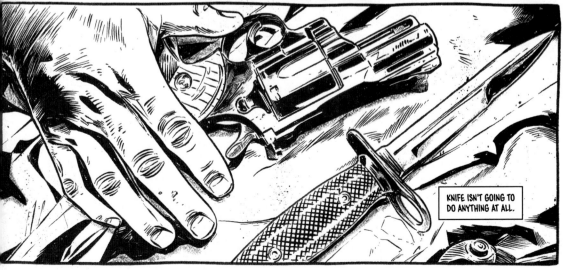

KNIFE ISN'T GOING TO DO ANYTHING AT ALL.

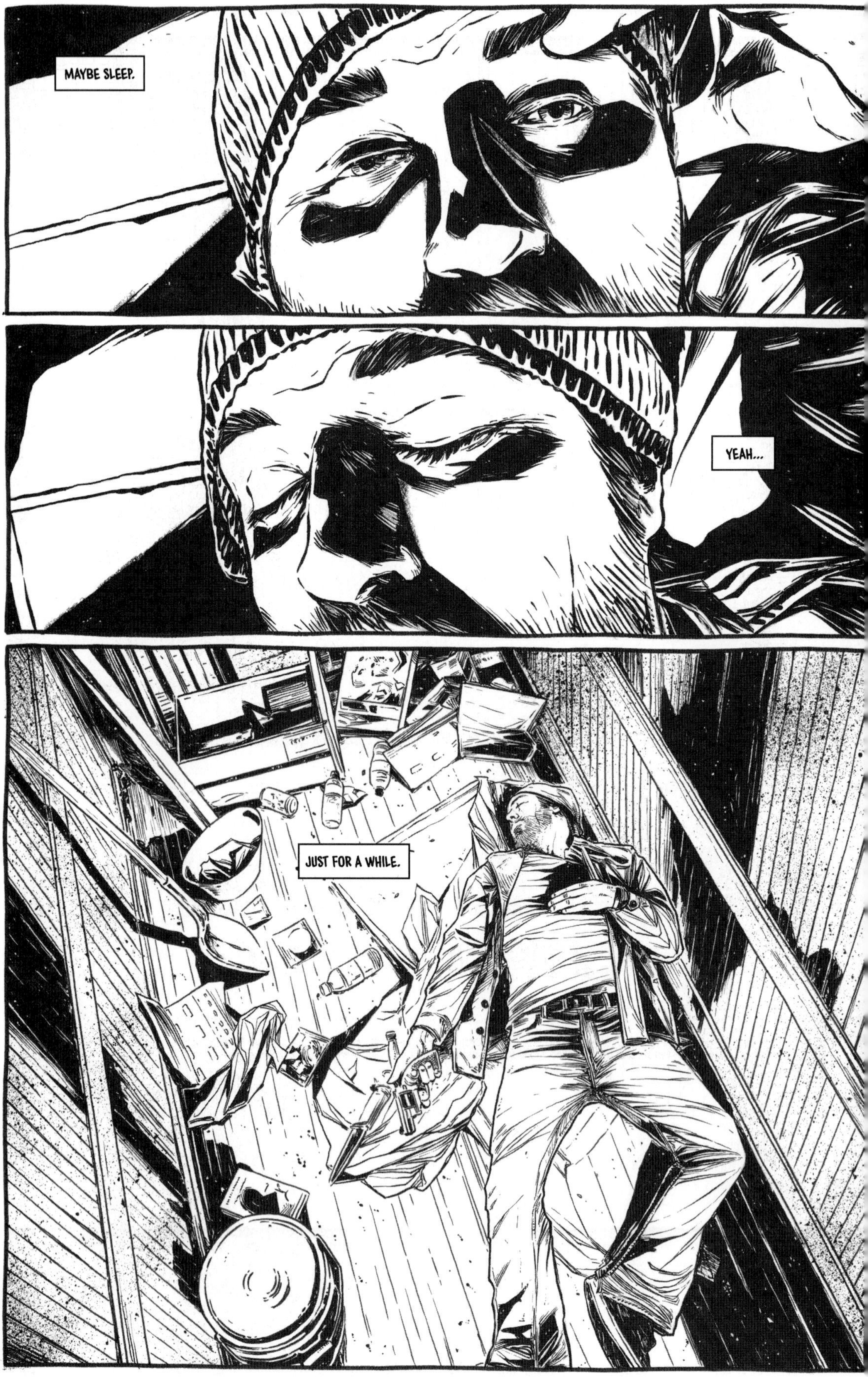
MAYBE SLEEP.
YEAH...
JUST FOR A WHILE.

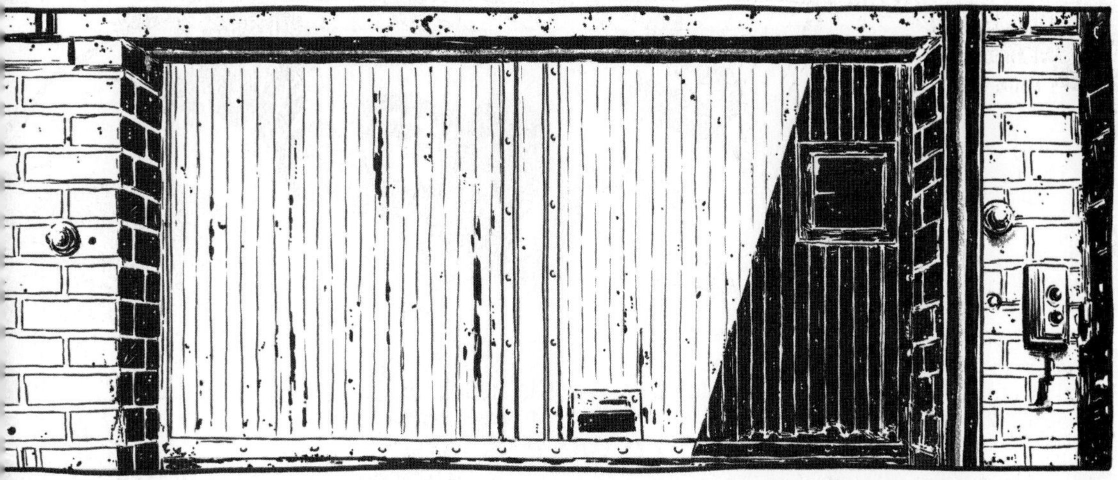

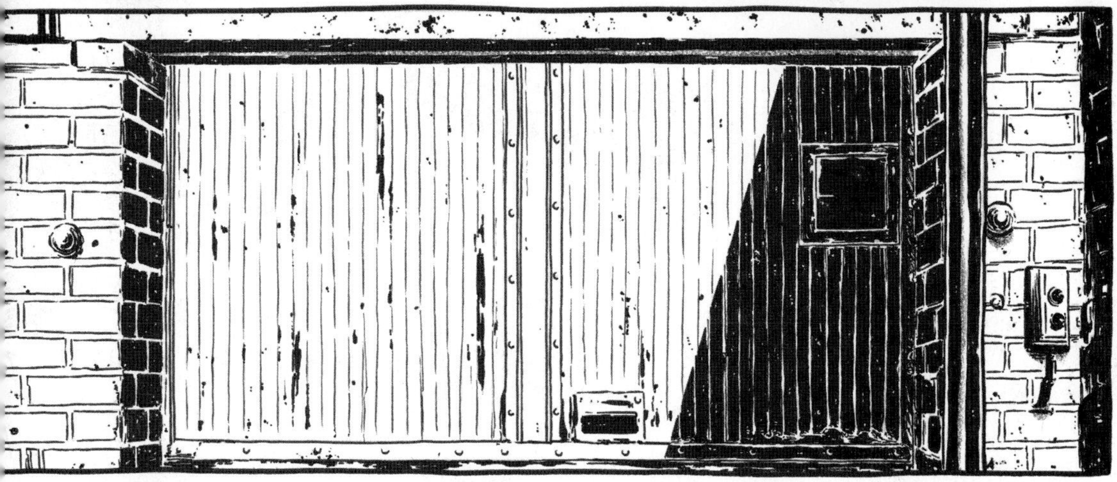

THE SHAFT

BY JEREMY HAUN

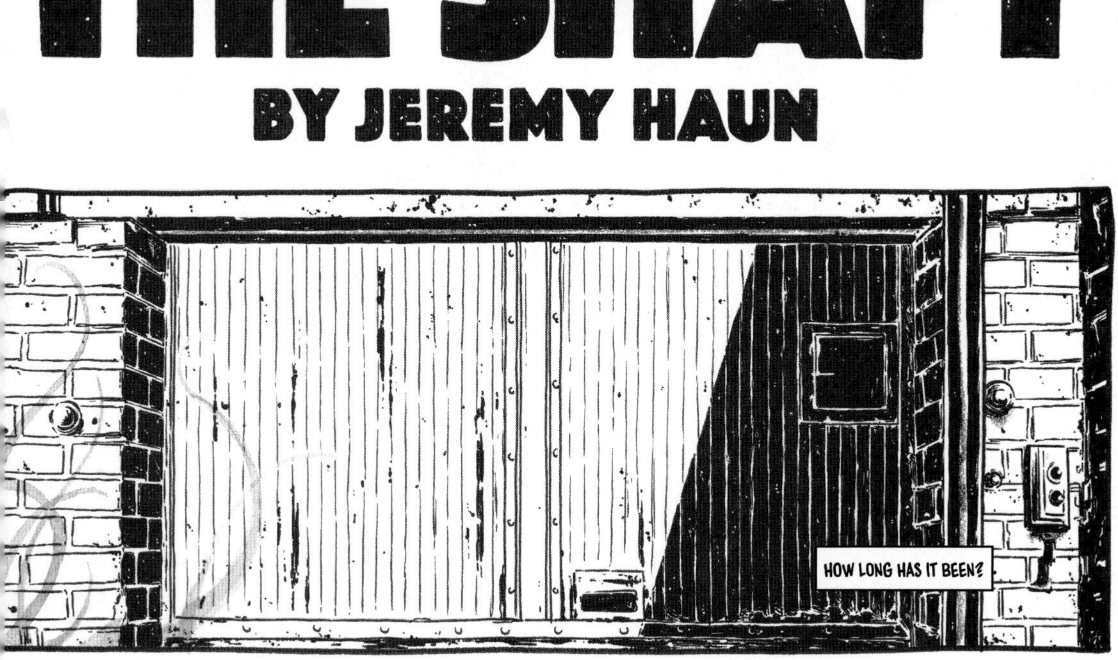
HOW LONG HAS IT BEEN?

ONE SUMMER NIGHT

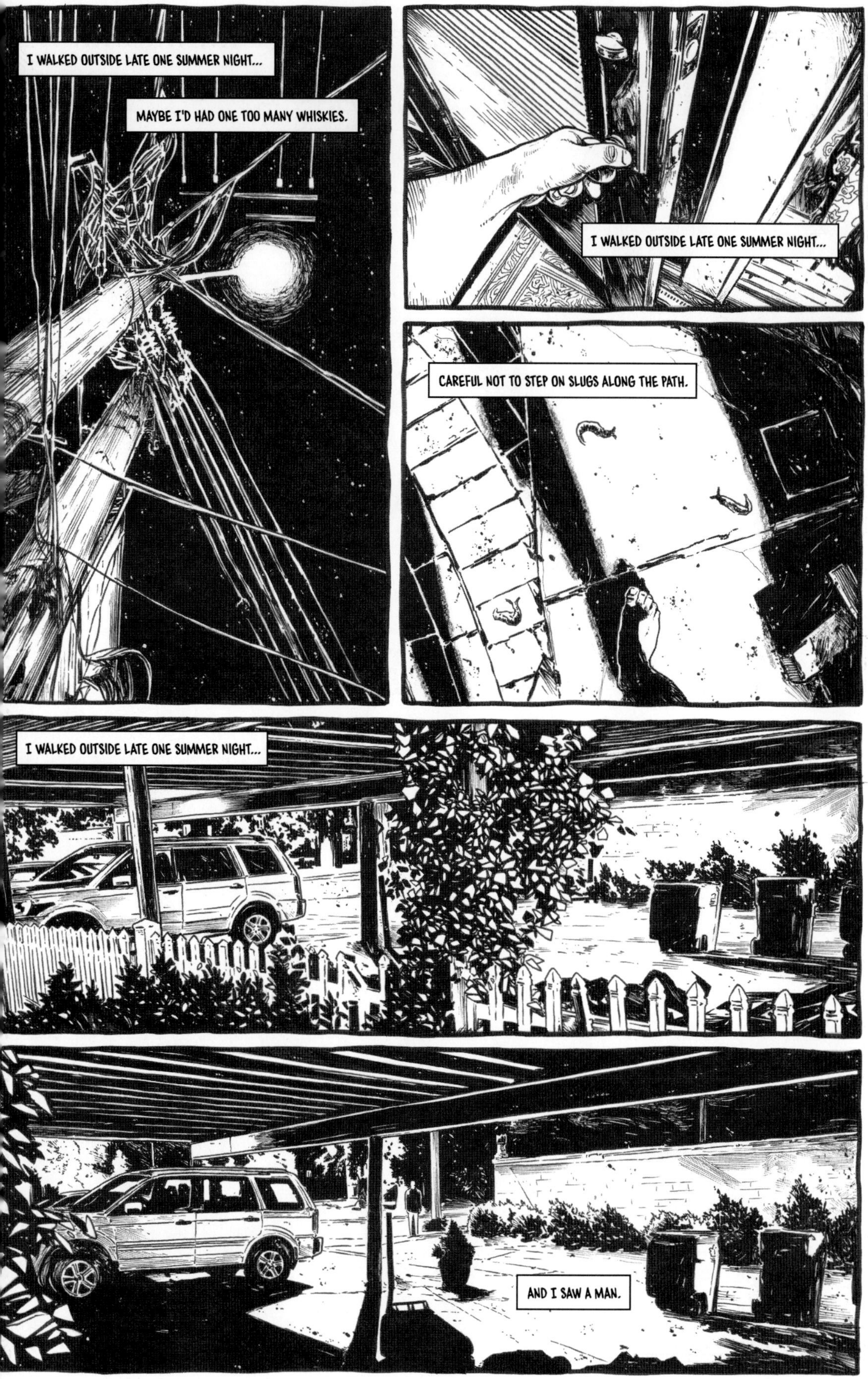
I WALKED OUTSIDE LATE ONE SUMMER NIGHT...
MAYBE I'D HAD ONE TOO MANY WHISKIES.
I WALKED OUTSIDE LATE ONE SUMMER NIGHT...
CAREFUL NOT TO STEP ON SLUGS ALONG THE PATH.
I WALKED OUTSIDE LATE ONE SUMMER NIGHT...
AND I SAW A MAN.

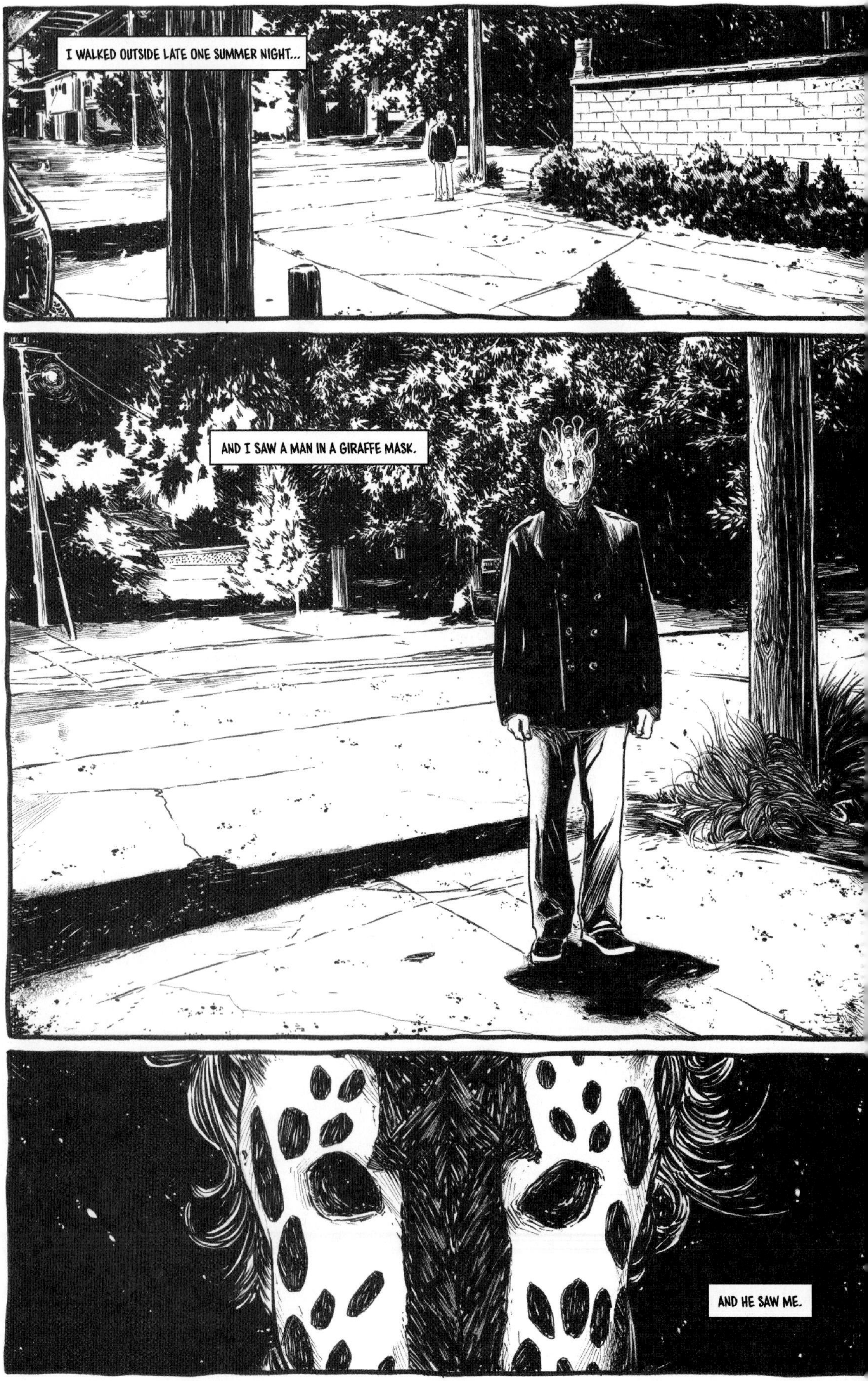
I WALKED OUTSIDE LATE ONE SUMMER NIGHT...
AND I SAW A MAN IN A GIRAFFE MASK.
AND HE SAW ME.

THE MONDAY
AFTER MONDAY

BOORAAAAAAA
THERE IT IS AGAIN...
MONDAY...
IS IT?
MAYBE.
NEW YORK TIMES SQUARE
Rockefeller 5TH AVENUE
Greenwich Village LEXINGTON
CENTRAL PARK Tribeca
7TH AVENUE Broadway
BROOKLYN BRIDGE 34TH
ROOSEVELT BRYANT PARK
Columbus Circle
Square SOHO

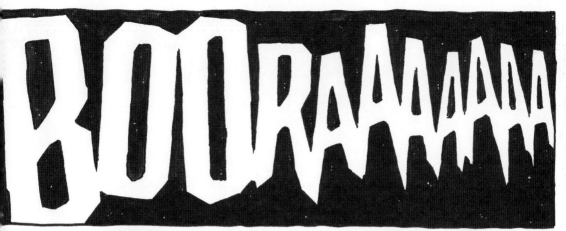

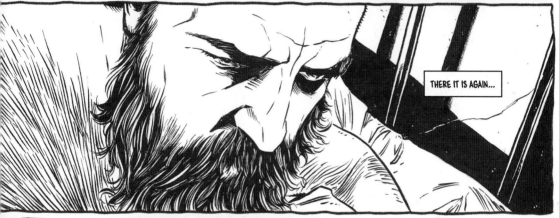

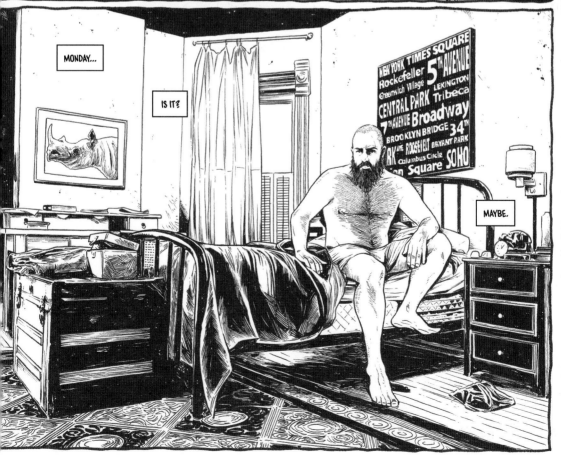

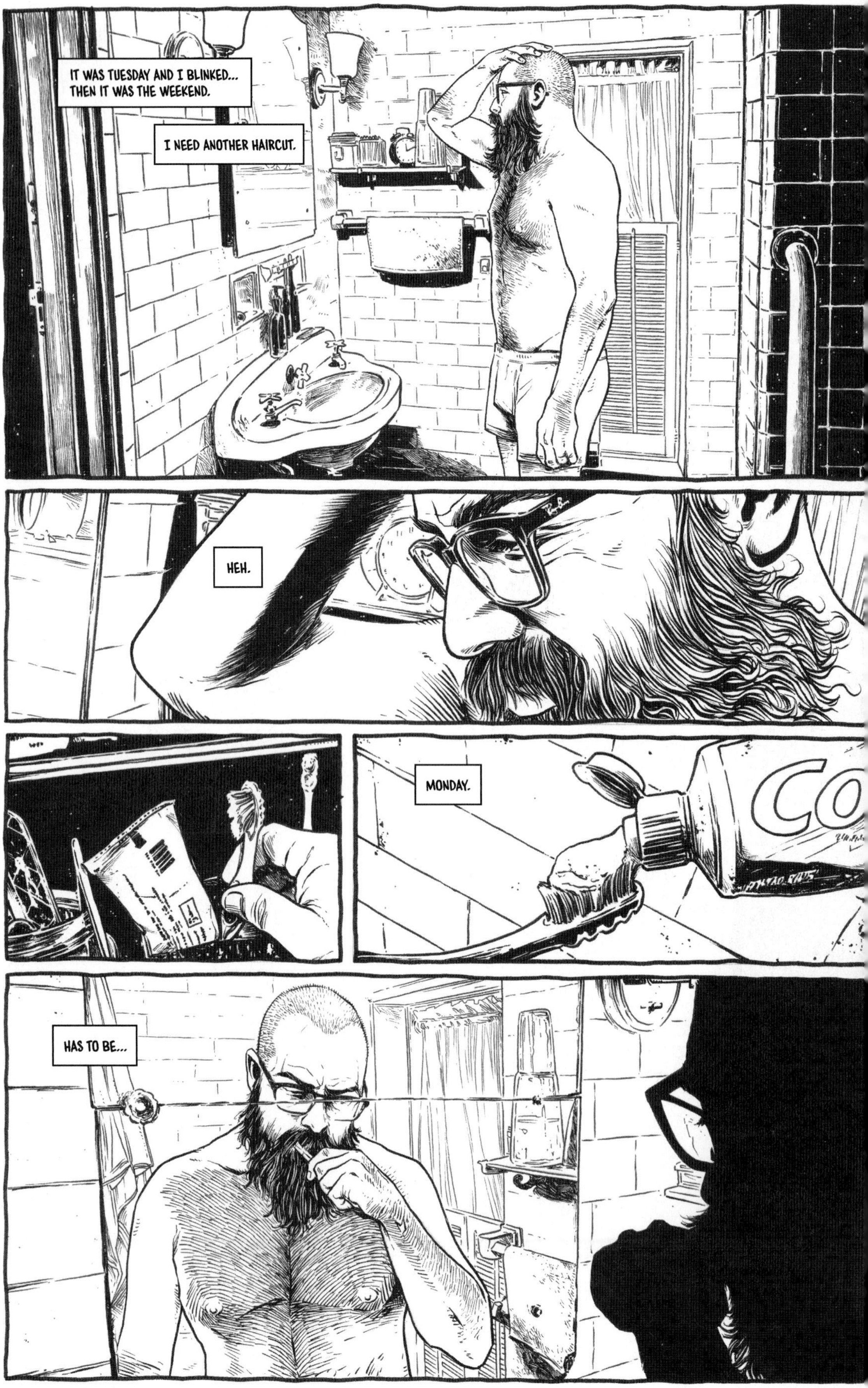
IT WAS TUESDAY AND I BLINKED... THEN IT WAS THE WEEKEND.
I NEED ANOTHER HAIRCUT.
HEH.
MONDAY.
HAS TO BE...

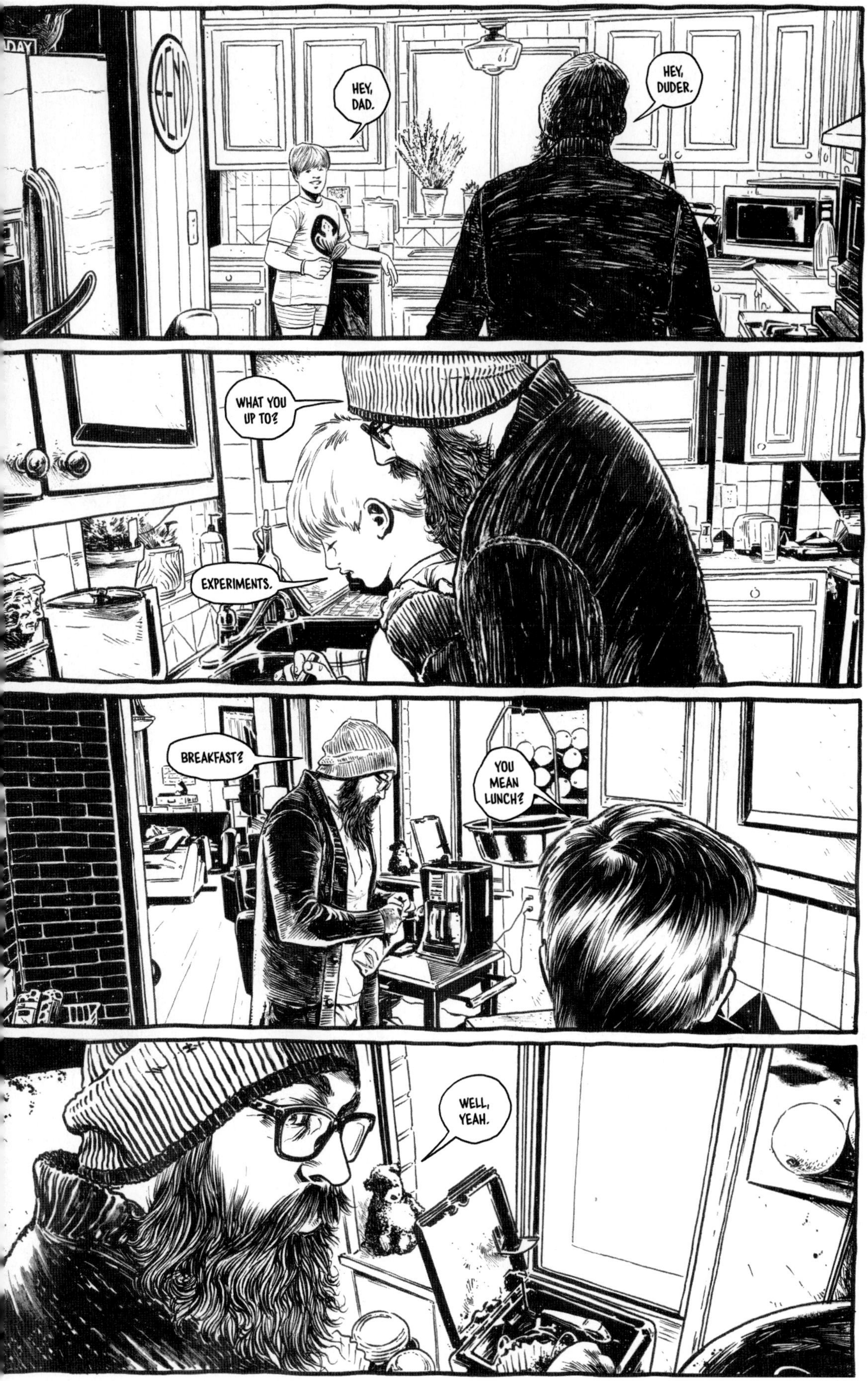
HEY, DAD.
HEY, DUDER.
WHAT YOU UP TO?
EXPERIMENTS.
BREAKFAST?
YOU MEAN LUNCH?
WELL, YEAH.

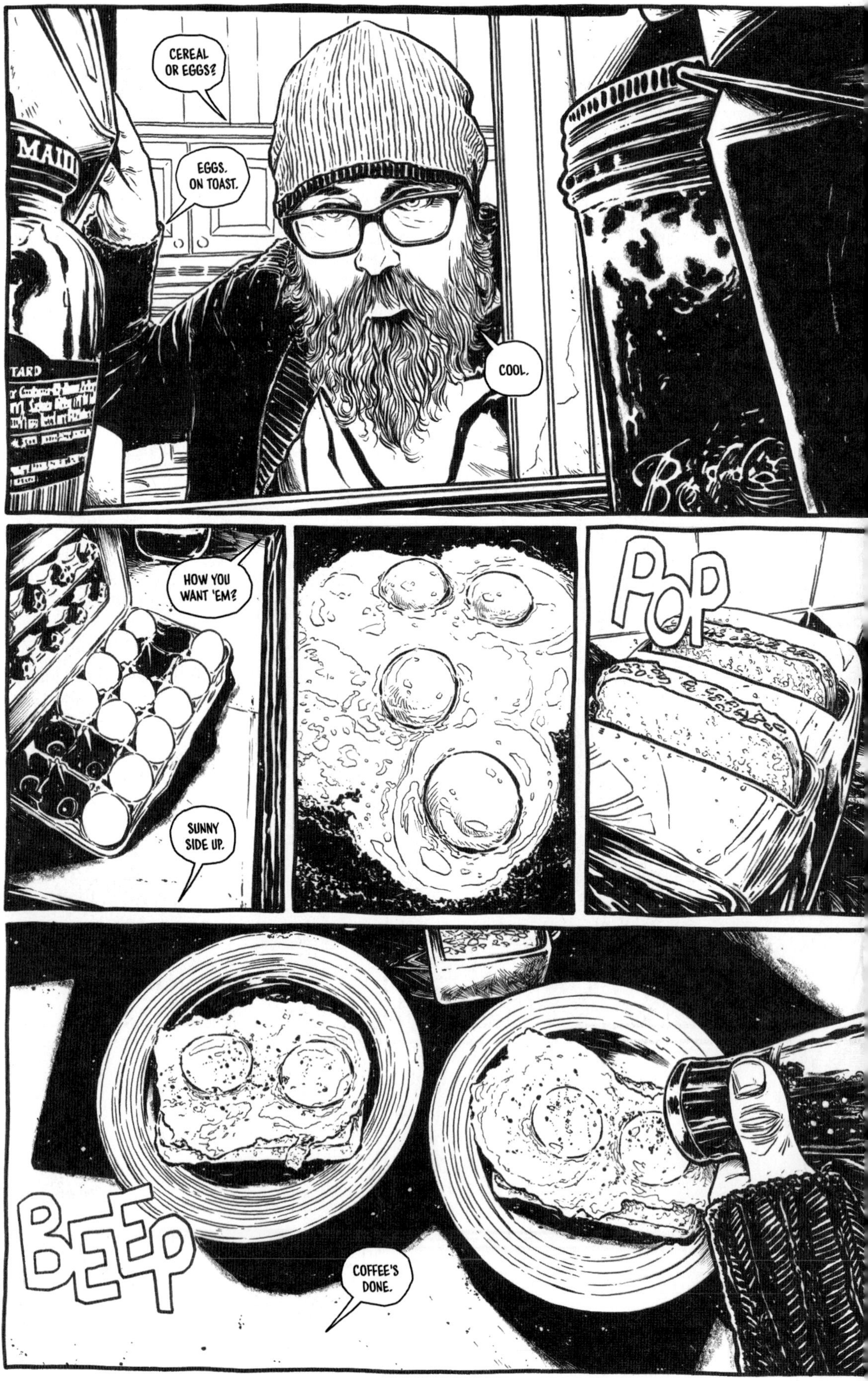
CEREAL OR EGGS?
EGGS. ON TOAST.
COOL.
HOW YOU WANT 'EM?
SUNNY SIDE UP.
POP
BEEP
COFFEE'S DONE.

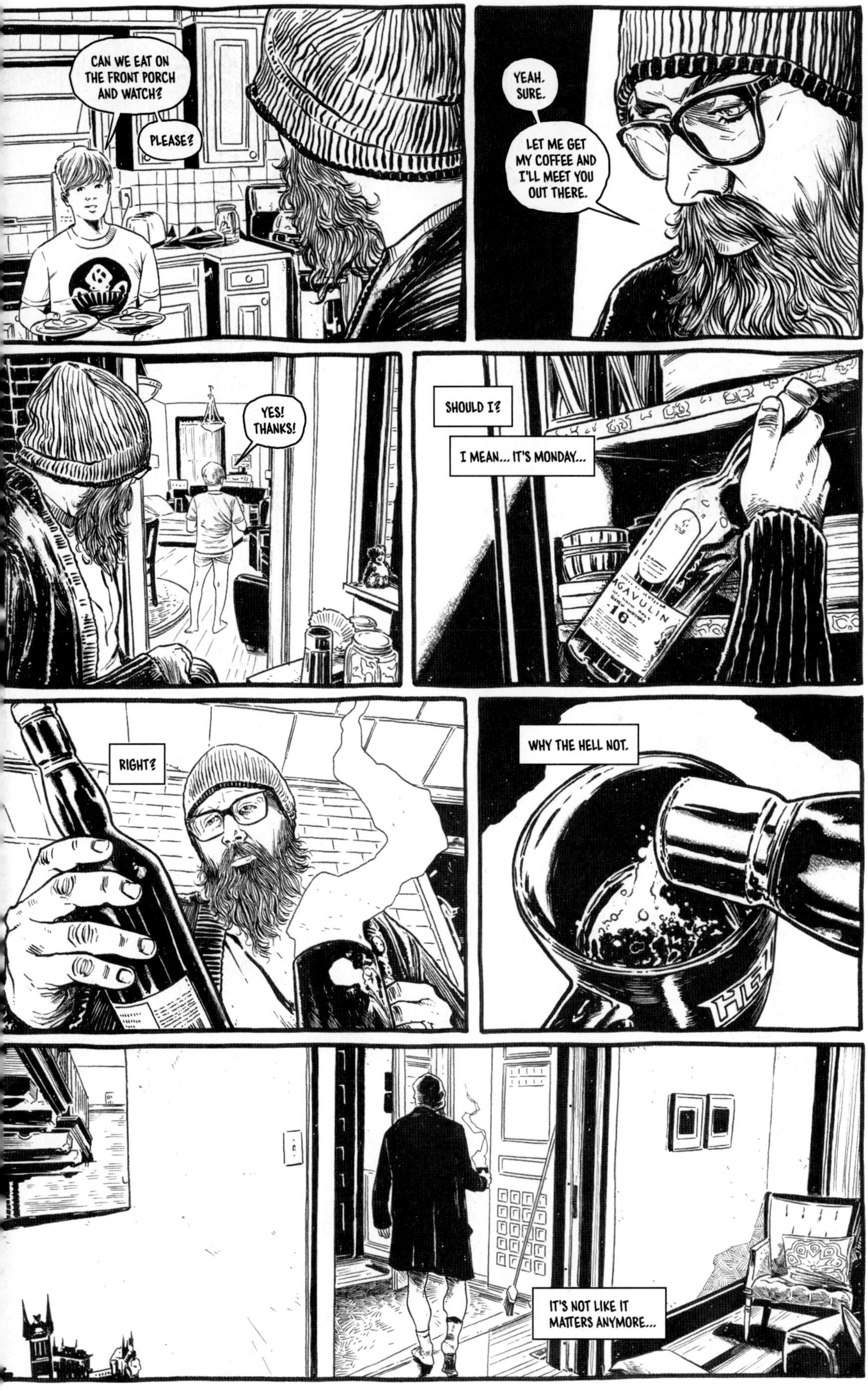
CAN WE EAT ON THE FRONT PORCH AND WATCH?
PLEASE?
YEAH. SURE.
LET ME GET MY COFFEE AND I'LL MEET YOU OUT THERE.
YES! THANKS!
SHOULD I?
I MEAN... IT'S MONDAY...
RIGHT?
WHY THE HELL NOT.
IT'S NOT LIKE IT MATTERS ANYMORE...

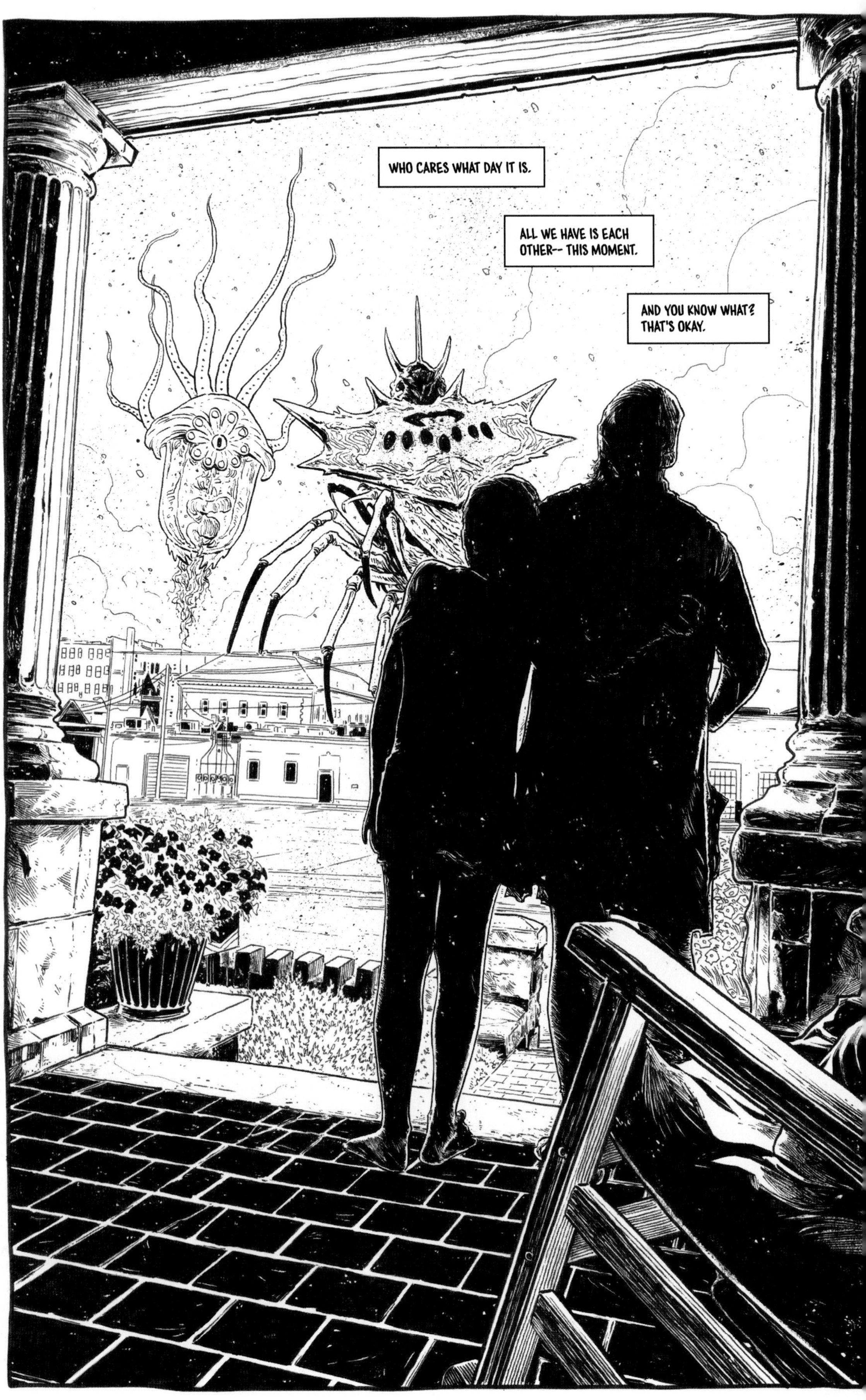
WHO CARES WHAT DAY IT IS.
ALL WE HAVE IS EACH OTHER-- THIS MOMENT.
AND YOU KNOW WHAT? THAT'S OKAY.

THE IMPORTANCE OF MAKING LISTS

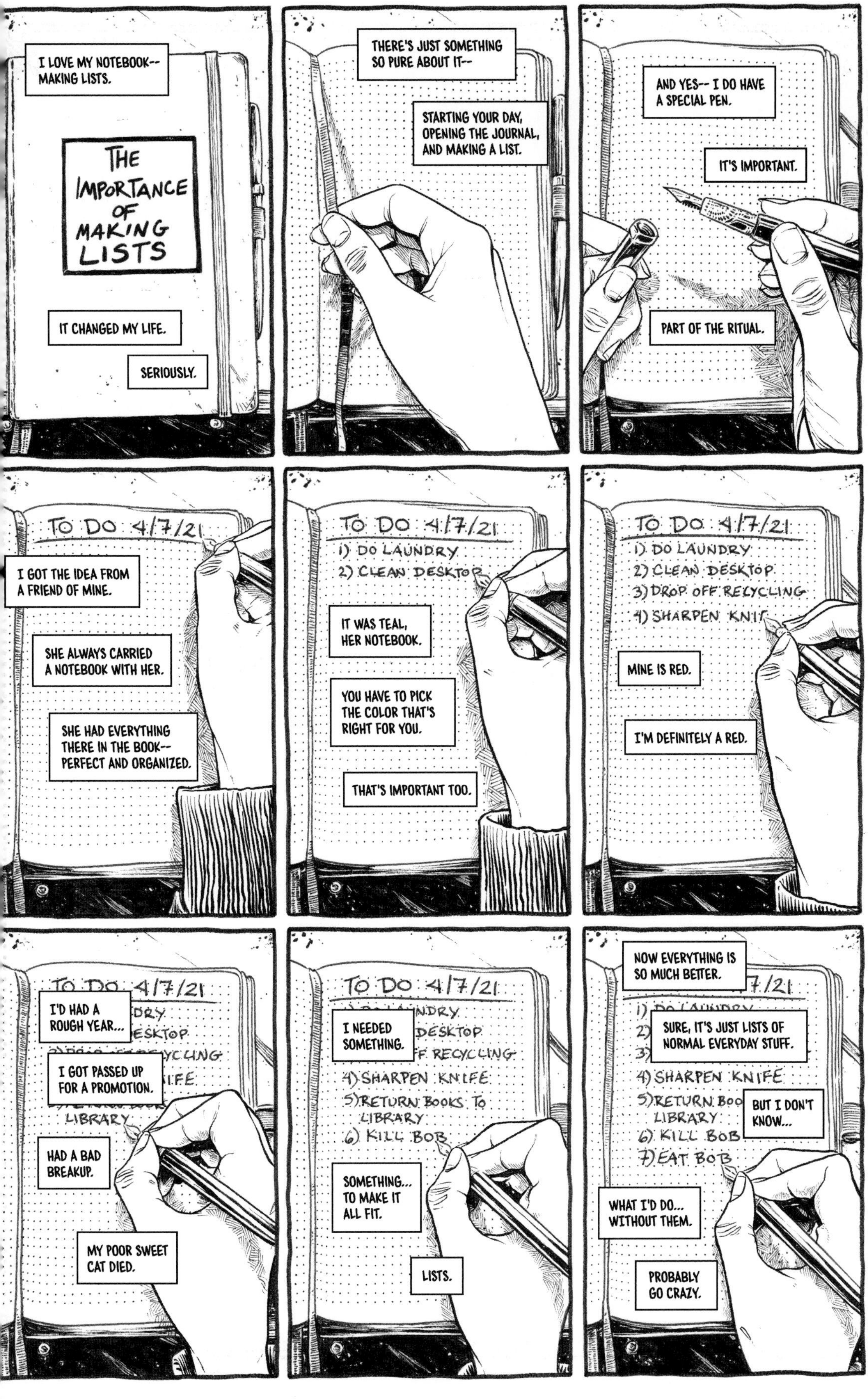
I LOVE MY NOTEBOOK--
MAKING LISTS.
THE IMPORTANCE OF MAKING LISTS
IT CHANGED MY LIFE.
SERIOUSLY.
THERE'S JUST SOMETHING SO PURE ABOUT IT--
STARTING YOUR DAY, OPENING THE JOURNAL, AND MAKING A LIST.
AND YES-- I DO HAVE A SPECIAL PEN.
IT'S IMPORTANT.
PART OF THE RITUAL.
TO DO 4/7/21
I GOT THE IDEA FROM A FRIEND OF MINE.
SHE ALWAYS CARRIED A NOTEBOOK WITH HER.
SHE HAD EVERYTHING THERE IN THE BOOK-- PERFECT AND ORGANIZED.
TO DO 4/7/21
1) DO LAUNDRY
2) CLEAN DESKTOP
IT WAS TEAL, HER NOTEBOOK.
YOU HAVE TO PICK THE COLOR THAT'S RIGHT FOR YOU.
THAT'S IMPORTANT TOO.
TO DO 4/7/21
1) DO LAUNDRY
2) CLEAN DESKTOP
3) DROP OFF RECYCLING
4) SHARPEN KNIF
MINE IS RED.
I'M DEFINITELY A RED.
I'D HAD A ROUGH YEAR...
I GOT PASSED UP FOR A PROMOTION.
HAD A BAD BREAKUP.
MY POOR SWEET CAT DIED.
TO DO 4/7/21
4) SHARPEN KNIFE
5) RETURN BOOKS TO LIBRARY
6) KILL BOB
I NEEDED SOMETHING.
SOMETHING... TO MAKE IT ALL FIT.
LISTS.
NOW EVERYTHING IS SO MUCH BETTER.
SURE, IT'S JUST LISTS OF NORMAL EVERYDAY STUFF.
4) SHARPEN KNIFE
5) RETURN BOO
LIBRARY
6) KILL BOB
7) EAT BOB
BUT I DON'T KNOW...
WHAT I'D DO... WITHOUT THEM.
PROBABLY GO CRAZY.

ALL THE STARS

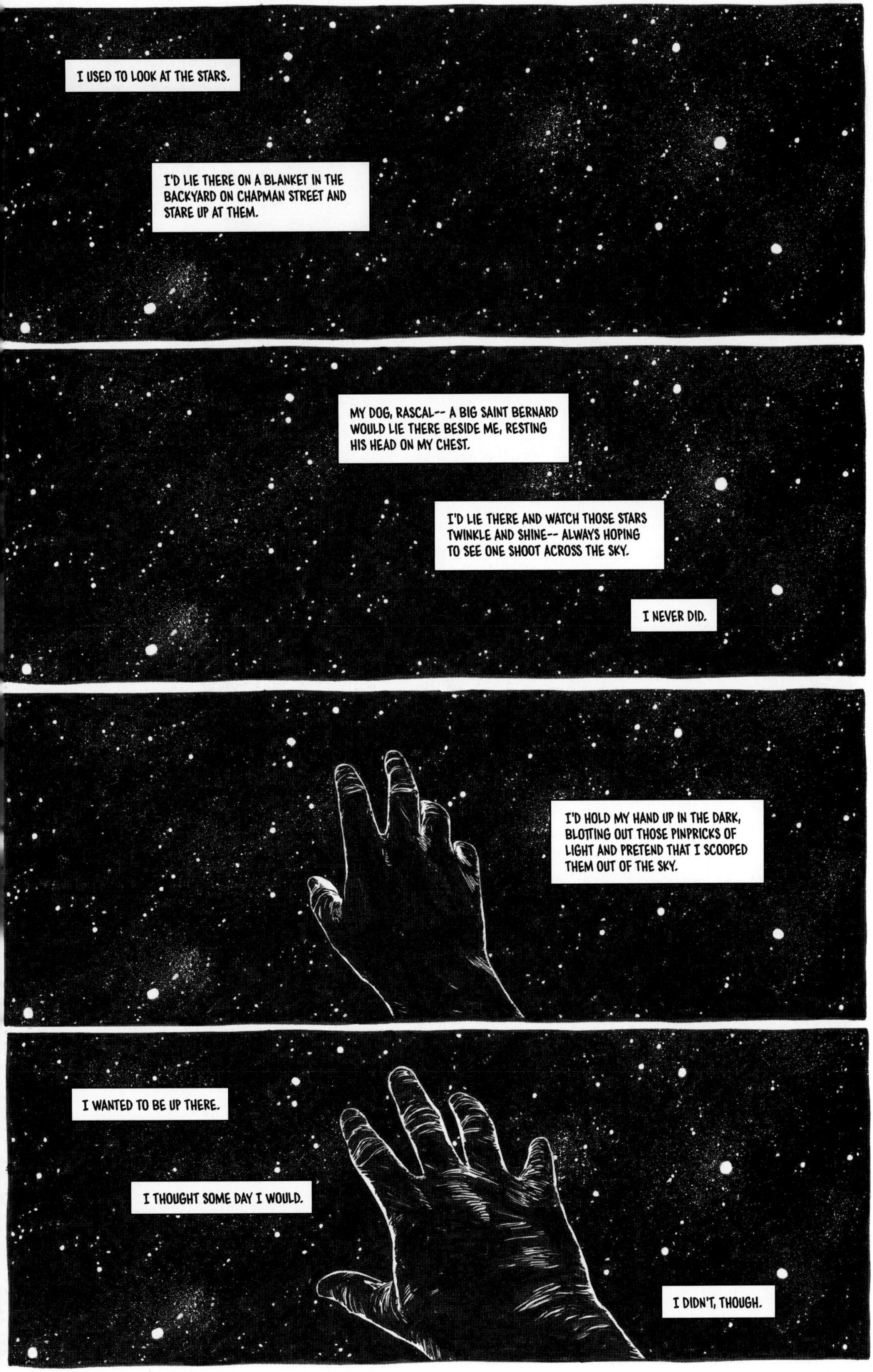
I USED TO LOOK AT THE STARS.
I'D LIE THERE ON A BLANKET IN THE BACKYARD ON CHAPMAN STREET AND STARE UP AT THEM.
MY DOG, RASCAL-- A BIG SAINT BERNARD WOULD LIE THERE BESIDE ME, RESTING HIS HEAD ON MY CHEST.
I'D LIE THERE AND WATCH THOSE STARS TWINKLE AND SHINE-- ALWAYS HOPING TO SEE ONE SHOOT ACROSS THE SKY.
I NEVER DID.
I'D HOLD MY HAND UP IN THE DARK, BLOTTING OUT THOSE PINPRICKS OF LIGHT AND PRETEND THAT I SCOOPED THEM OUT OF THE SKY.
I WANTED TO BE UP THERE.
I THOUGHT SOME DAY I WOULD.
I DIDN'T, THOUGH.

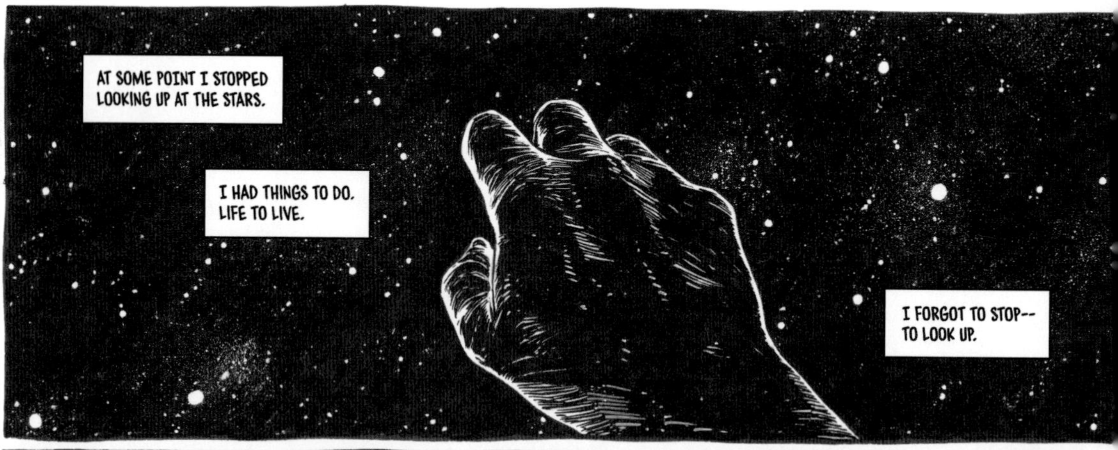
AT SOME POINT I STOPPED LOOKING UP AT THE STARS.
I HAD THINGS TO DO. LIFE TO LIVE.
I FORGOT TO STOP-- TO LOOK UP.

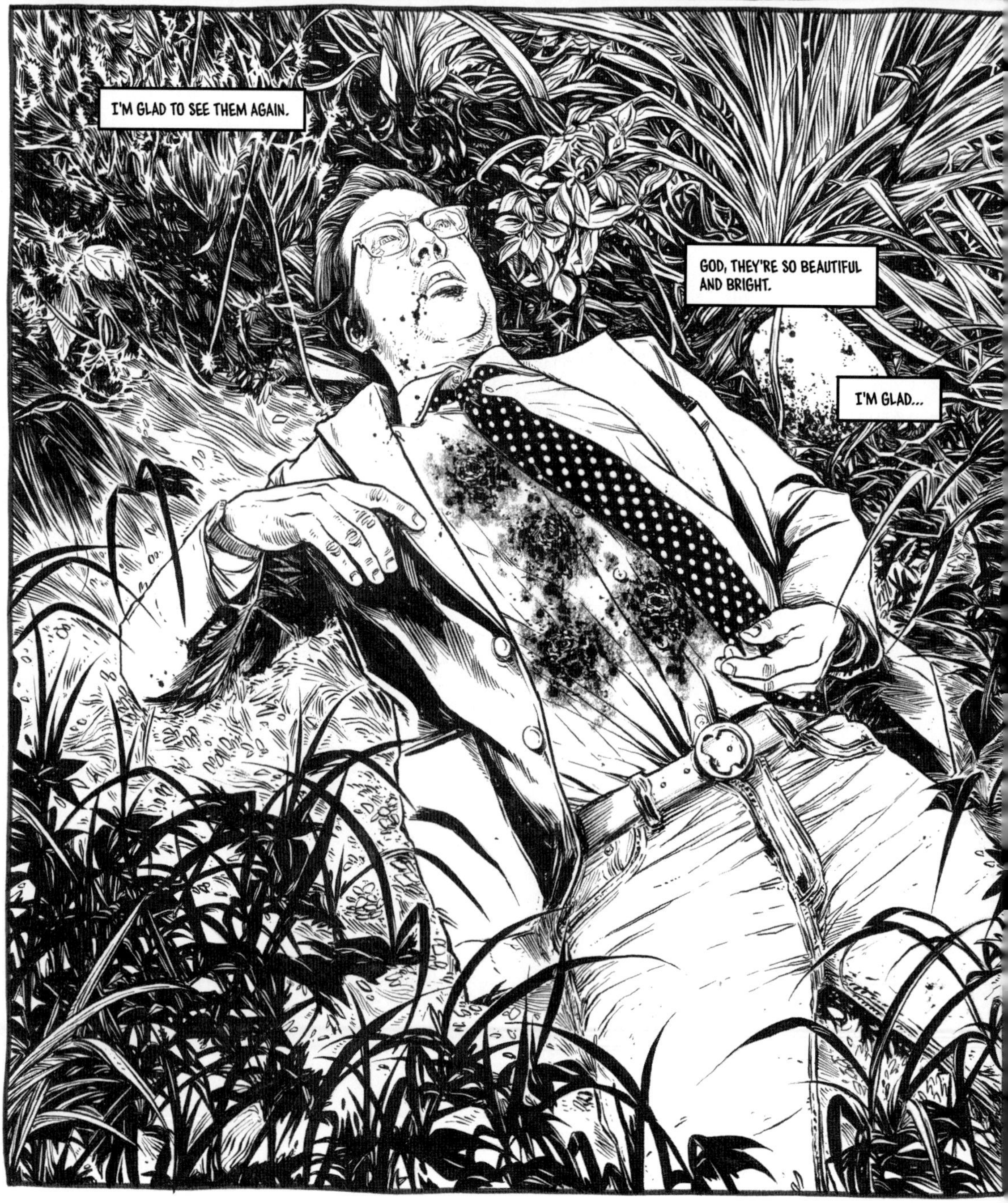
I'M GLAD TO SEE THEM AGAIN.
GOD, THEY'RE SO BEAUTIFUL AND BRIGHT.
I'M GLAD...

THE PRIVATE

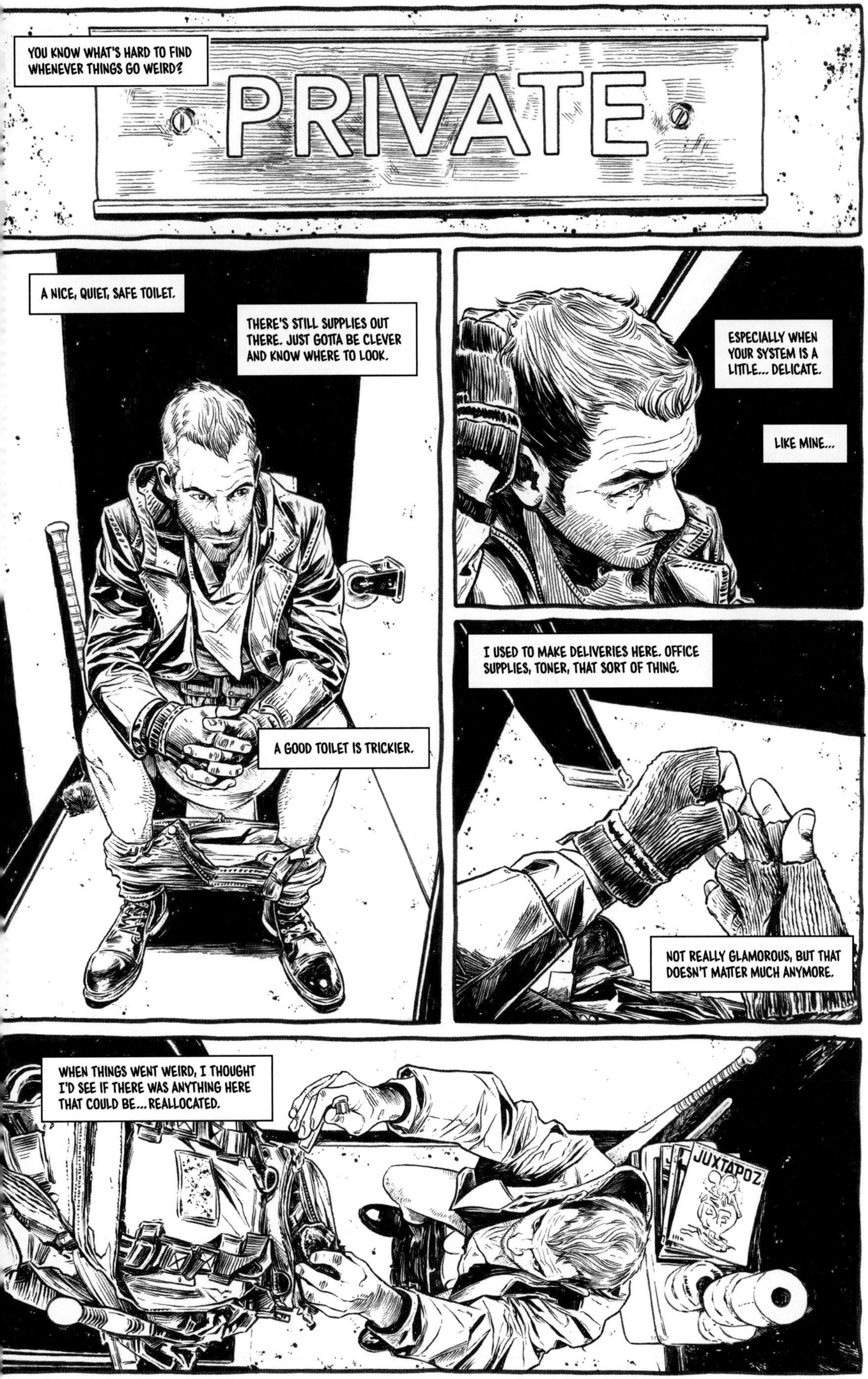
YOU KNOW WHAT'S HARD TO FIND WHENEVER THINGS GO WEIRD?
PRIVATE
A NICE, QUIET, SAFE TOILET.
THERE'S STILL SUPPLIES OUT THERE. JUST GOTTA BE CLEVER AND KNOW WHERE TO LOOK.
A GOOD TOILET IS TRICKIER.
ESPECIALLY WHEN YOUR SYSTEM IS A LITTLE... DELICATE.
LIKE MINE...
I USED TO MAKE DELIVERIES HERE. OFFICE SUPPLIES, TONER, THAT SORT OF THING.
NOT REALLY GLAMOROUS, BUT THAT DOESN'T MATTER MUCH ANYMORE.
WHEN THINGS WENT WEIRD, I THOUGHT I'D SEE IF THERE WAS ANYTHING HERE THAT COULD BE... REALLOCATED.
JUXTAPOZ

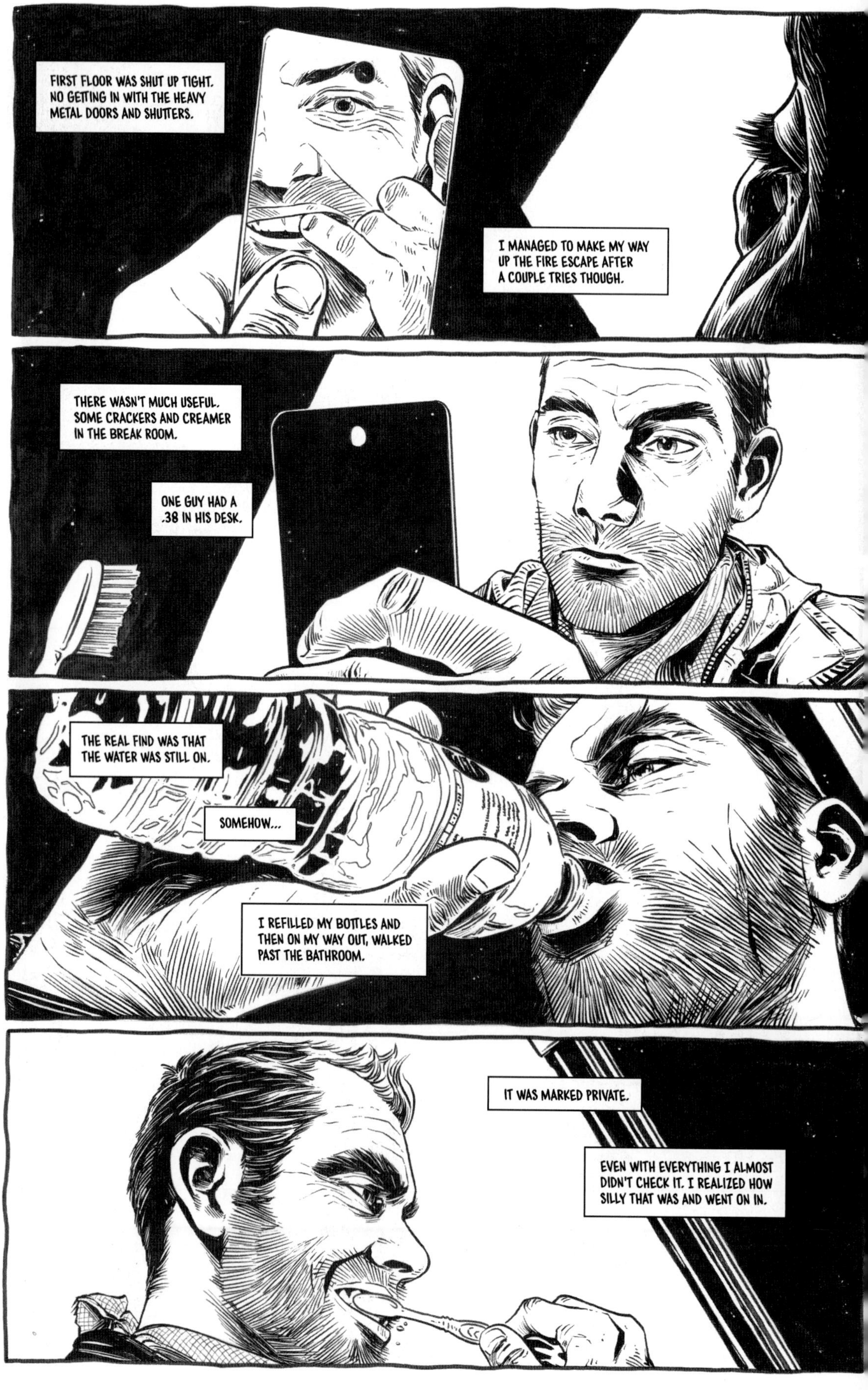
FIRST FLOOR WAS SHUT UP TIGHT. NO GETTING IN WITH THE HEAVY METAL DOORS AND SHUTTERS.
I MANAGED TO MAKE MY WAY UP THE FIRE ESCAPE AFTER A COUPLE TRIES THOUGH.
THERE WASN'T MUCH USEFUL. SOME CRACKERS AND CREAMER IN THE BREAK ROOM.
ONE GUY HAD A .38 IN HIS DESK.
THE REAL FIND WAS THAT THE WATER WAS STILL ON.
SOMEHOW...
I REFILLED MY BOTTLES AND THEN ON MY WAY OUT, WALKED PAST THE BATHROOM.
IT WAS MARKED PRIVATE.
EVEN WITH EVERYTHING I ALMOST DIDN'T CHECK IT. I REALIZED HOW SILLY THAT WAS AND WENT ON IN.

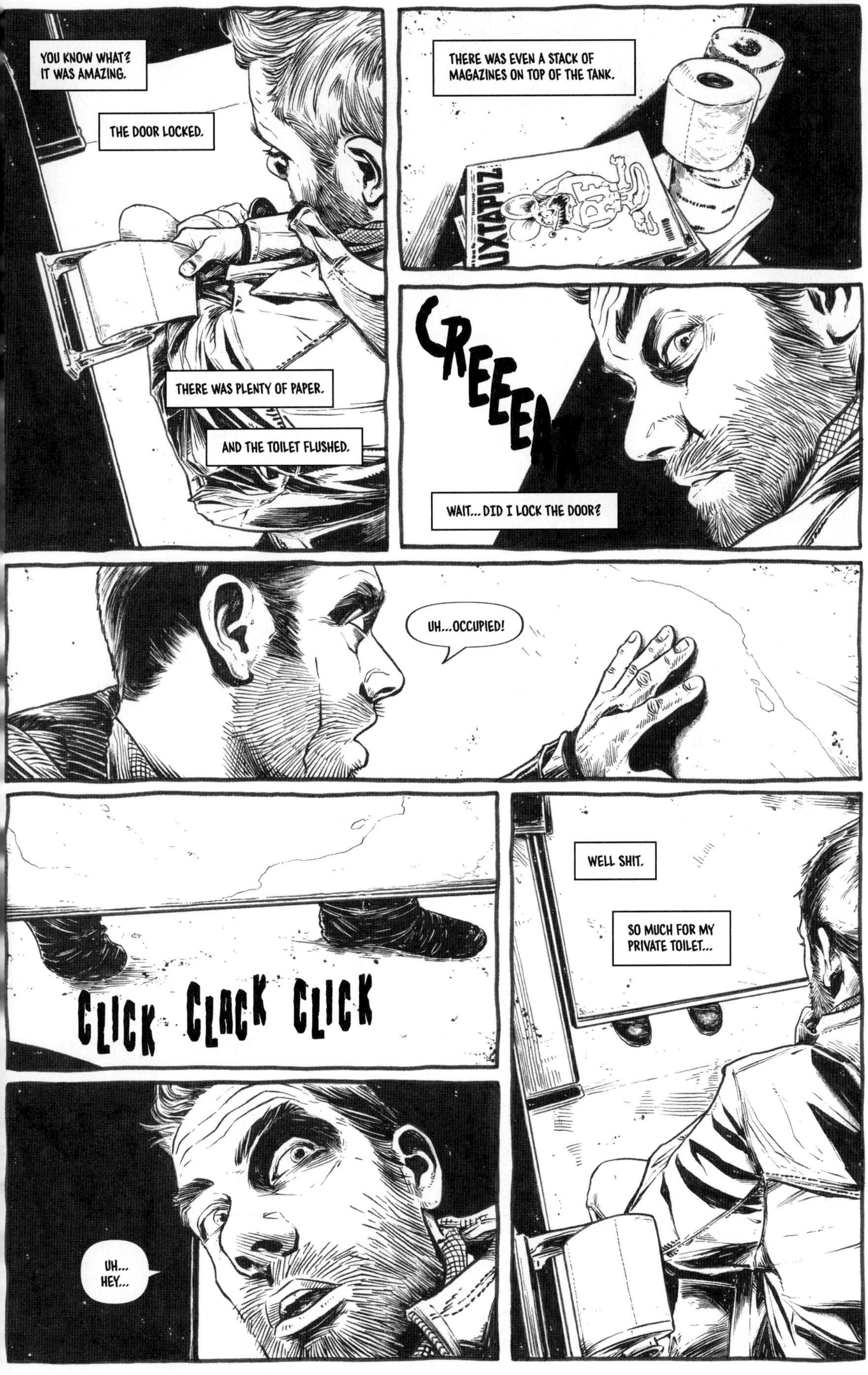
YOU KNOW WHAT? IT WAS AMAZING.
THE DOOR LOCKED.
THERE WAS PLENTY OF PAPER.
AND THE TOILET FLUSHED.
THERE WAS EVEN A STACK OF MAGAZINES ON TOP OF THE TANK.
JUXTAPOZ
CREEEEAK
WAIT... DID I LOCK THE DOOR?
UH...OCCUPIED!
CLICK CLACK CLICK
UH... HEY...
WELL SHIT.
SO MUCH FOR MY PRIVATE TOILET...

THE CLASS OF 1894

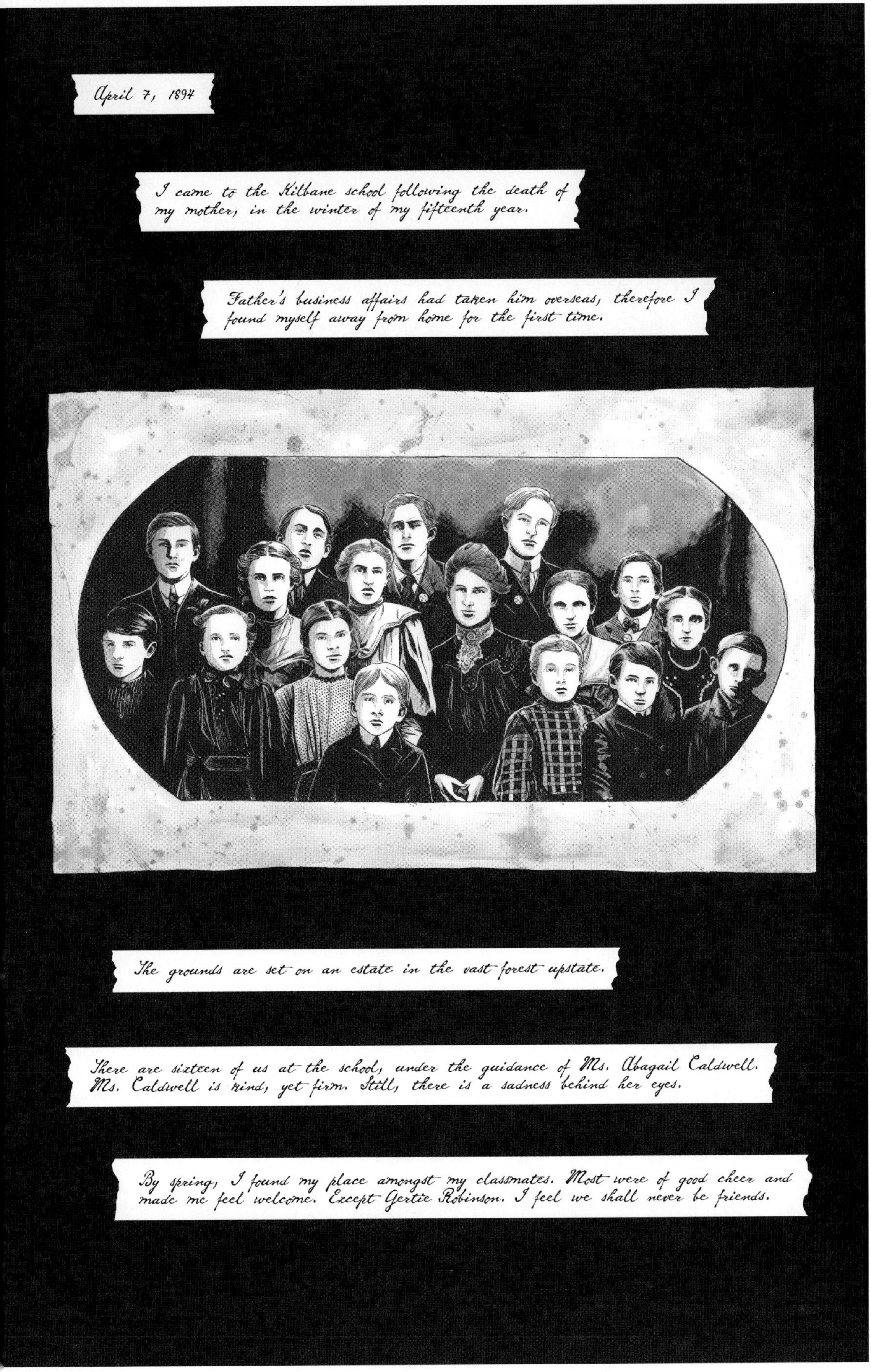
April 7, 1894
I came to the Kilbane school following the death of my mother, in the winter of my fifteenth year.
Father's business affairs had taken him overseas, therefore I found myself away from home for the first time.
The grounds are set on an estate in the vast forest upstate.
There are sixteen of us at the school, under the guidance of Ms. Abagail Caldwell. Ms. Caldwell is kind, yet firm. Still, there is a sadness behind her eyes.
By spring, I found my place amongst my classmates. Most were of good cheer and made me feel welcome. Except Gertie Robinson. I feel we shall never be friends.

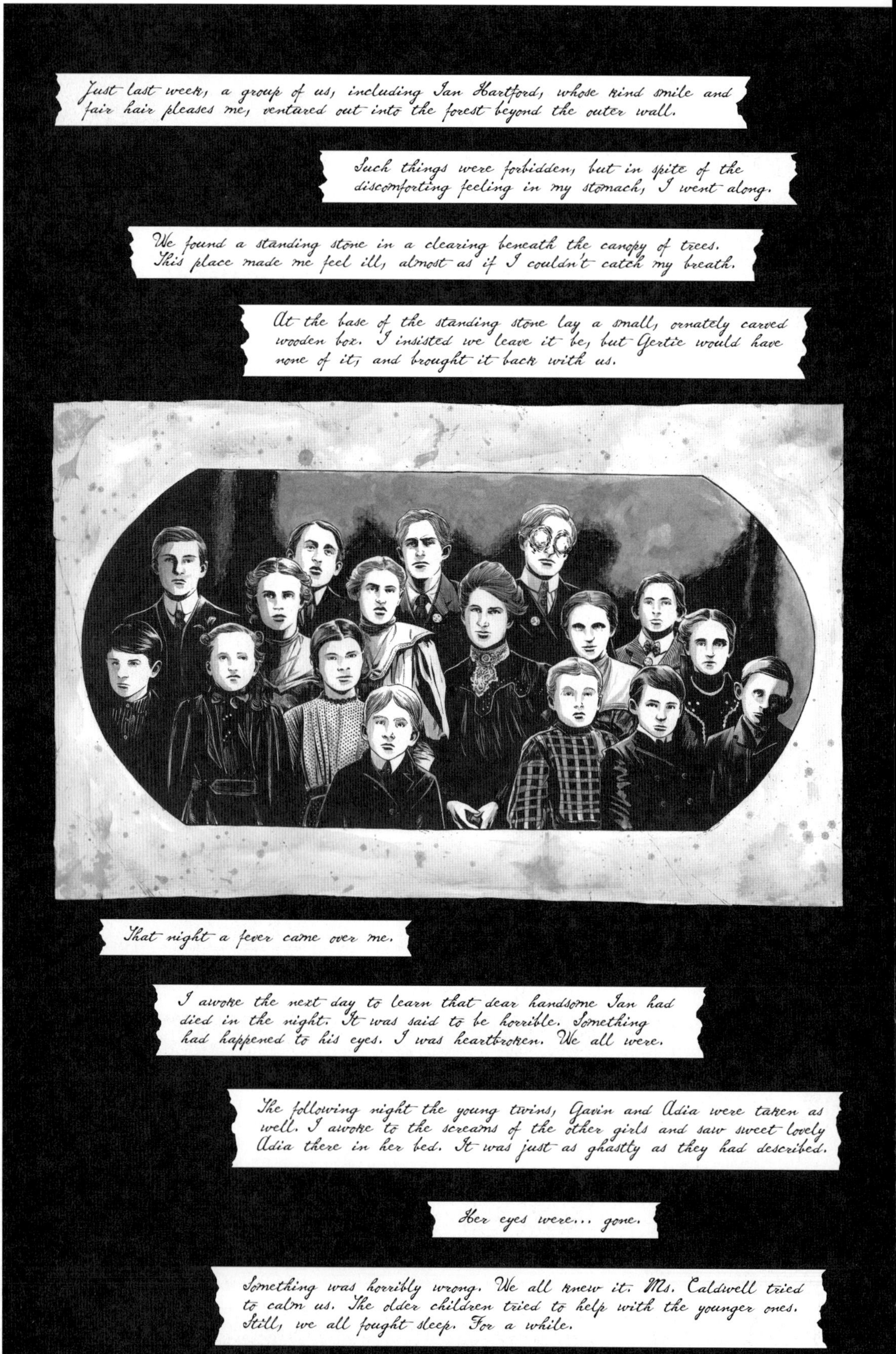
Just last week, a group of us, including Ian Hartford, whose kind smile and fair hair pleases me, ventured out into the forest beyond the outer wall.
Such things were forbidden, but in spite of the discomforting feeling in my stomach, I went along.
We found a standing stone in a clearing beneath the canopy of trees. This place made me feel ill, almost as if I couldn't catch my breath.
At the base of the standing stone lay a small, ornately carved wooden box. I insisted we leave it be, but Gertie would have none of it, and brought it back with us.
That night a fever came over me.
I awoke the next day to learn that dear handsome Ian had died in the night. It was said to be horrible. Something had happened to his eyes. I was heartbroken. We all were.
The following night the young twins, Gavin and Adia were taken as well. I awoke to the screams of the other girls and saw sweet lovely Adia there in her bed. It was just as ghastly as they had described.
Her eyes were... gone.
Something was horribly wrong. We all knew it. Ms. Caldwell tried to calm us. The older children tried to help with the younger ones. Still, we all fought sleep. For a while.

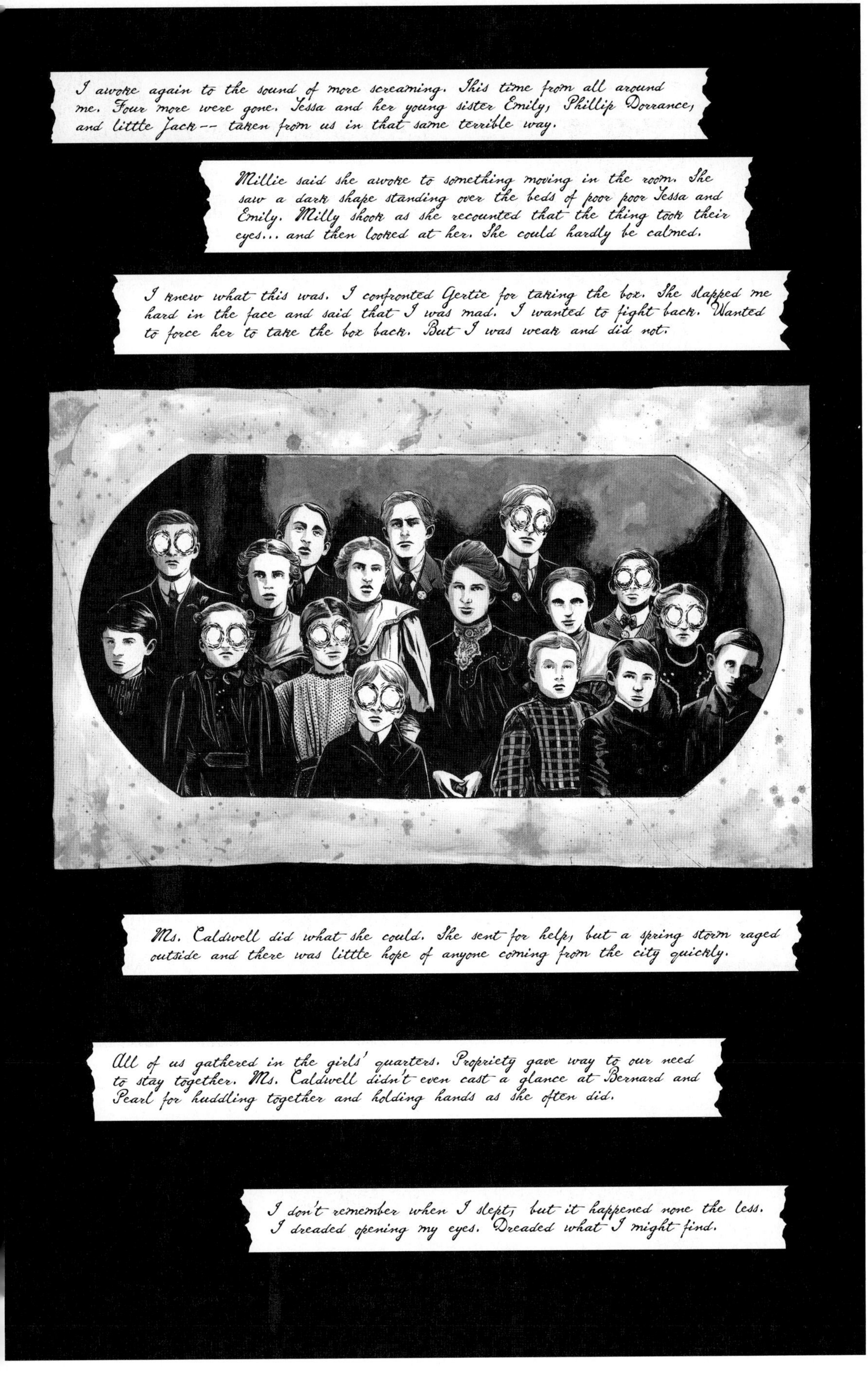
I awoke again to the sound of more screaming. This time from all around me. Four more were gone. Tessa and her young sister Emily, Phillip Dorrance, and little Jack-- taken from us in that same terrible way.
Millie said she awoke to something moving in the room. She saw a dark shape standing over the beds of poor poor Tessa and Emily. Milly shook as she recounted that the thing took their eyes... and then looked at her. She could hardly be calmed.
I knew what this was. I confronted Gertie for taking the box. She slapped me hard in the face and said that I was mad. I wanted to fight back. Wanted to force her to take the box back. But I was weak and did not.
Ms. Caldwell did what she could. She sent for help, but a spring storm raged outside and there was little hope of anyone coming from the city quickly.
All of us gathered in the girls' quarters. Propriety gave way to our need to stay together. Ms. Caldwell didn't even cast a glance at Bernard and Pearl for huddling together and holding hands as she often did.
I don't remember when I slept, but it happened none the less. I dreaded opening my eyes. Dreaded what I might find.

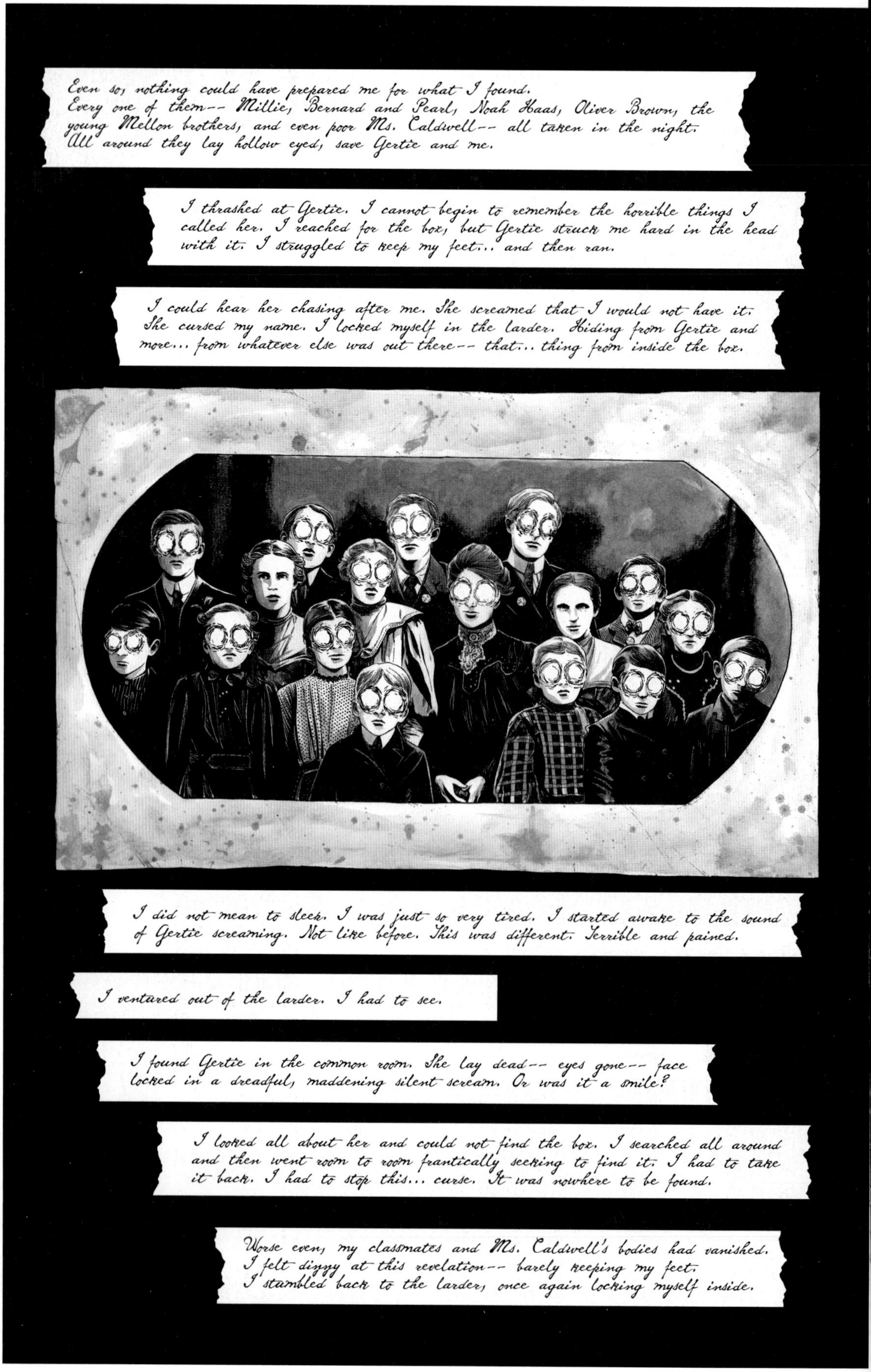
Even so, nothing could have prepared me for what I found. Every one of them-- Millie, Bernard and Pearl, Noah Haas, Oliver Brown, the young Mellon brothers, and even poor Ms. Caldwell-- all taken in the night. All around they lay hollow eyed, save Gertie and me.
I thrashed at Gertie. I cannot begin to remember the horrible things I called her. I reached for the box, but Gertie struck me hard in the head with it. I struggled to keep my feet... and then ran.
I could hear her chasing after me. She screamed that I would not have it. She cursed my name. I locked myself in the larder. Hiding from Gertie and more... from whatever else was out there-- that... thing from inside the box.
I did not mean to sleep. I was just so very tired. I started awake to the sound of Gertie screaming. Not like before. This was different. Terrible and pained.
I ventured out of the larder. I had to see.
I found Gertie in the common room. She lay dead-- eyes gone-- face locked in a dreadful, maddening silent scream. Or was it a smile?
I looked all about her and could not find the box. I searched all around and then went room to room frantically seeking to find it. I had to take it back. I had to stop this... curse. It was nowhere to be found.
Worse even, my classmates and Ms. Caldwell's bodies had vanished. I felt dizzy at this revelation-- barely keeping my feet. I stumbled back to the larder, once again locking myself inside.

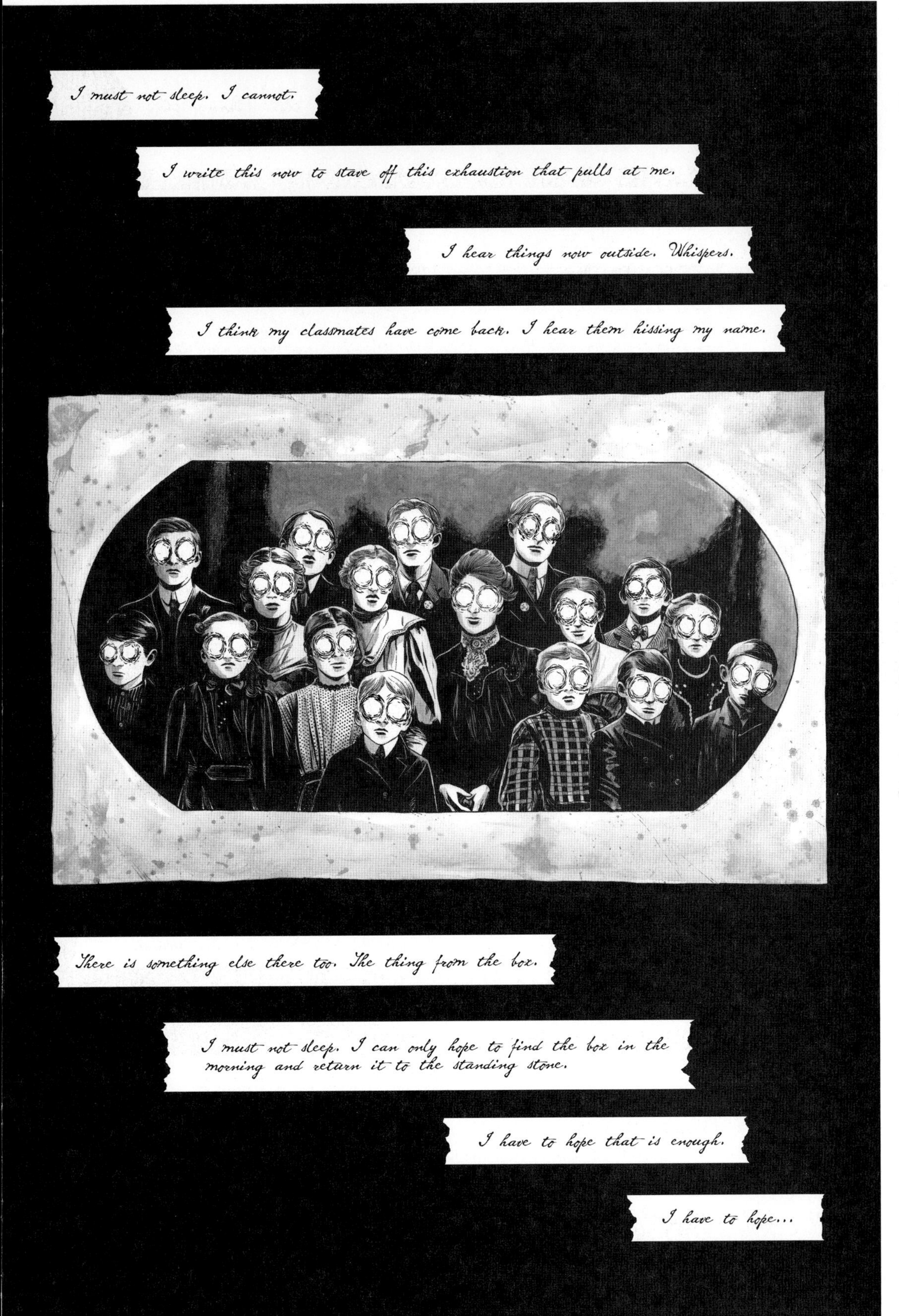
I must not sleep. I cannot.
I write this now to stave off this exhaustion that pulls at me.
I hear things now outside. Whispers.
I think my classmates have come back. I hear them hissing my name.
There is something else there too. The thing from the box.
I must not sleep. I can only hope to find the box in the morning and return it to the standing stone.
I have to hope that is enough.
I have to hope...

KIT-CAT

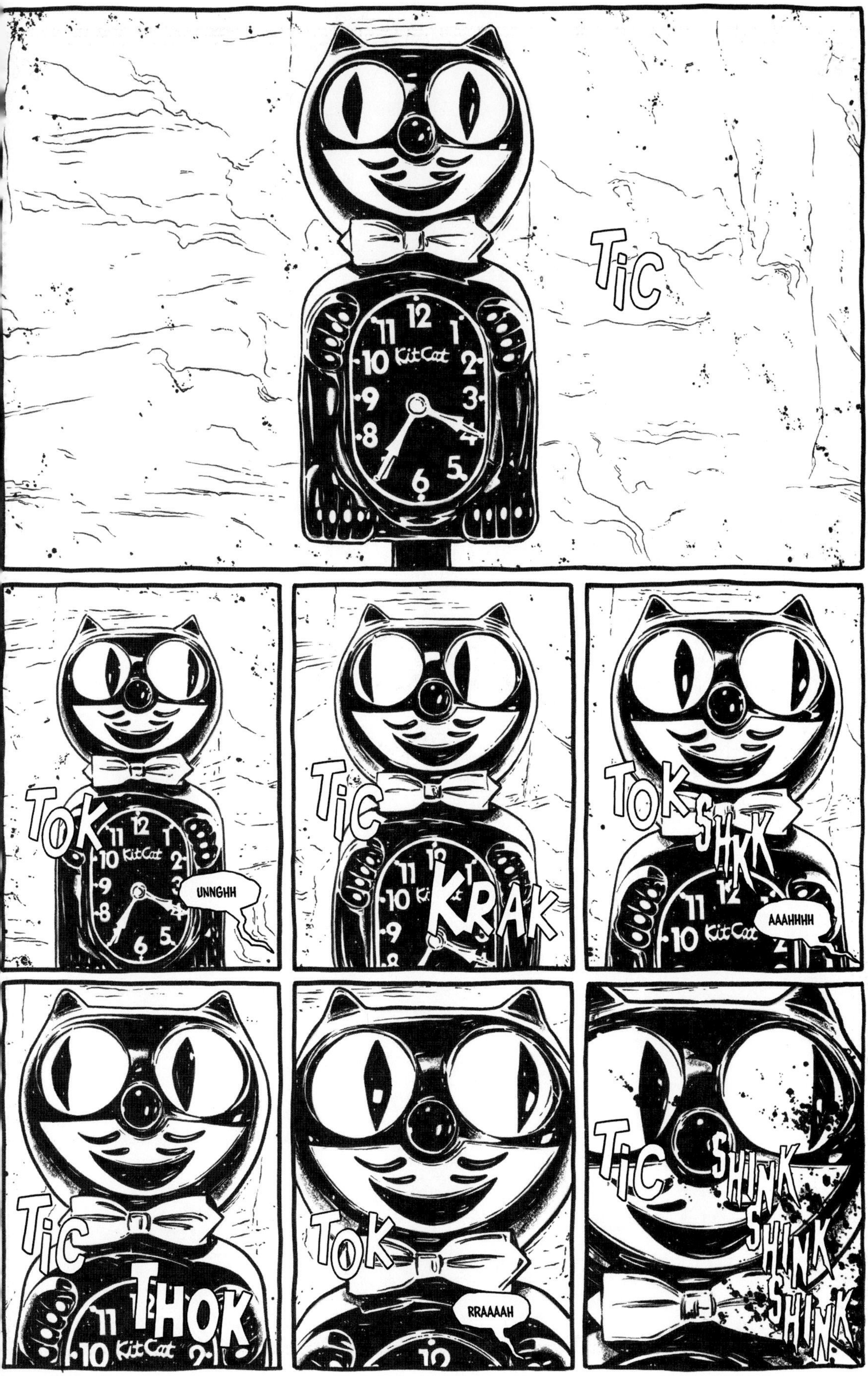
TIC
TOK
UNNGHH
TIC
KRAK
TOK
SHKK
AAAHHHH
TIC
THOK
TOK
RRAAAAH
TIC
SHINK
SHINK
SHINK

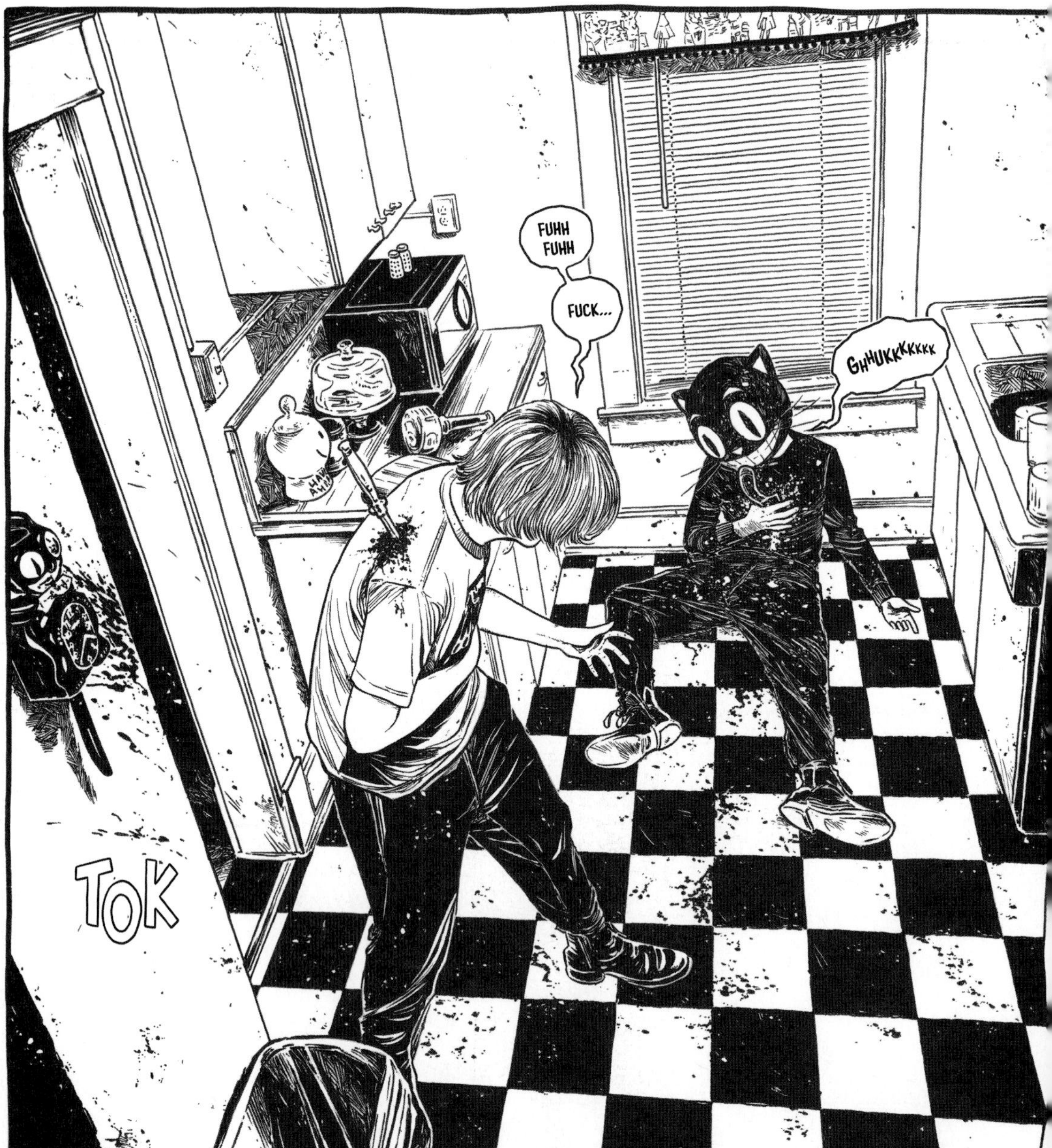
FUHH
FUHH
FUCK...
GHHUKKKKKK
TOK

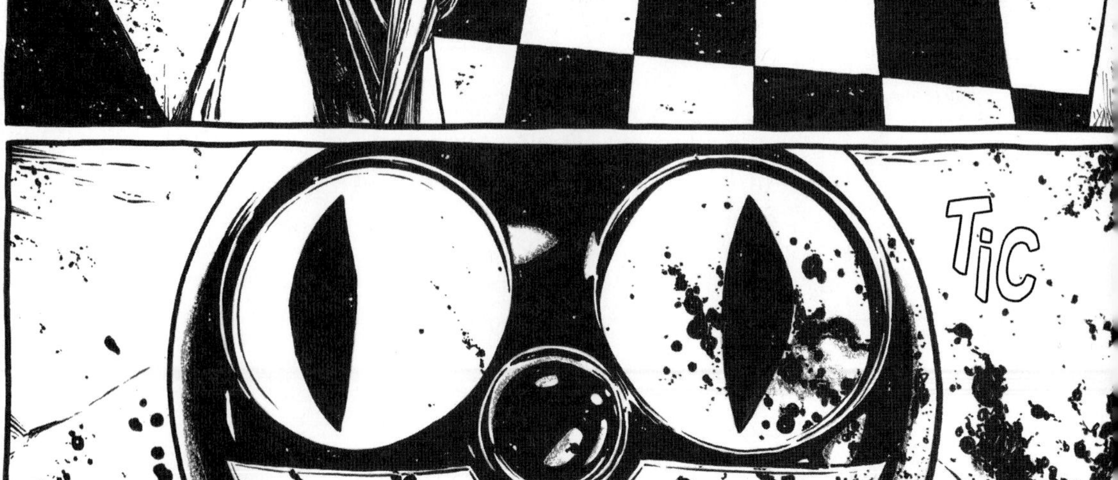
TIC

SABBATICAL AT THE ELMS

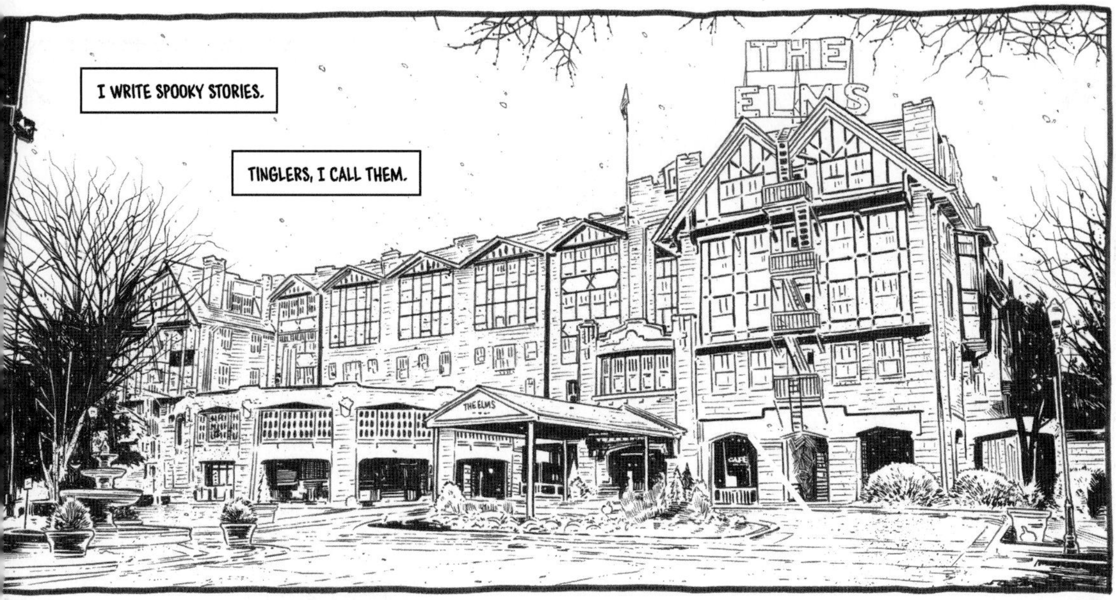
I WRITE SPOOKY STORIES.
TINGLERS, I CALL THEM.
THE ELMS

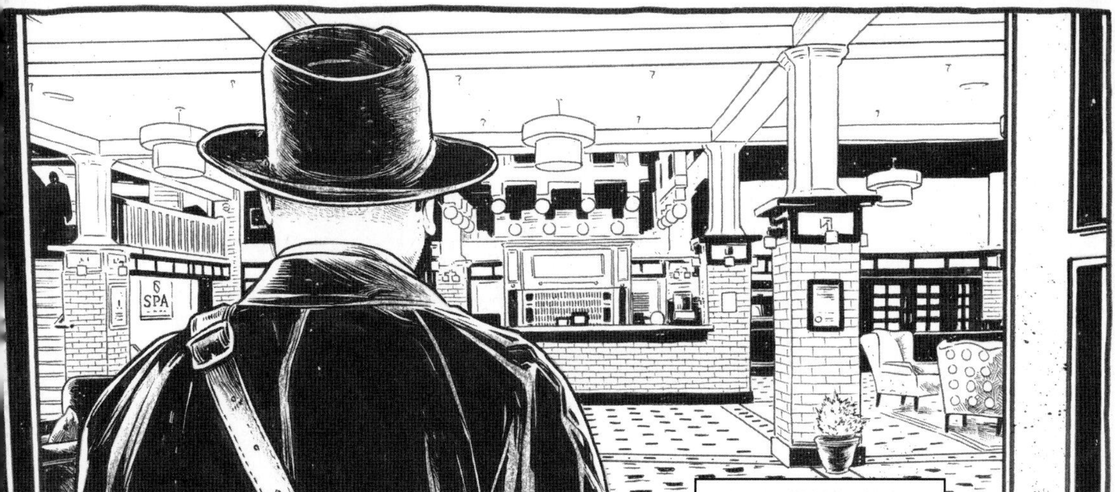
SPA
NOT SUPER HIGHBROW THINGS--
JUST LITERARY ENOUGH TO FEEL
GOOD ABOUT IT ALL.

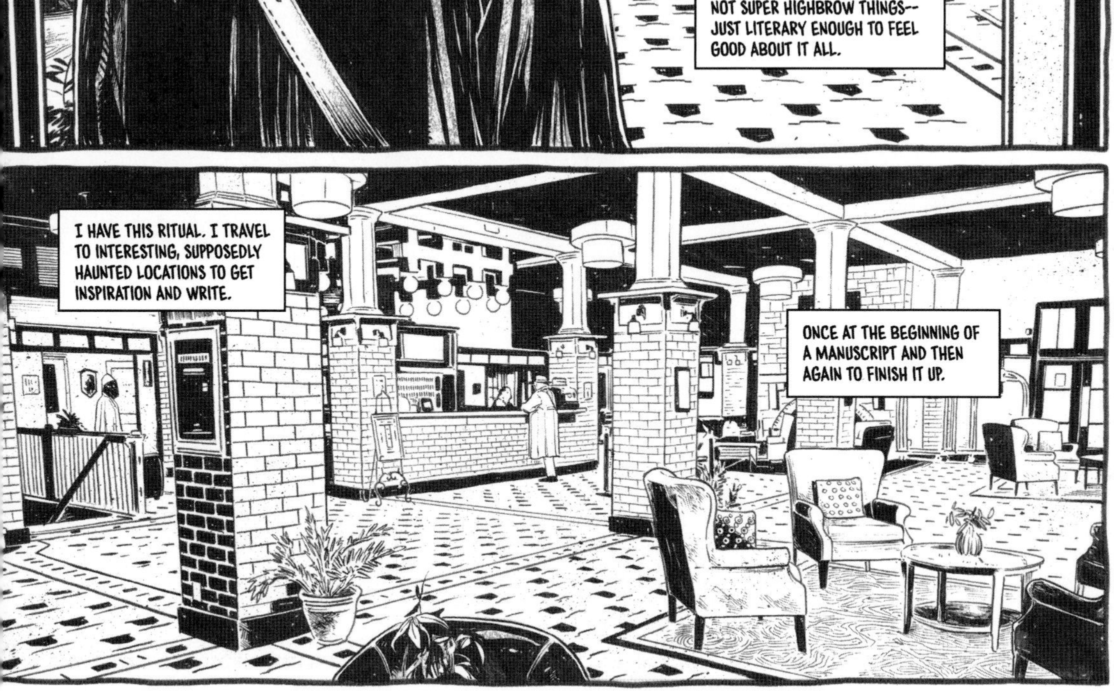
I HAVE THIS RITUAL. I TRAVEL TO INTERESTING, SUPPOSEDLY HAUNTED LOCATIONS TO GET INSPIRATION AND WRITE.
ONCE AT THE BEGINNING OF A MANUSCRIPT AND THEN AGAIN TO FINISH IT UP.

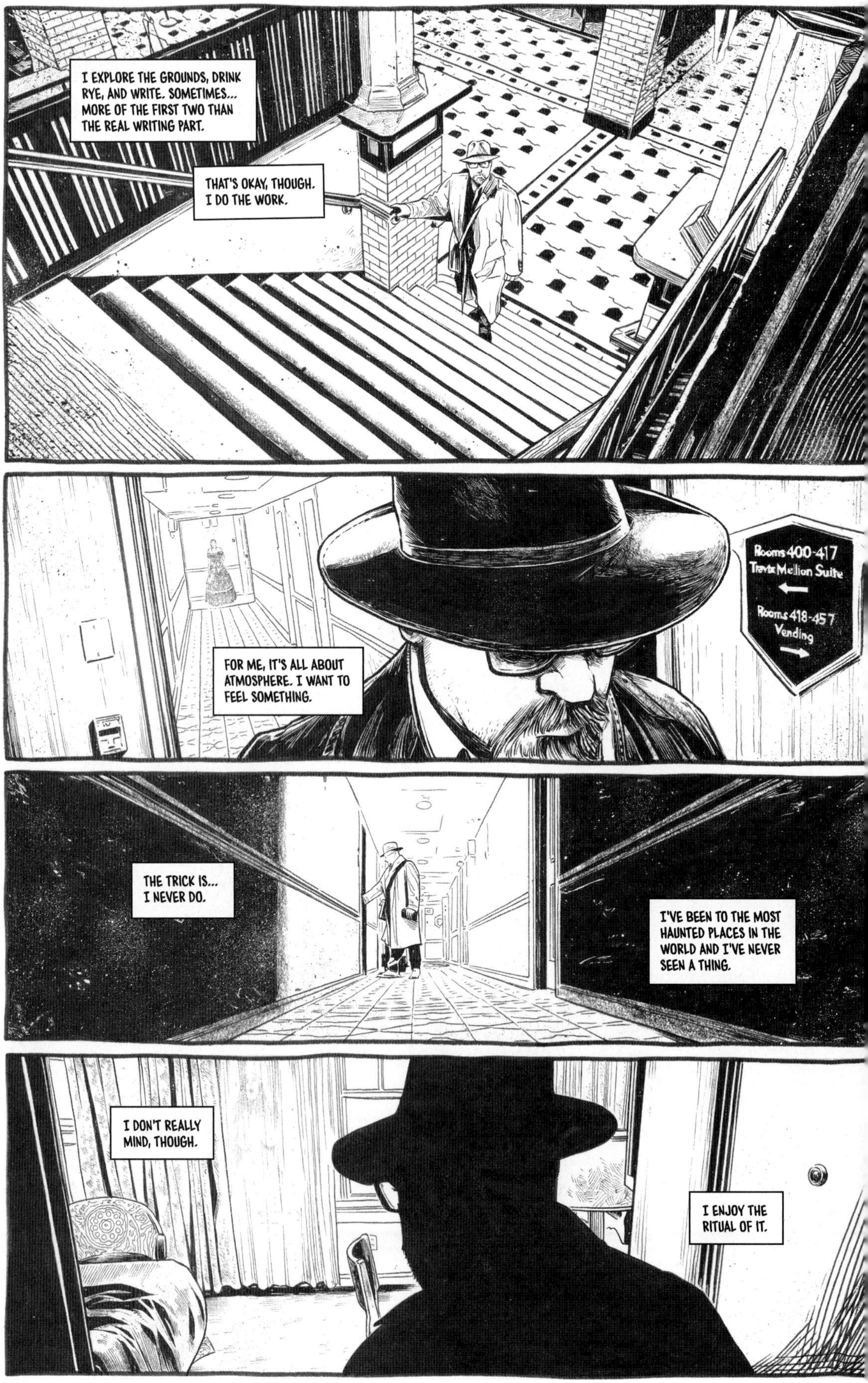
I EXPLORE THE GROUNDS, DRINK RYE, AND WRITE. SOMETIMES... MORE OF THE FIRST TWO THAN THE REAL WRITING PART.
THAT'S OKAY, THOUGH. I DO THE WORK.
Rooms 400-417
Travis Mellion Suite
Rooms 418-457
Vending
FOR ME, IT'S ALL ABOUT ATMOSPHERE. I WANT TO FEEL SOMETHING.
THE TRICK IS... I NEVER DO.
I'VE BEEN TO THE MOST HAUNTED PLACES IN THE WORLD AND I'VE NEVER SEEN A THING.
I DON'T REALLY MIND, THOUGH.
I ENJOY THE RITUAL OF IT.

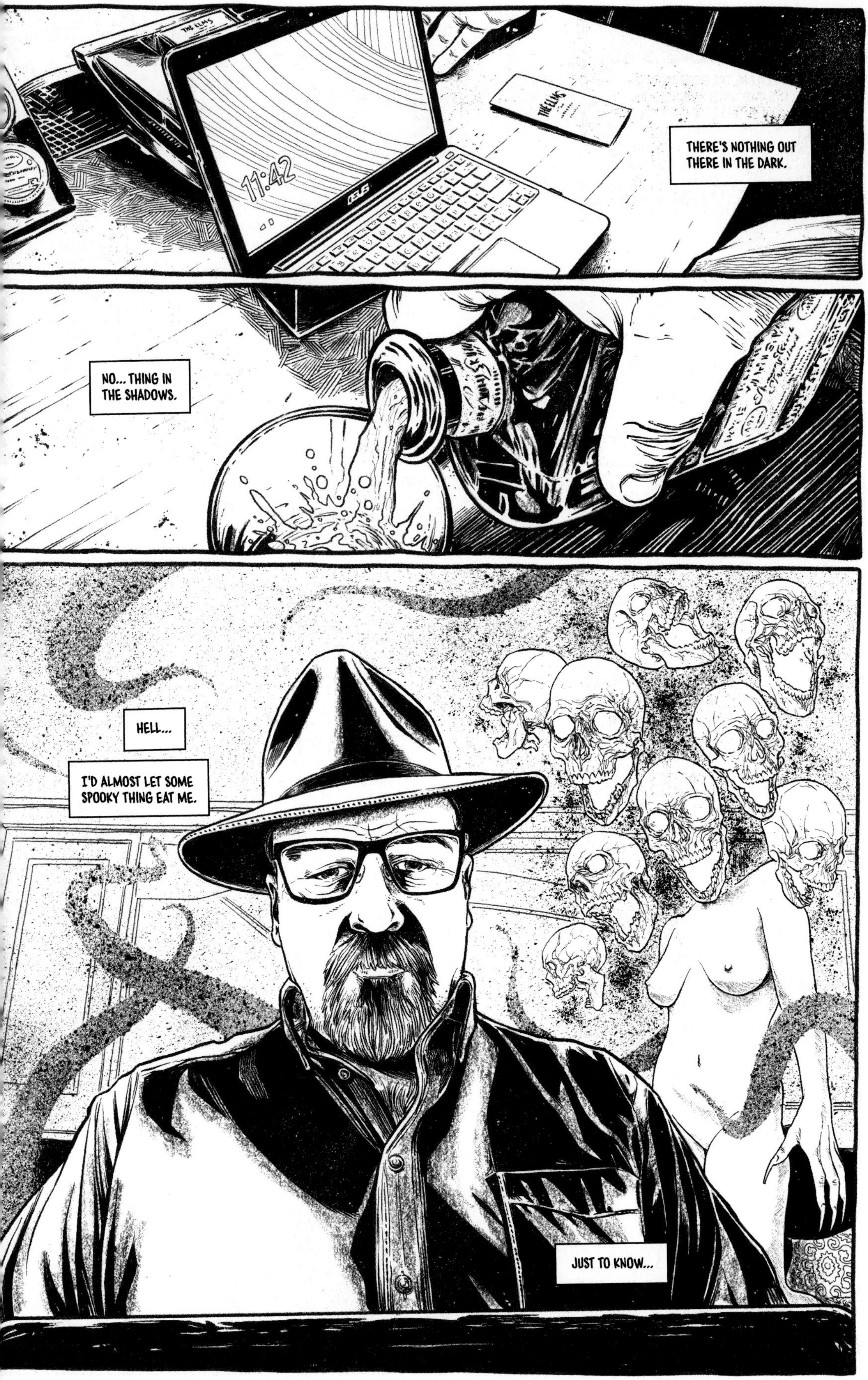
THE ELMS
11:42
THERE'S NOTHING OUT THERE IN THE DARK.
NO... THING IN THE SHADOWS.
HELL...
I'D ALMOST LET SOME SPOOKY THING EAT ME.
JUST TO KNOW...

THE PACKAGE

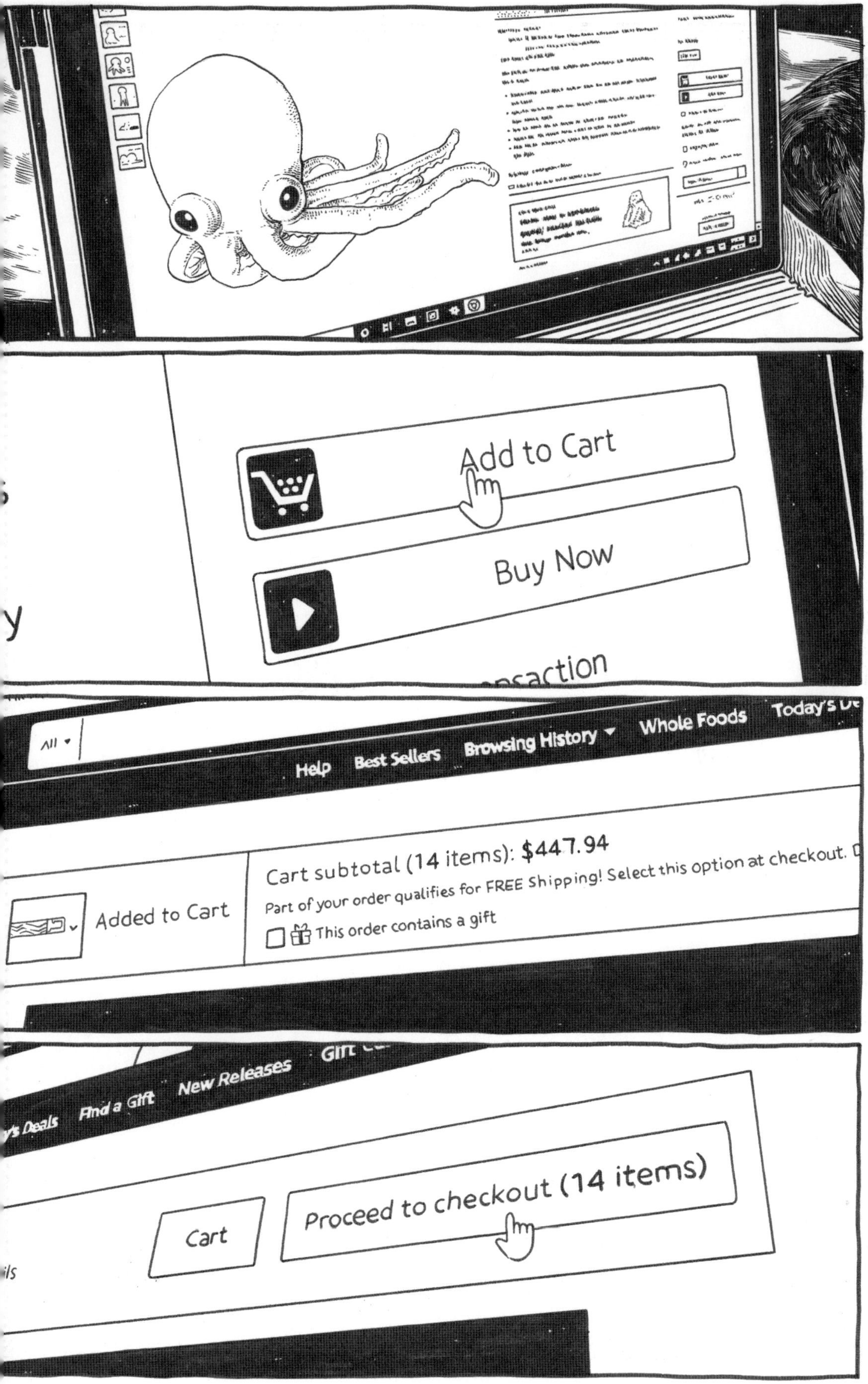
Add to Cart
Buy Now
All
Help
Best Sellers
Browsing History
Whole Foods
Added to Cart
Cart subtotal (14 items): $447.94
Part of your order qualifies for FREE Shipping! Select this option at checkout.
This order contains a gift
Find a Gift
New Releases
Cart
Proceed to checkout (14 items)

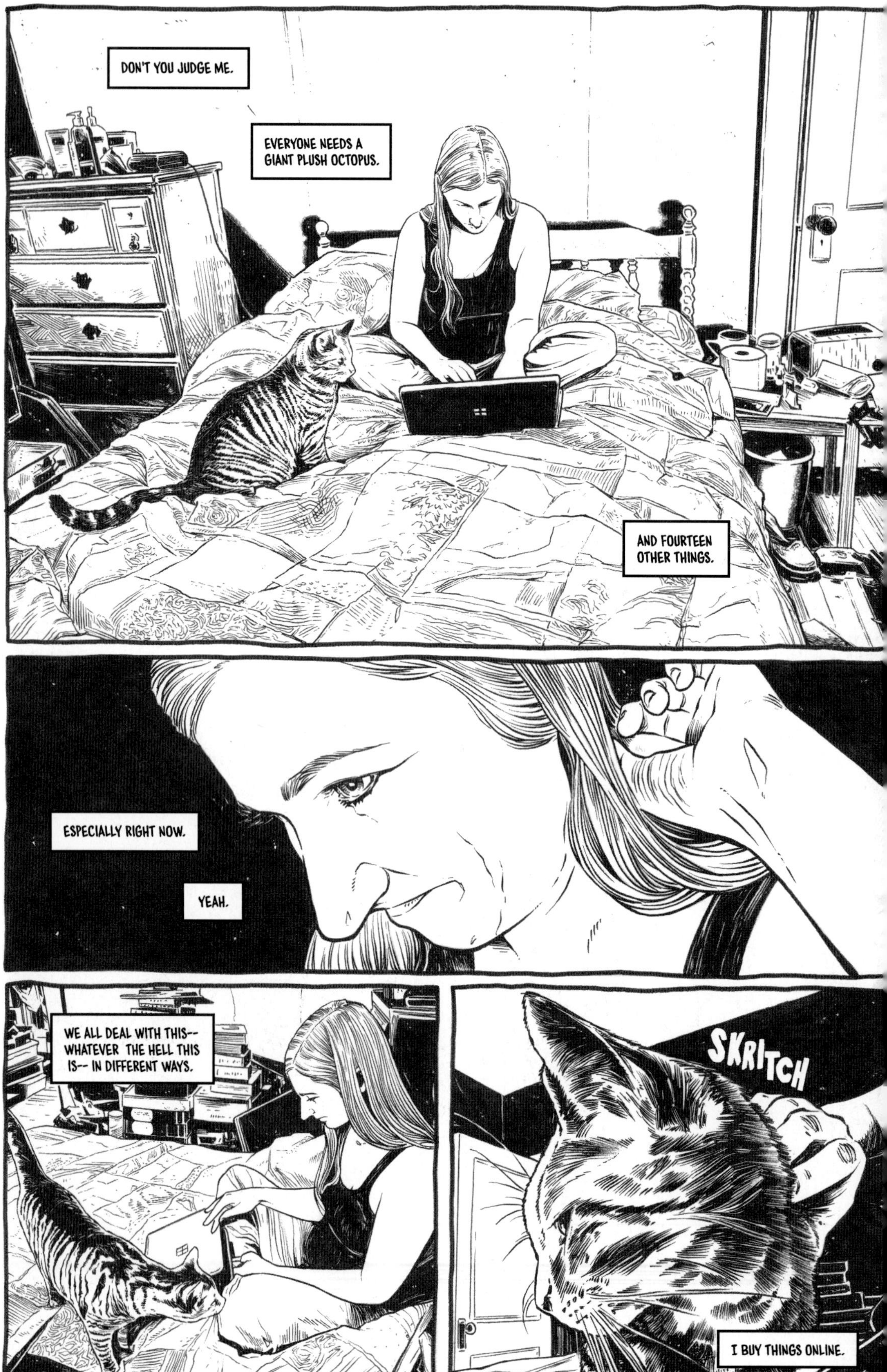
DON'T YOU JUDGE ME.
EVERYONE NEEDS A GIANT PLUSH OCTOPUS.
AND FOURTEEN OTHER THINGS.
ESPECIALLY RIGHT NOW.
YEAH.
WE ALL DEAL WITH THIS-- WHATEVER THE HELL THIS IS-- IN DIFFERENT WAYS.
SKRITCH
I BUY THINGS ONLINE.

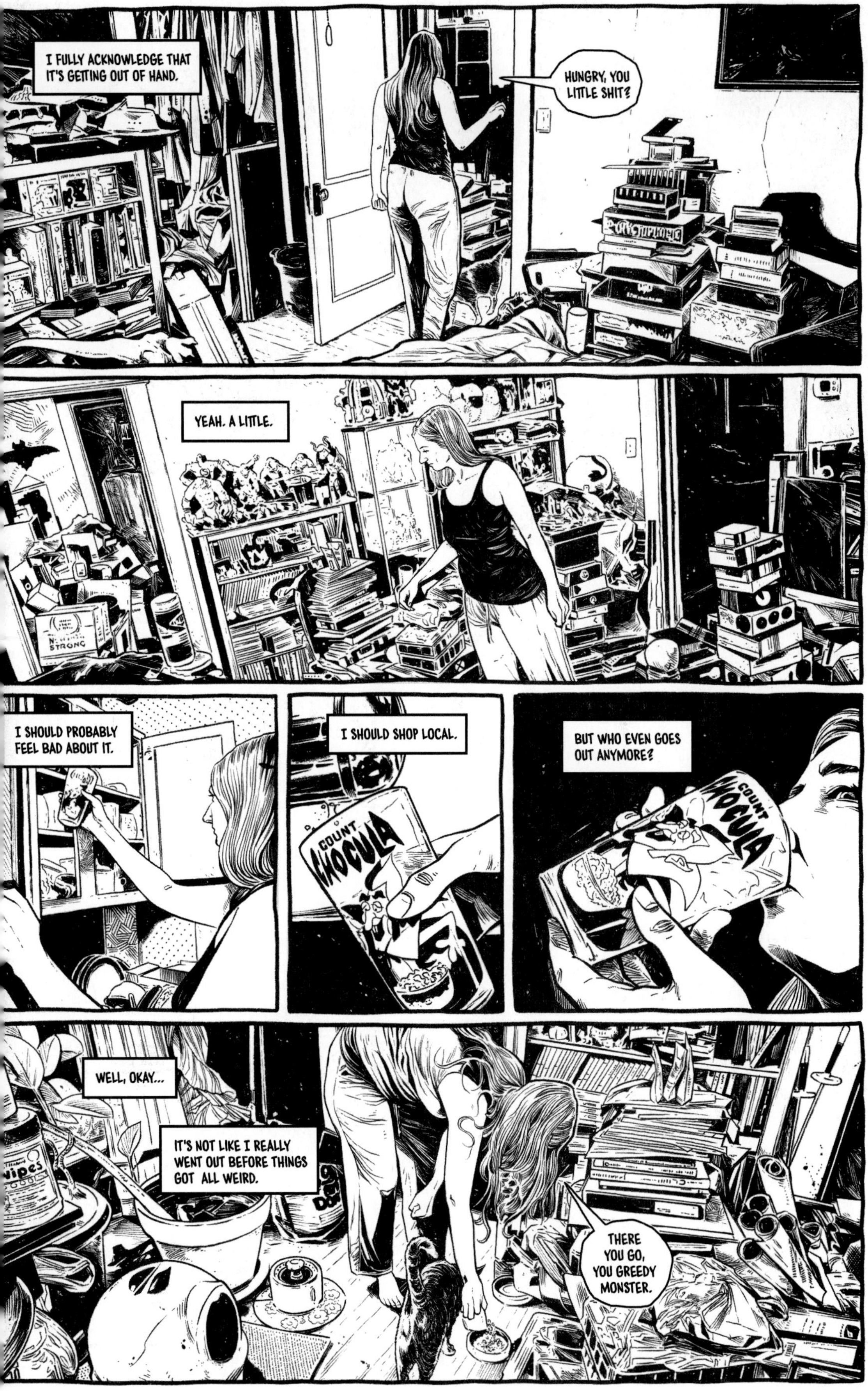
I FULLY ACKNOWLEDGE THAT IT'S GETTING OUT OF HAND.
HUNGRY, YOU LITTLE SHIT?
YEAH. A LITTLE.
I SHOULD PROBABLY FEEL BAD ABOUT IT.
I SHOULD SHOP LOCAL.
BUT WHO EVEN GOES OUT ANYMORE?
COUNT CHOCULA
WELL, OKAY...
IT'S NOT LIKE I REALLY WENT OUT BEFORE THINGS GOT ALL WEIRD.
THERE YOU GO, YOU GREEDY MONSTER.

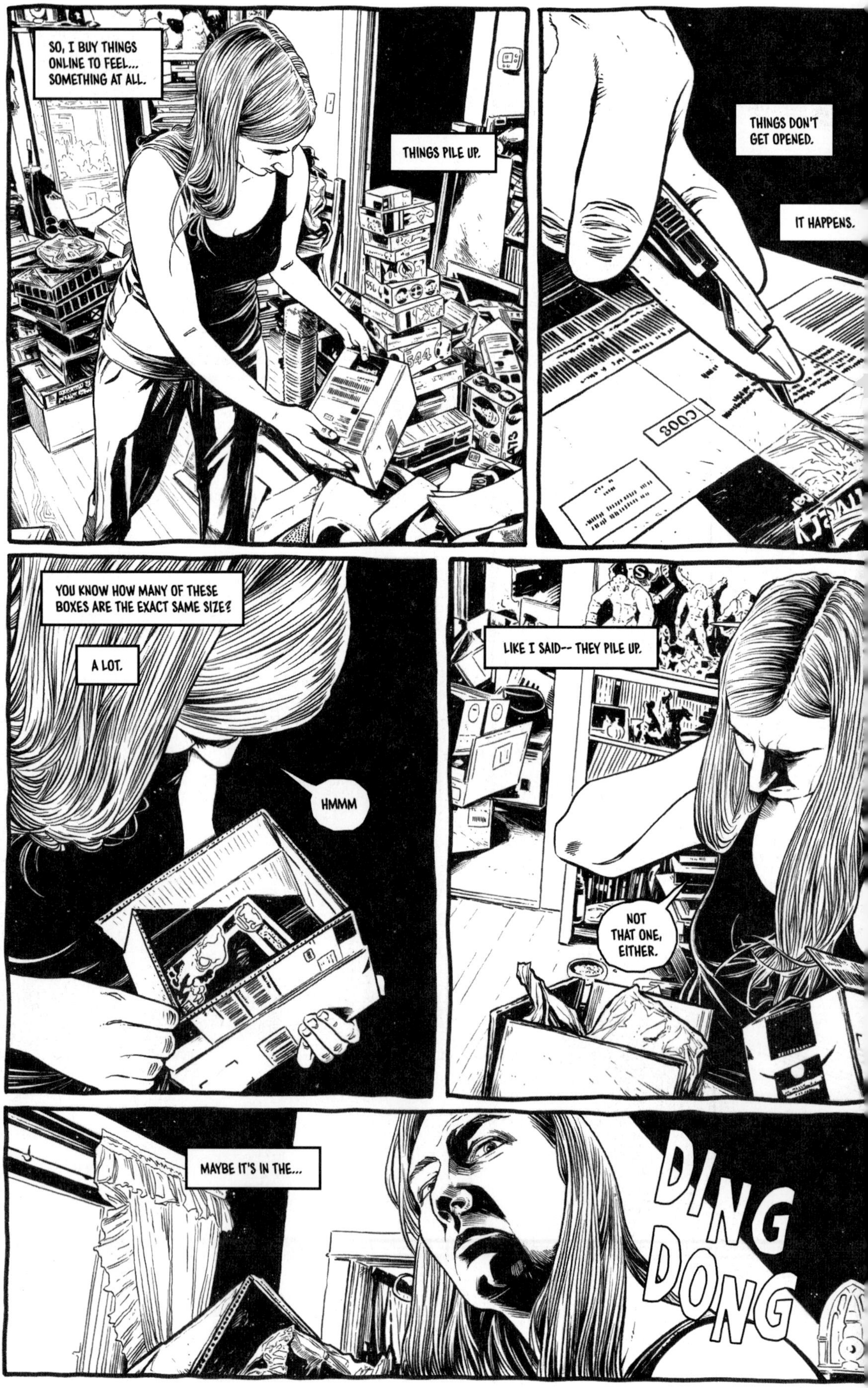
SO, I BUY THINGS ONLINE TO FEEL... SOMETHING AT ALL.
THINGS PILE UP.
THINGS DON'T GET OPENED.
IT HAPPENS.
YOU KNOW HOW MANY OF THESE BOXES ARE THE EXACT SAME SIZE?
A LOT.
HMMM
LIKE I SAID-- THEY PILE UP.
NOT THAT ONE, EITHER.
MAYBE IT'S IN THE...
DING DONG

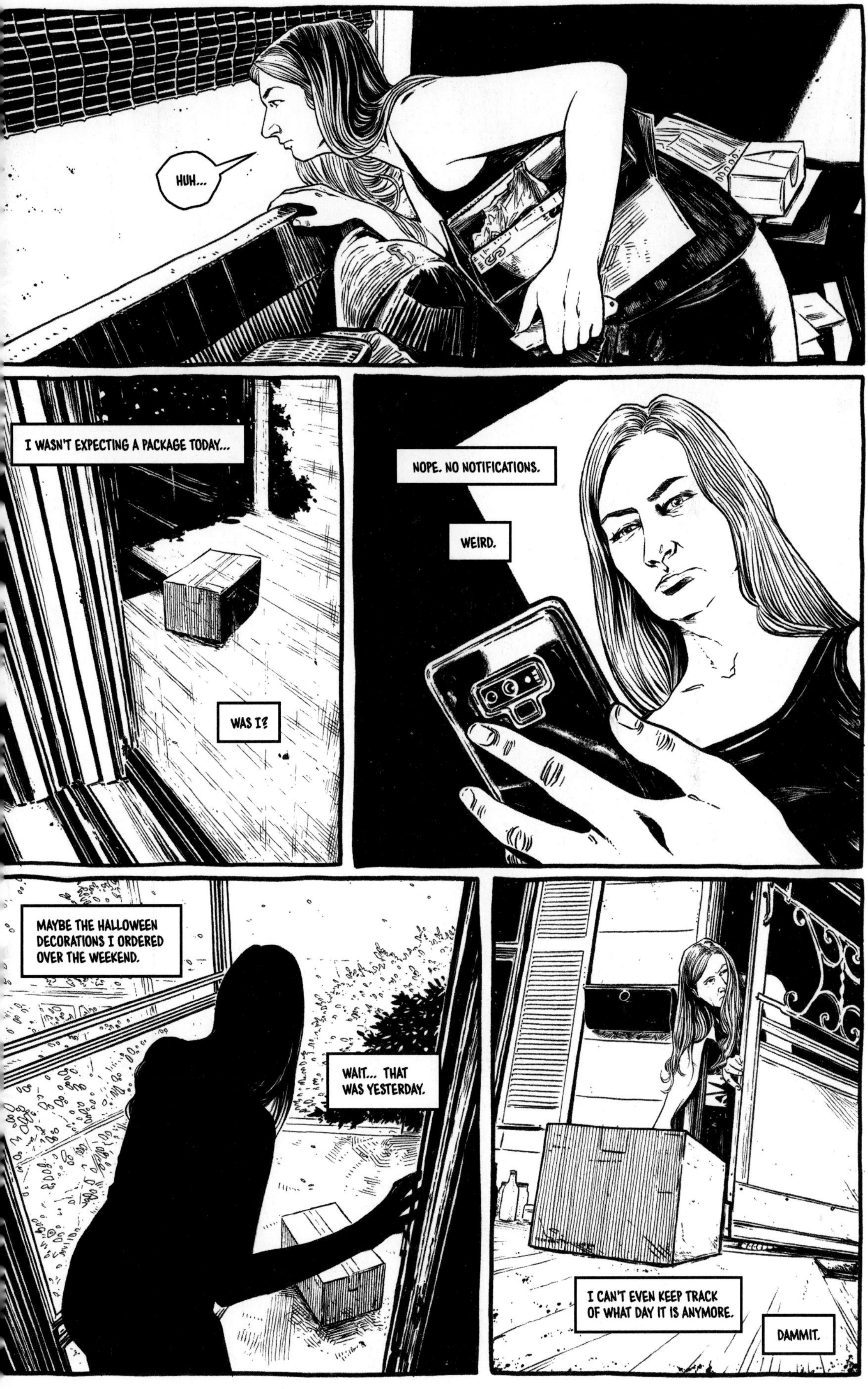
HUH...
I WASN'T EXPECTING A PACKAGE TODAY...
WAS I?
NOPE. NO NOTIFICATIONS.
WEIRD.
MAYBE THE HALLOWEEN DECORATIONS I ORDERED OVER THE WEEKEND.
WAIT... THAT WAS YESTERDAY.
I CAN'T EVEN KEEP TRACK OF WHAT DAY IT IS ANYMORE.
DAMMIT.

HMM...

HEAVIER THAN IT LOOKS...

I DID ORDER THOSE BOOKS.

BUT I DON'T THINK THEY'D BE THIS BIG.

SHOULD I RECORD THIS UNBOXING?

NAH.

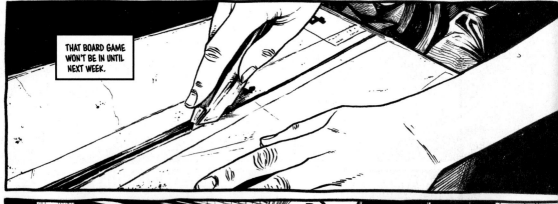

THAT BOARD GAME WON'T BE IN UNTIL NEXT WEEK.

WHAT'S THAT...

WEIRD SMELL?

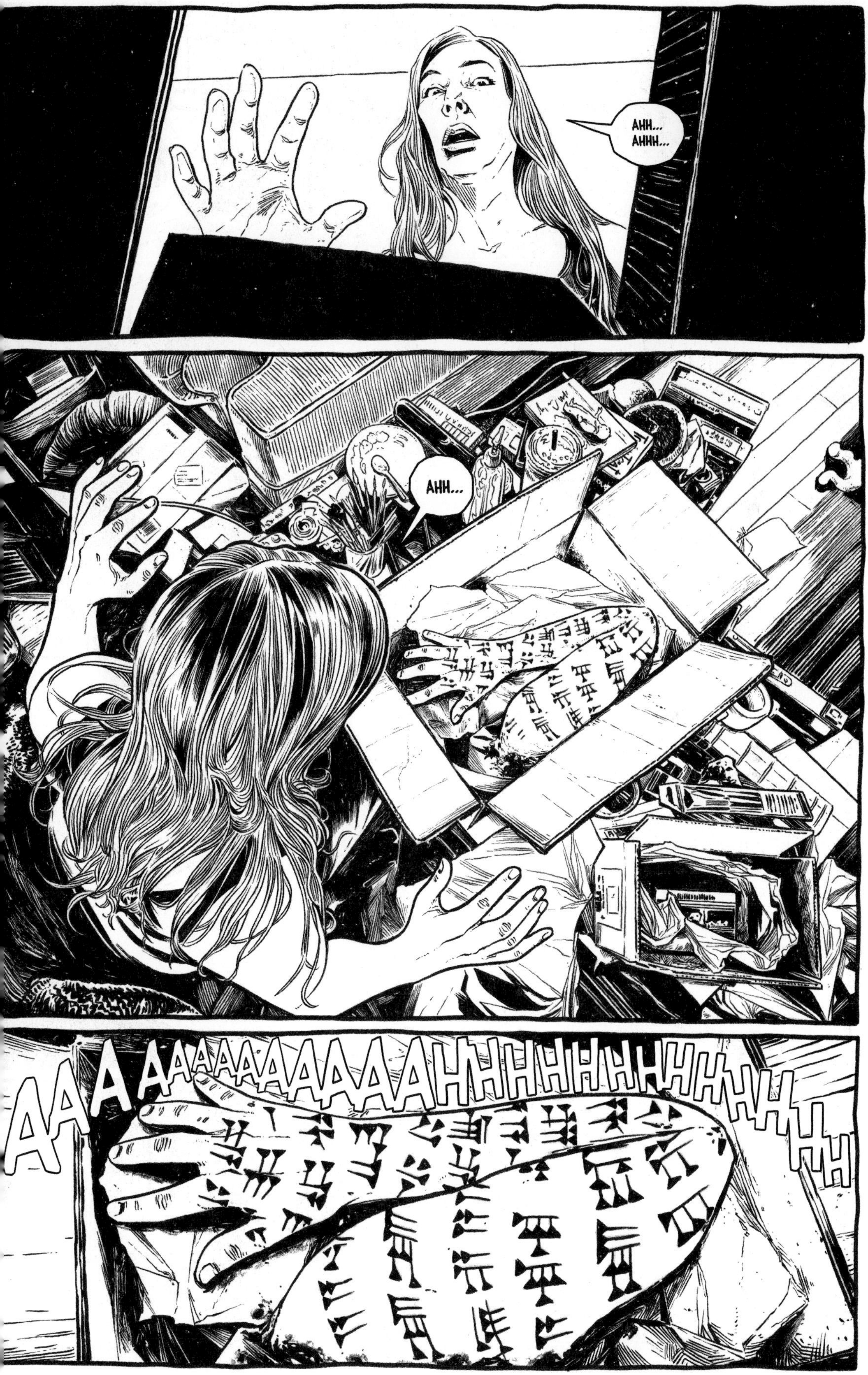
AHH... AHHH...
AHH...
AAAAAAAAAAAAAAAAHHHHHHHHHHHHHHHHHH

THE OLD-FASHIONED

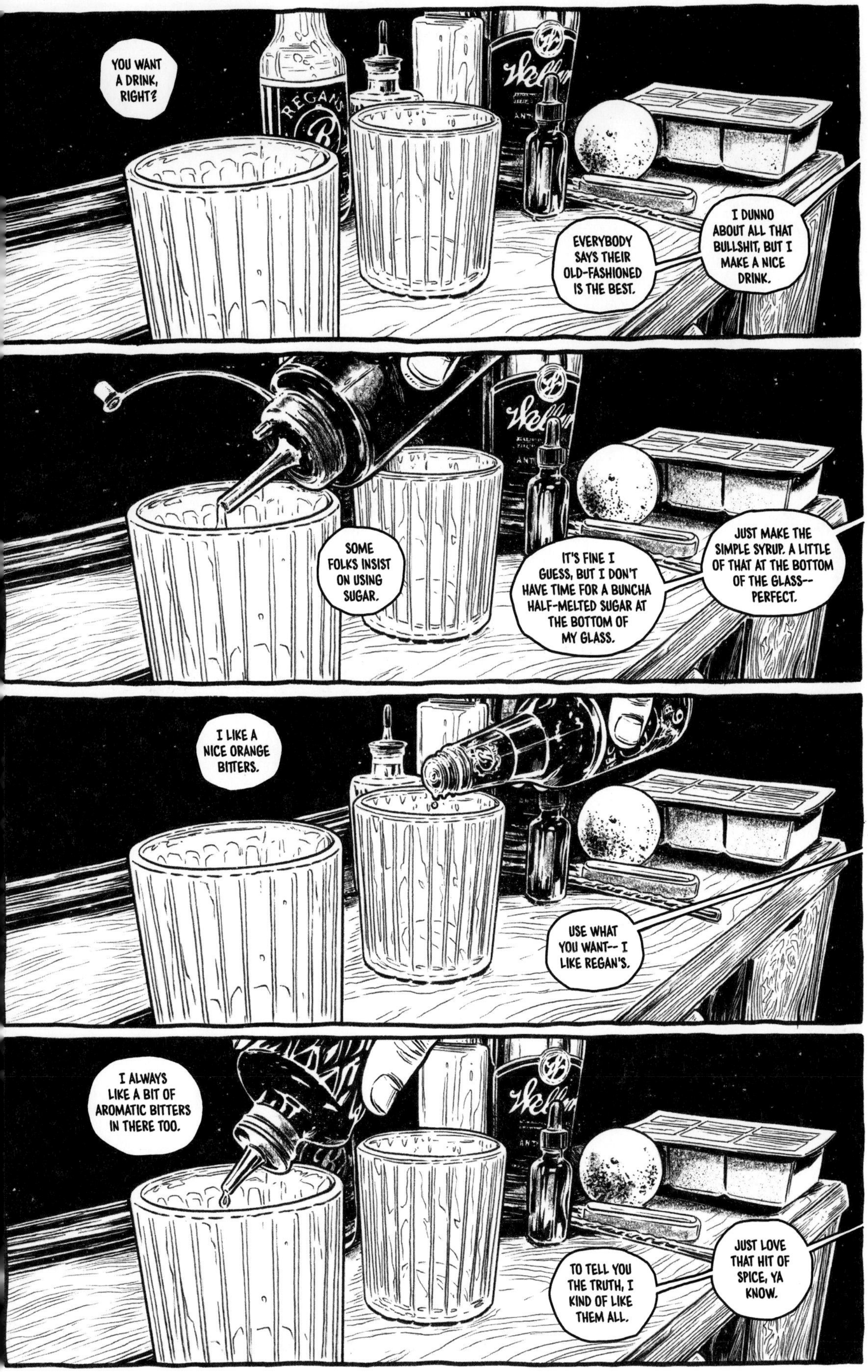
YOU WANT A DRINK, RIGHT?
EVERYBODY SAYS THEIR OLD-FASHIONED IS THE BEST.
I DUNNO ABOUT ALL THAT BULLSHIT, BUT I MAKE A NICE DRINK.
SOME FOLKS INSIST ON USING SUGAR.
IT'S FINE I GUESS, BUT I DON'T HAVE TIME FOR A BUNCHA HALF-MELTED SUGAR AT THE BOTTOM OF MY GLASS.
JUST MAKE THE SIMPLE SYRUP. A LITTLE OF THAT AT THE BOTTOM OF THE GLASS-- PERFECT.
I LIKE A NICE ORANGE BITTERS.
USE WHAT YOU WANT-- I LIKE REGAN'S.
I ALWAYS LIKE A BIT OF AROMATIC BITTERS IN THERE TOO.
TO TELL YOU THE TRUTH, I KIND OF LIKE THEM ALL.
JUST LOVE THAT HIT OF SPICE, YA KNOW.

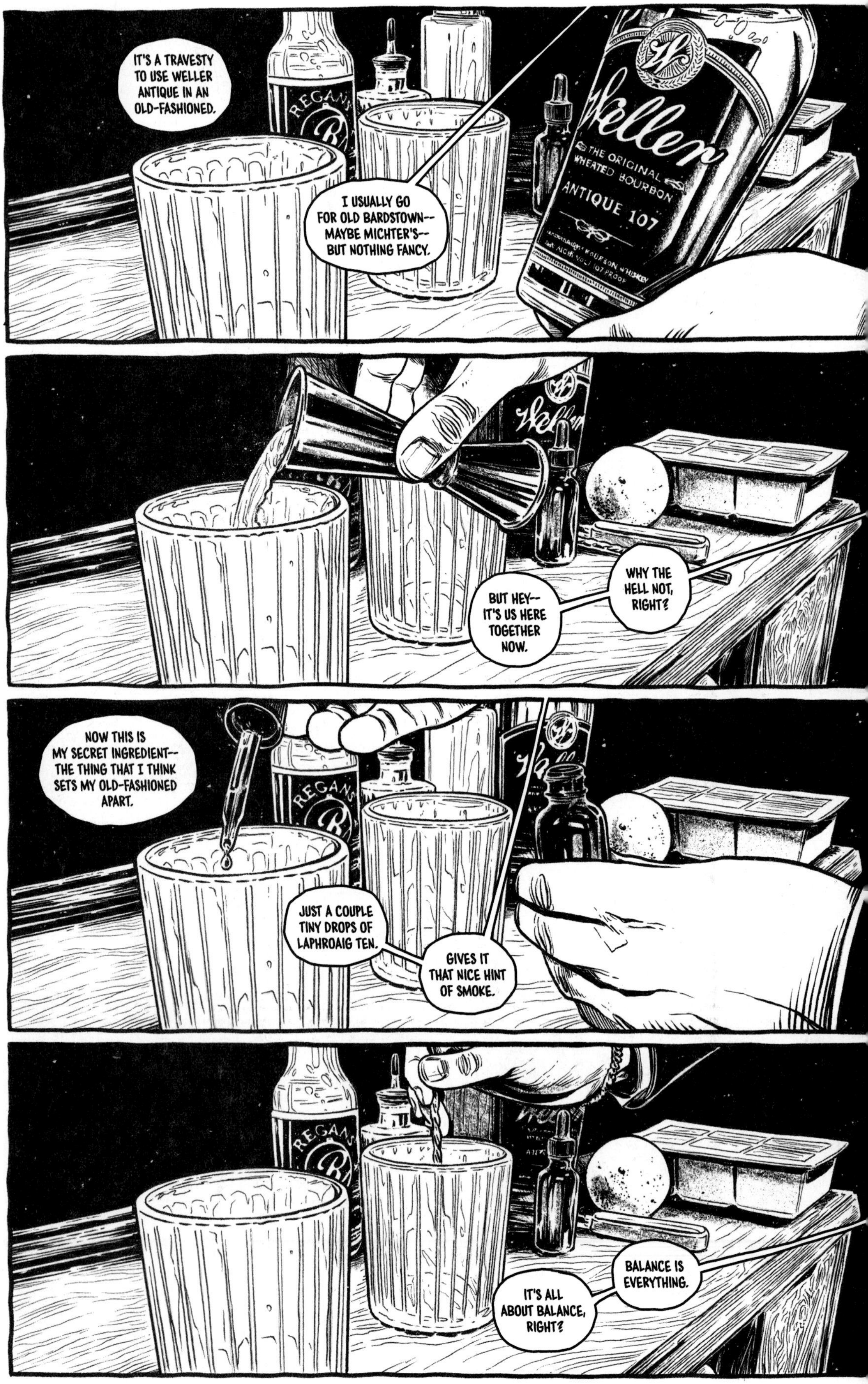
IT'S A TRAVESTY TO USE WELLER ANTIQUE IN AN OLD-FASHIONED.
I USUALLY GO FOR OLD BARDSTOWN-- MAYBE MICHTER'S-- BUT NOTHING FANCY.
REGANS
Weller
THE ORIGINAL WHEATED BOURBON
ANTIQUE 107
BUT HEY-- IT'S US HERE TOGETHER NOW.
WHY THE HELL NOT, RIGHT?
NOW THIS IS MY SECRET INGREDIENT-- THE THING THAT I THINK SETS MY OLD-FASHIONED APART.
JUST A COUPLE TINY DROPS OF LAPHROAIG TEN.
GIVES IT THAT NICE HINT OF SMOKE.
IT'S ALL ABOUT BALANCE, RIGHT?
BALANCE IS EVERYTHING.

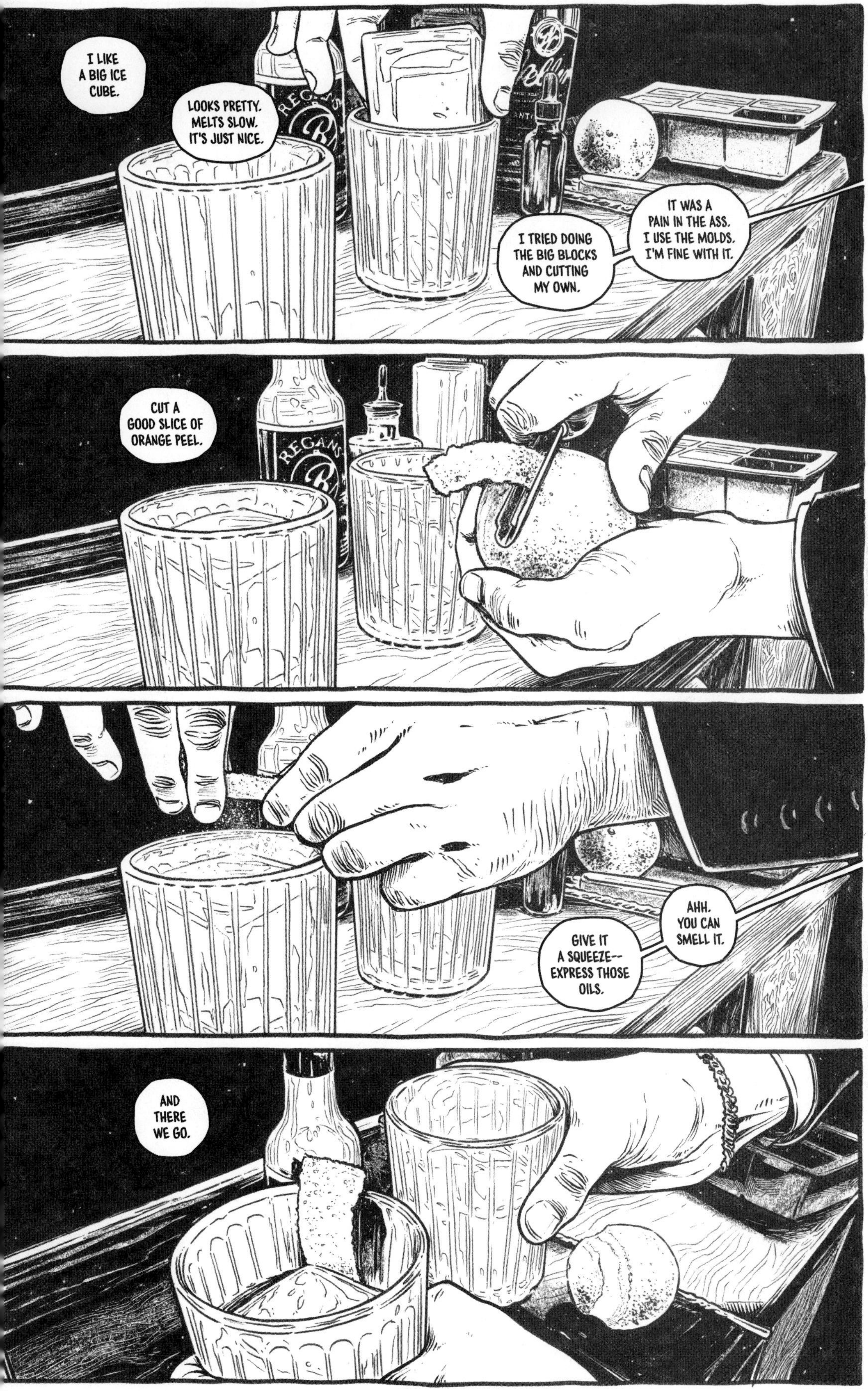

I LIKE A BIG ICE CUBE.
LOOKS PRETTY. MELTS SLOW. IT'S JUST NICE.
I TRIED DOING THE BIG BLOCKS AND CUTTING MY OWN.
IT WAS A PAIN IN THE ASS. I USE THE MOLDS. I'M FINE WITH IT.
CUT A GOOD SLICE OF ORANGE PEEL.
GIVE IT A SQUEEZE-- EXPRESS THOSE OILS.
AHH. YOU CAN SMELL IT.
AND THERE WE GO.

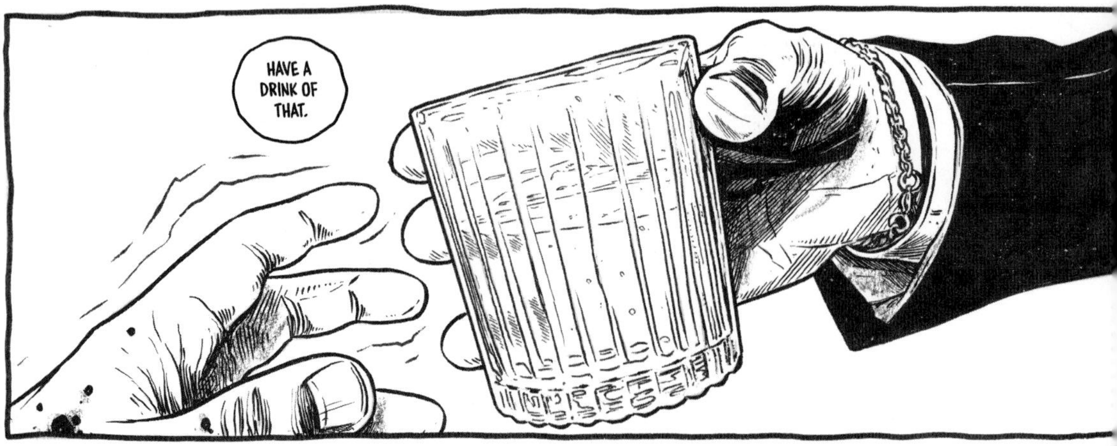
HAVE A DRINK OF THAT.

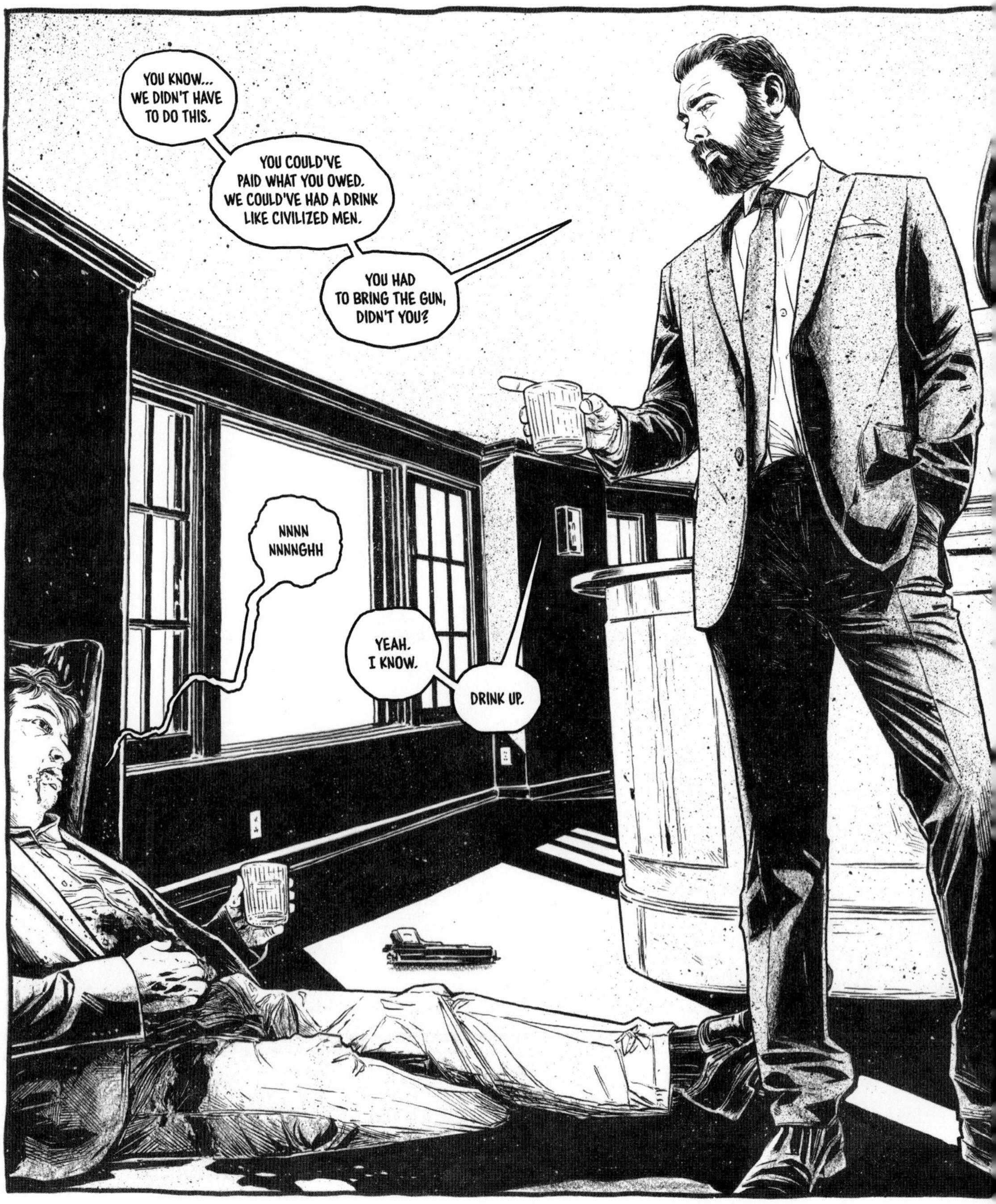
YOU KNOW... WE DIDN'T HAVE TO DO THIS.
YOU COULD'VE PAID WHAT YOU OWED. WE COULD'VE HAD A DRINK LIKE CIVILIZED MEN.
YOU HAD TO BRING THE GUN, DIDN'T YOU?
NNNN NNNNGHH
YEAH. I KNOW.
DRINK UP.

I Will Do
Dark Things

I LOOK OUT THERE-- AT THE WORLD OUTSIDE.
I SEE THE THINGS MOVING AND SOMETHING STIRS INSIDE OF ME.
COMMERCIAL SPACE FOR LEASE
I SHOULDN'T GO OUT THERE.
I SHOULDN'T.
IF I DO... THERE WILL BE NO END TO MY HORRORS.

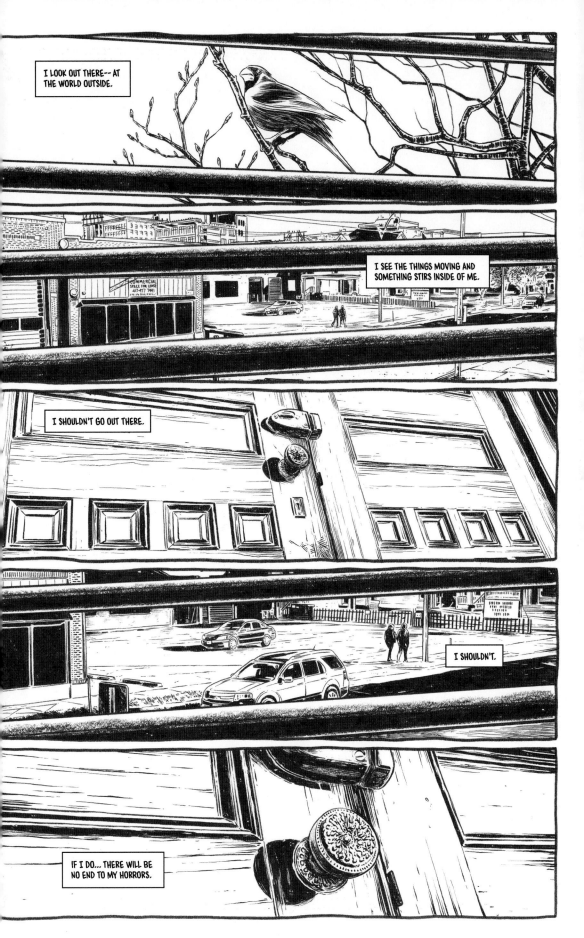

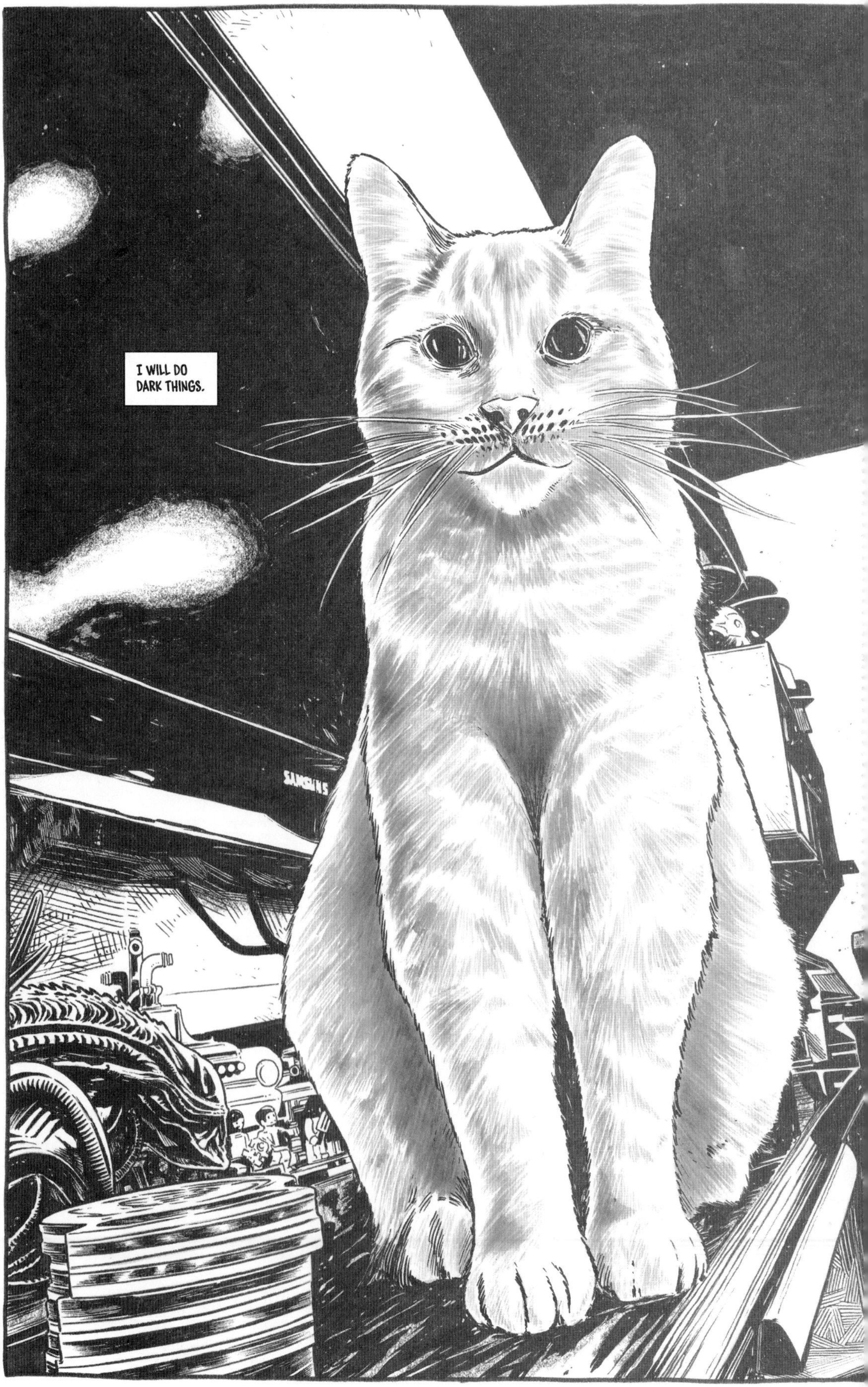
I WILL DO
DARK THINGS.

THE COIN

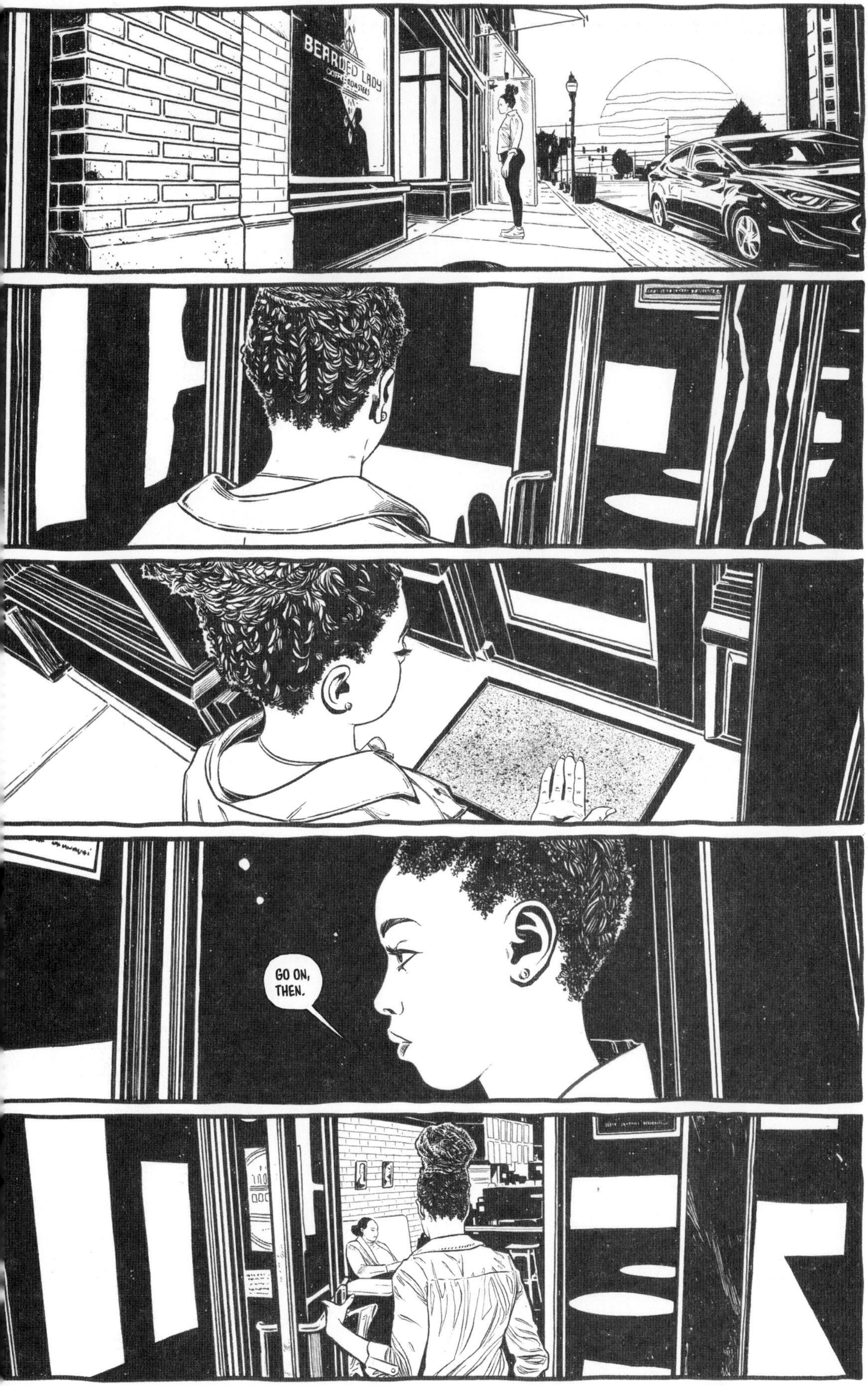
BEARDED LADY
COFFEE ROASTERS
GO ON, THEN.

SHIKK

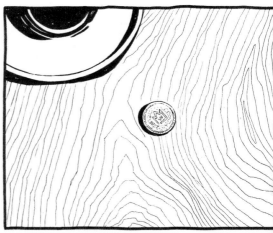

TELL ME ABOUT THE COIN.

OKAY...

BUT IS THAT REALLY THE THING YOU WANT TO ASK?

WH-WHERE IS MY FRIEND MALCOLM?

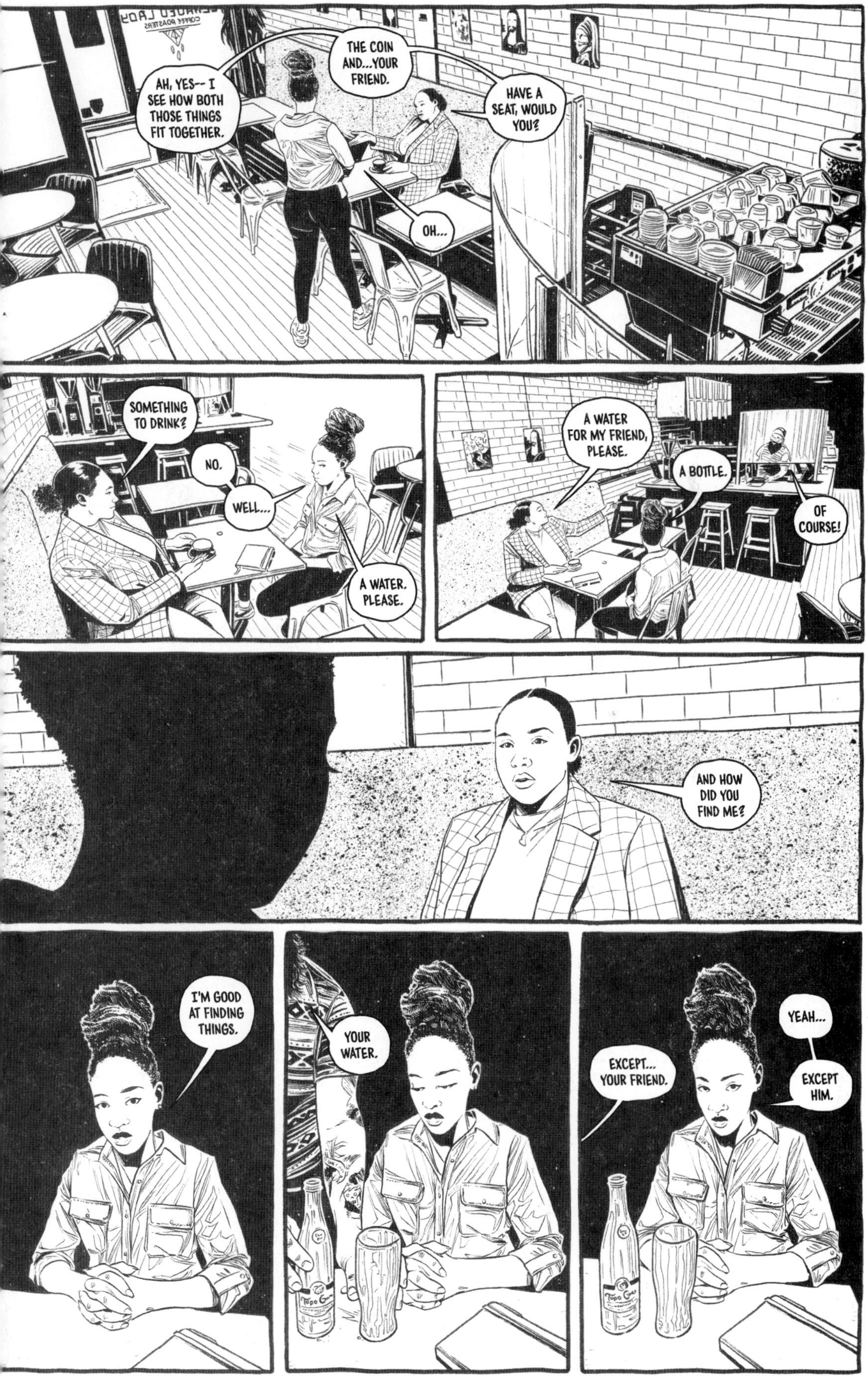
THE COIN AND...YOUR FRIEND.
AH, YES-- I SEE HOW BOTH THOSE THINGS FIT TOGETHER.
HAVE A SEAT, WOULD YOU?
OH...
SOMETHING TO DRINK?
NO.
WELL...
A WATER, PLEASE.
A WATER FOR MY FRIEND, PLEASE.
A BOTTLE.
OF COURSE!
AND HOW DID YOU FIND ME?
I'M GOOD AT FINDING THINGS.
YOUR WATER.
EXCEPT... YOUR FRIEND.
YEAH...
EXCEPT HIM.

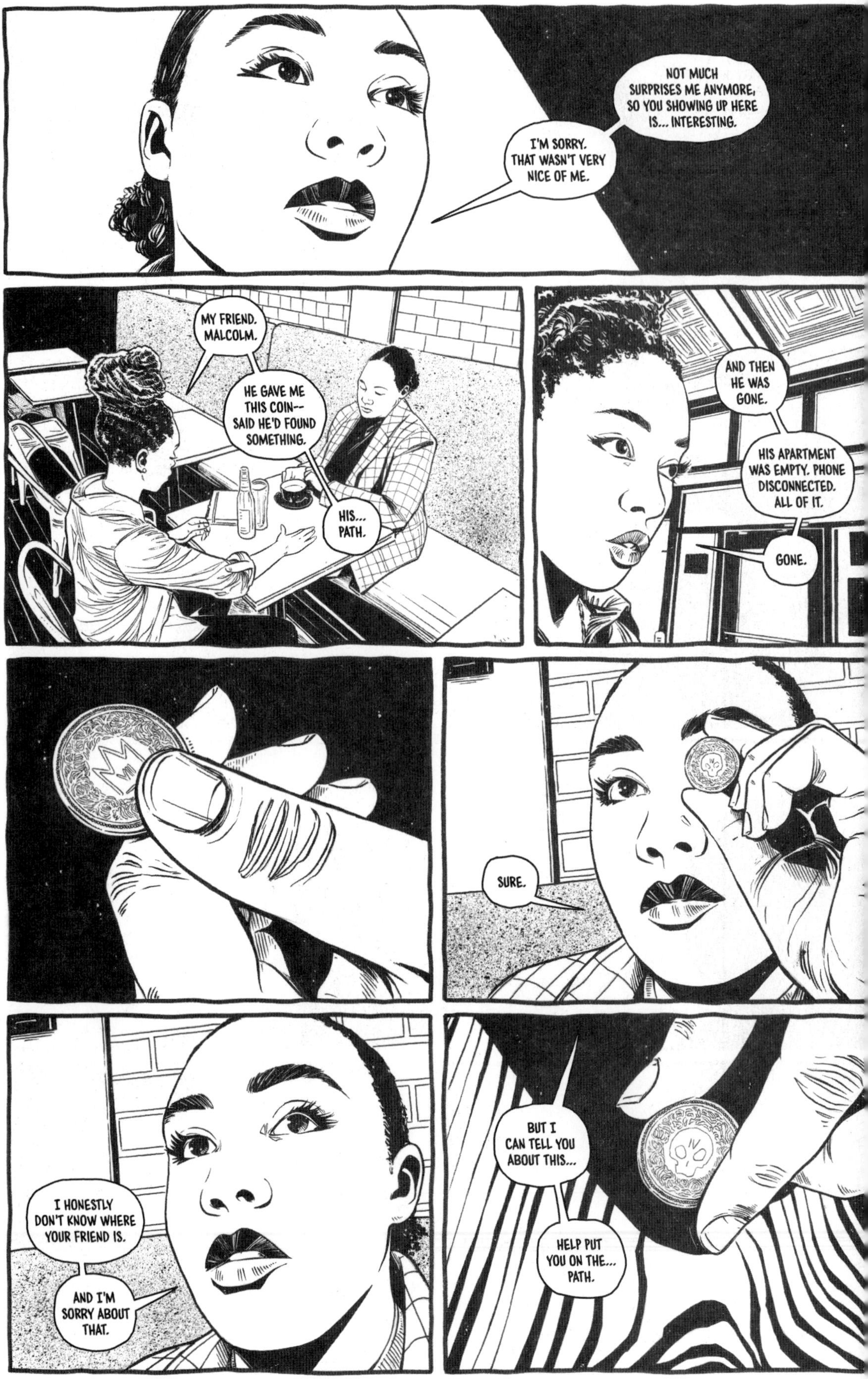
NOT MUCH SURPRISES ME ANYMORE, SO YOU SHOWING UP HERE IS... INTERESTING.
I'M SORRY. THAT WASN'T VERY NICE OF ME.
MY FRIEND. MALCOLM.
HE GAVE ME THIS COIN-- SAID HE'D FOUND SOMETHING.
HIS... PATH.
AND THEN HE WAS GONE.
HIS APARTMENT WAS EMPTY. PHONE DISCONNECTED. ALL OF IT.
GONE.
SURE.
I HONESTLY DON'T KNOW WHERE YOUR FRIEND IS.
AND I'M SORRY ABOUT THAT.
BUT I CAN TELL YOU ABOUT THIS...
HELP PUT YOU ON THE... PATH.

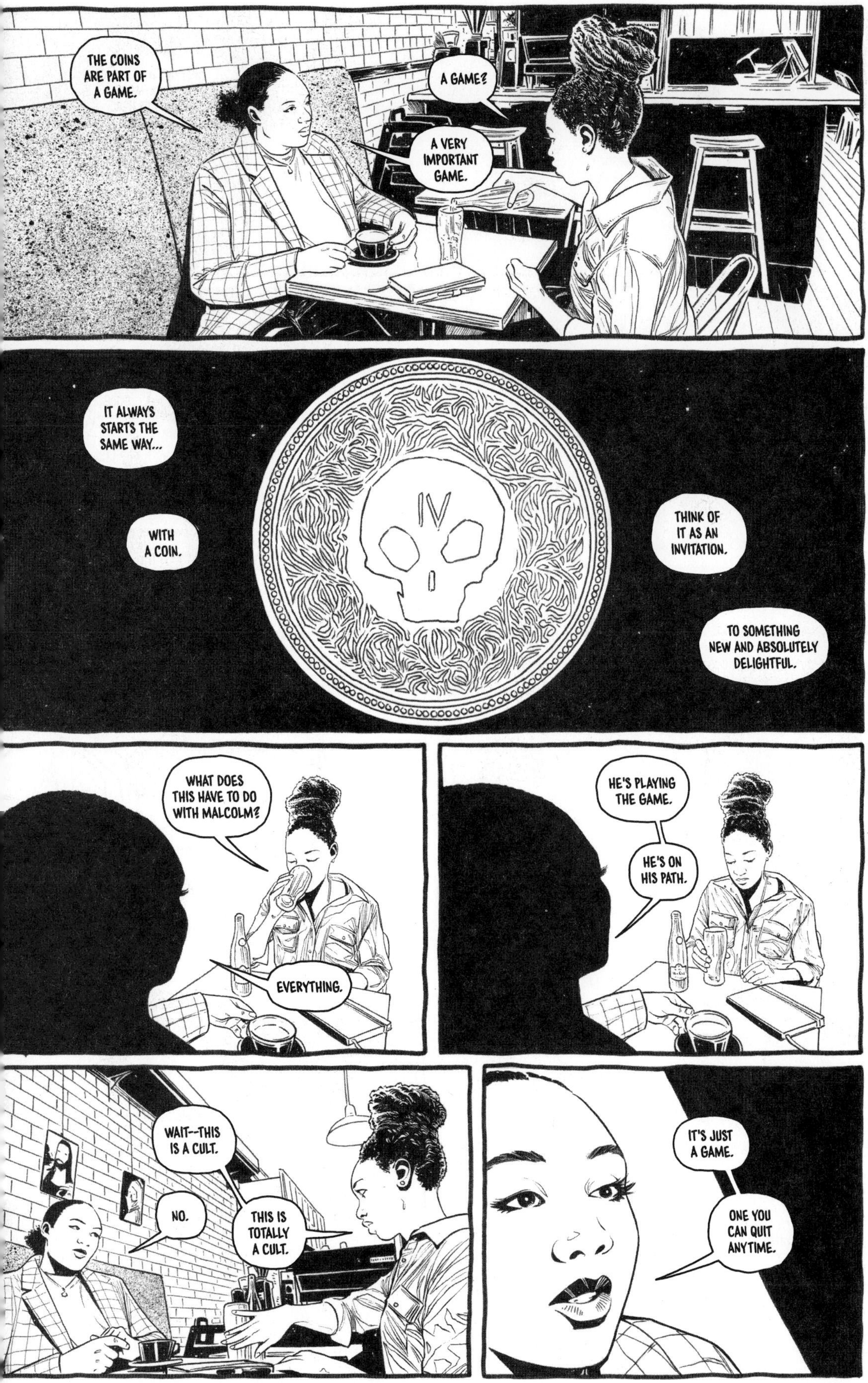
THE COINS ARE PART OF A GAME.
A GAME?
A VERY IMPORTANT GAME.
IT ALWAYS STARTS THE SAME WAY...
WITH A COIN.
IV
THINK OF IT AS AN INVITATION.
TO SOMETHING NEW AND ABSOLUTELY DELIGHTFUL.
WHAT DOES THIS HAVE TO DO WITH MALCOLM?
EVERYTHING.
HE'S PLAYING THE GAME.
HE'S ON HIS PATH.
WAIT--THIS IS A CULT.
NO.
THIS IS TOTALLY A CULT.
IT'S JUST A GAME.
ONE YOU CAN QUIT ANYTIME.

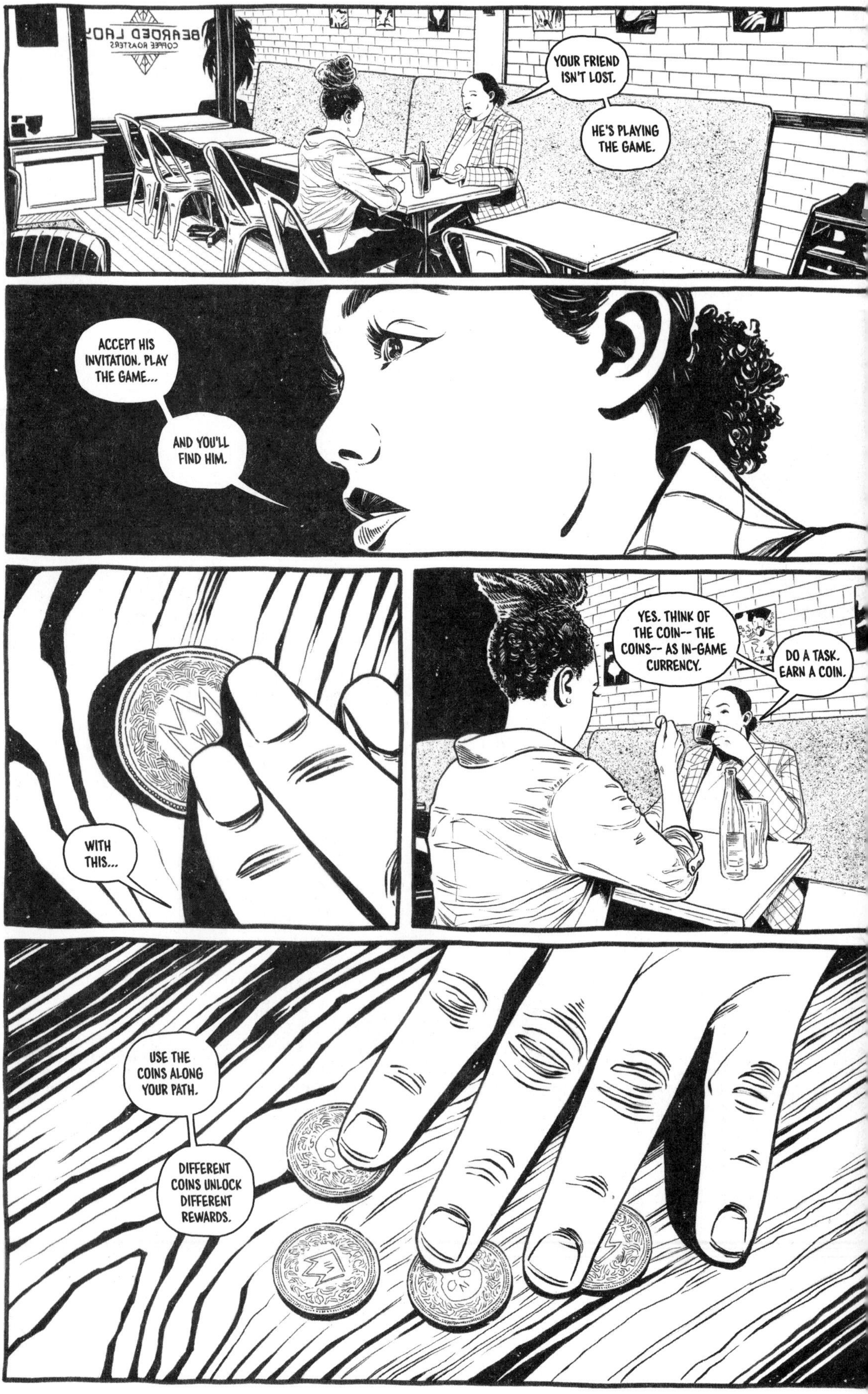
YOUR FRIEND ISN'T LOST.
HE'S PLAYING THE GAME.
ACCEPT HIS INVITATION. PLAY THE GAME...
AND YOU'LL FIND HIM.
WITH THIS...
YES. THINK OF THE COIN-- THE COINS-- AS IN-GAME CURRENCY.
DO A TASK. EARN A COIN.
USE THE COINS ALONG YOUR PATH.
DIFFERENT COINS UNLOCK DIFFERENT REWARDS.

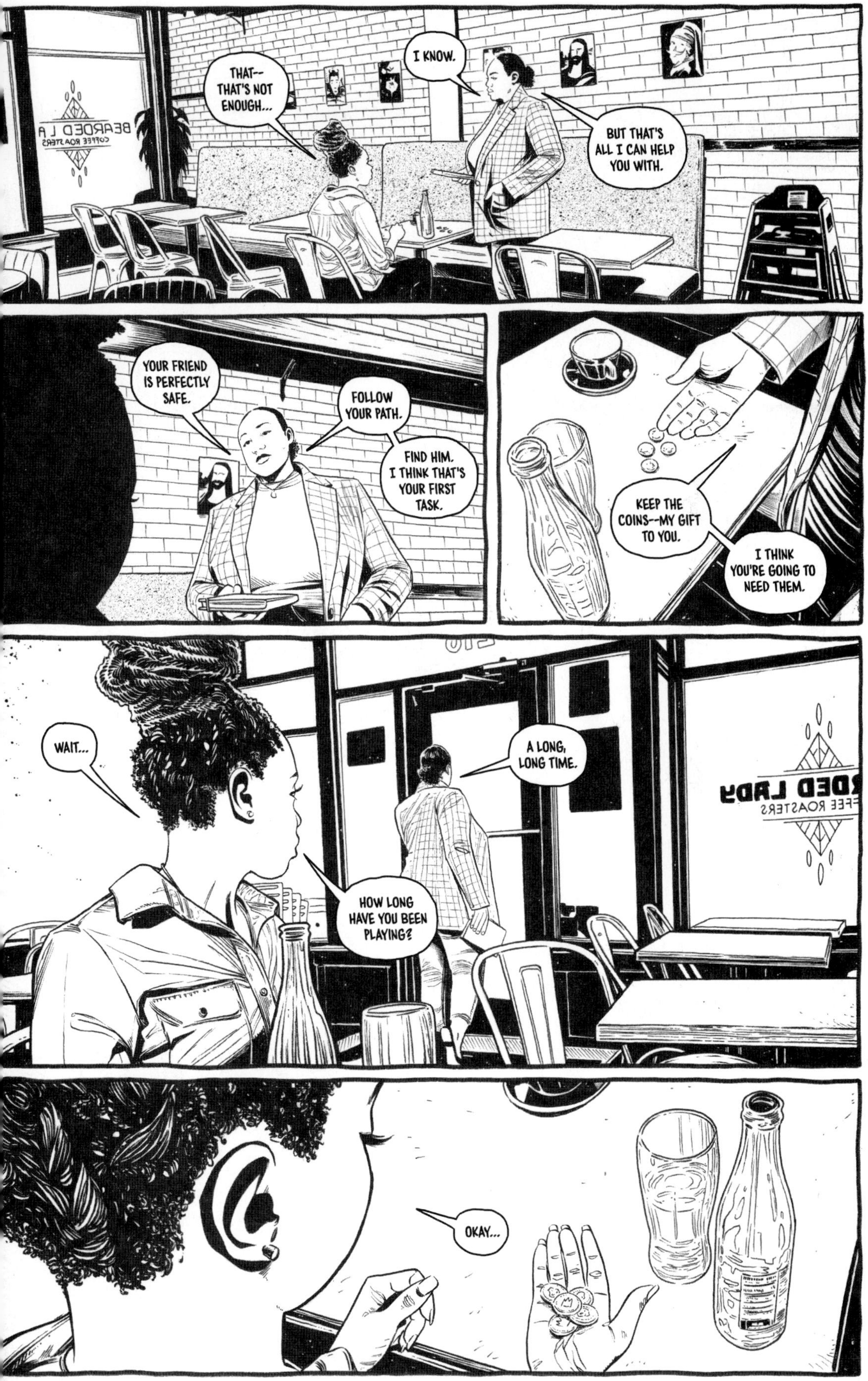
THAT--
THAT'S NOT ENOUGH...
I KNOW.
BUT THAT'S ALL I CAN HELP YOU WITH.
BEARDED L
COFFEE ROASTERS
YOUR FRIEND IS PERFECTLY SAFE.
FOLLOW YOUR PATH.
FIND HIM. I THINK THAT'S YOUR FIRST TASK.
KEEP THE COINS--MY GIFT TO YOU.
I THINK YOU'RE GOING TO NEED THEM.
WAIT...
A LONG, LONG TIME.
HOW LONG HAVE YOU BEEN PLAYING?
OKAY...

THE ARSENAL

OKAY...

I GUESS THIS IS IT.

I HOPE IT'S ENOUGH.

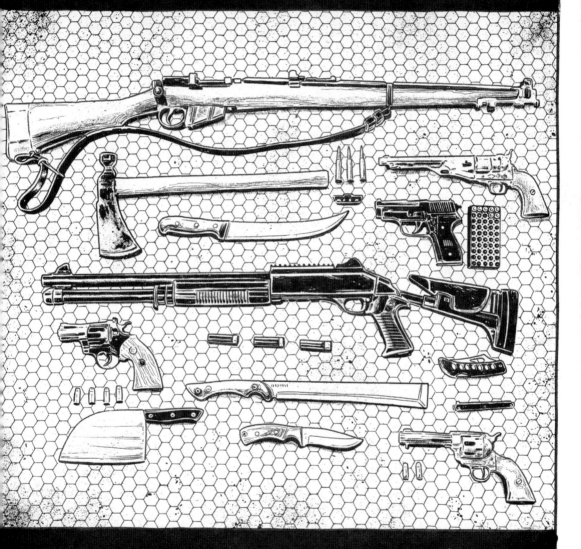

IT'S FUNNY... I NEVER EVEN LIKED
GUNS BEFORE ALL OF THIS--

BEFORE THEY CAME....

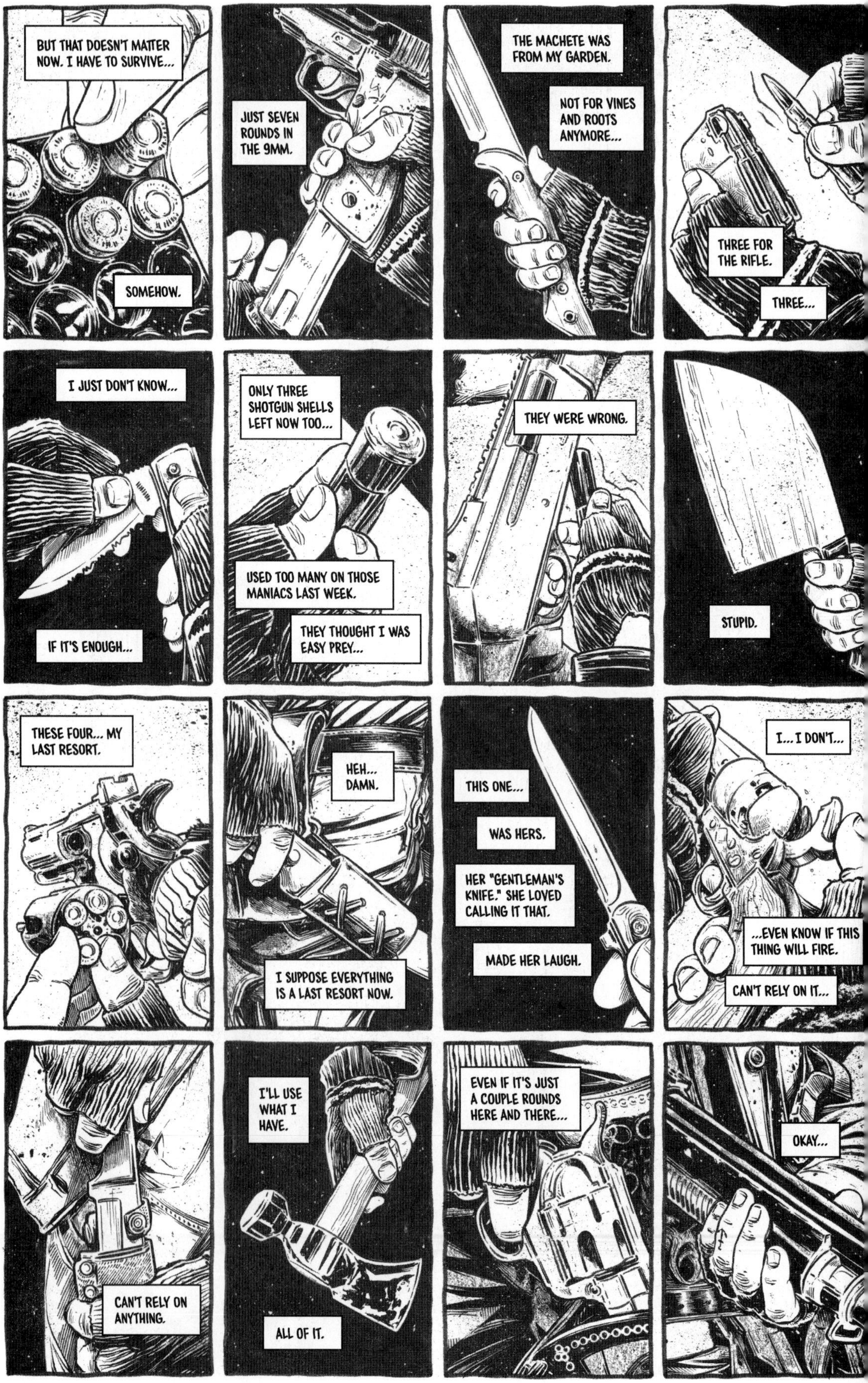
BUT THAT DOESN'T MATTER NOW. I HAVE TO SURVIVE...
SOMEHOW.
JUST SEVEN ROUNDS IN THE 9MM.
THE MACHETE WAS FROM MY GARDEN.
NOT FOR VINES AND ROOTS ANYMORE...
THREE FOR THE RIFLE.
THREE...
I JUST DON'T KNOW...
IF IT'S ENOUGH...
ONLY THREE SHOTGUN SHELLS LEFT NOW TOO...
USED TOO MANY ON THOSE MANIACS LAST WEEK.
THEY THOUGHT I WAS EASY PREY...
THEY WERE WRONG.
STUPID.
THESE FOUR... MY LAST RESORT.
HEH... DAMN.
I SUPPOSE EVERYTHING IS A LAST RESORT NOW.
THIS ONE...
WAS HERS.
HER "GENTLEMAN'S KNIFE." SHE LOVED CALLING IT THAT.
MADE HER LAUGH.
I... I DON'T...
...EVEN KNOW IF THIS THING WILL FIRE.
CAN'T RELY ON IT...
CAN'T RELY ON ANYTHING.
I'LL USE WHAT I HAVE.
ALL OF IT.
EVEN IF IT'S JUST A COUPLE ROUNDS HERE AND THERE...
OKAY...

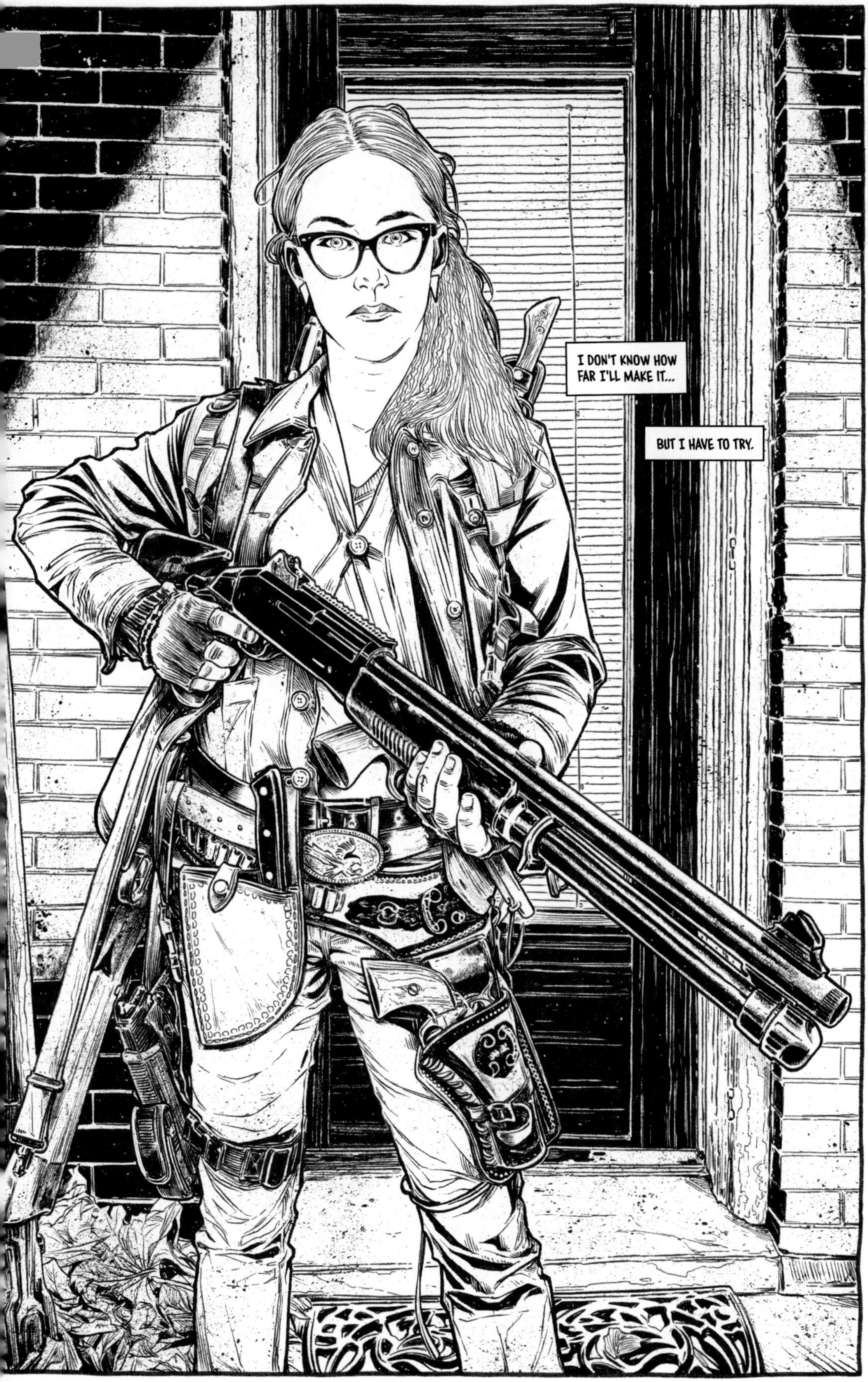
I DON'T KNOW HOW FAR I'LL MAKE IT...
BUT I HAVE TO TRY.

STILL IN HERE

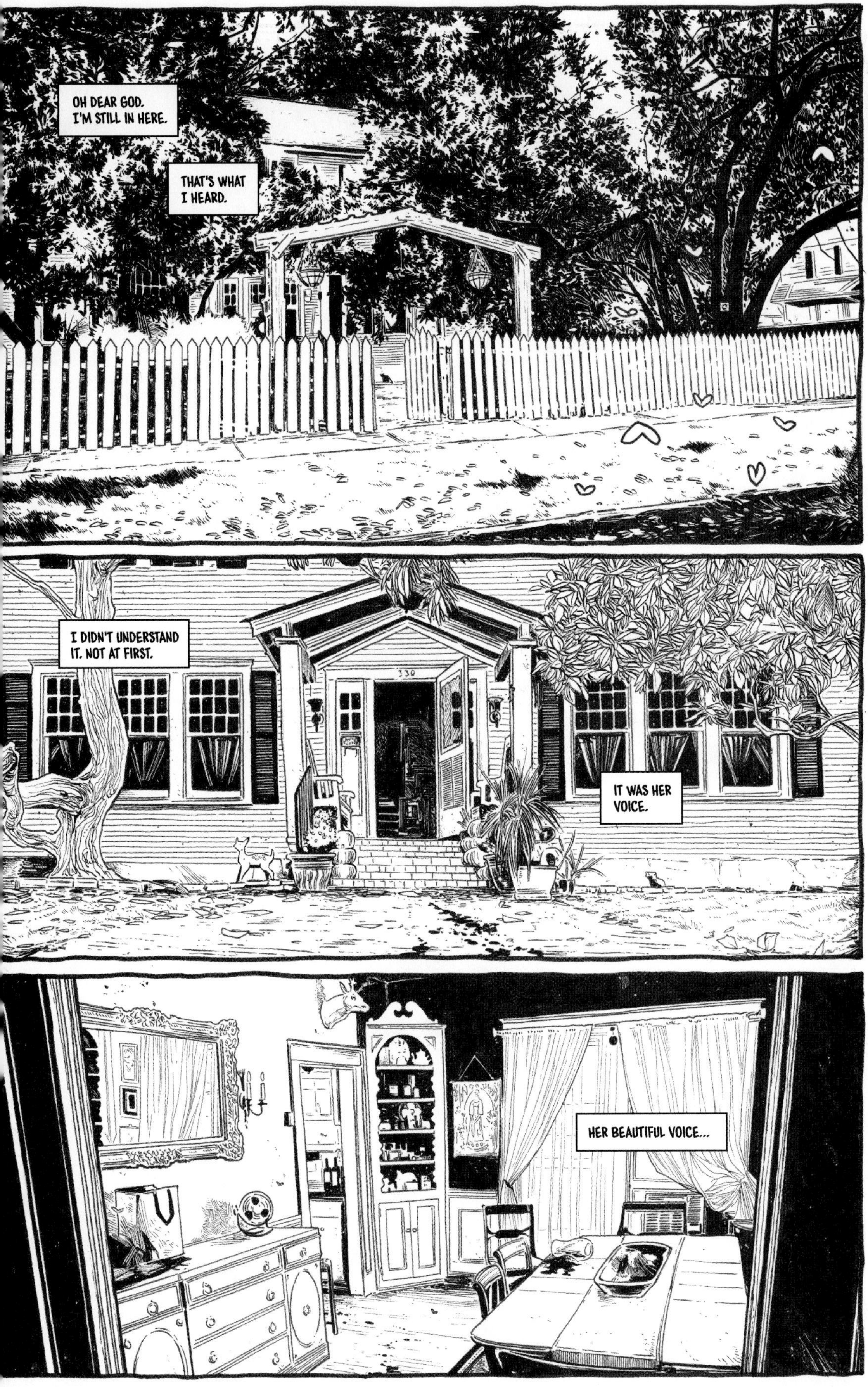
OH DEAR GOD. I'M STILL IN HERE.
THAT'S WHAT I HEARD.
I DIDN'T UNDERSTAND IT. NOT AT FIRST.
IT WAS HER VOICE.
HER BEAUTIFUL VOICE...

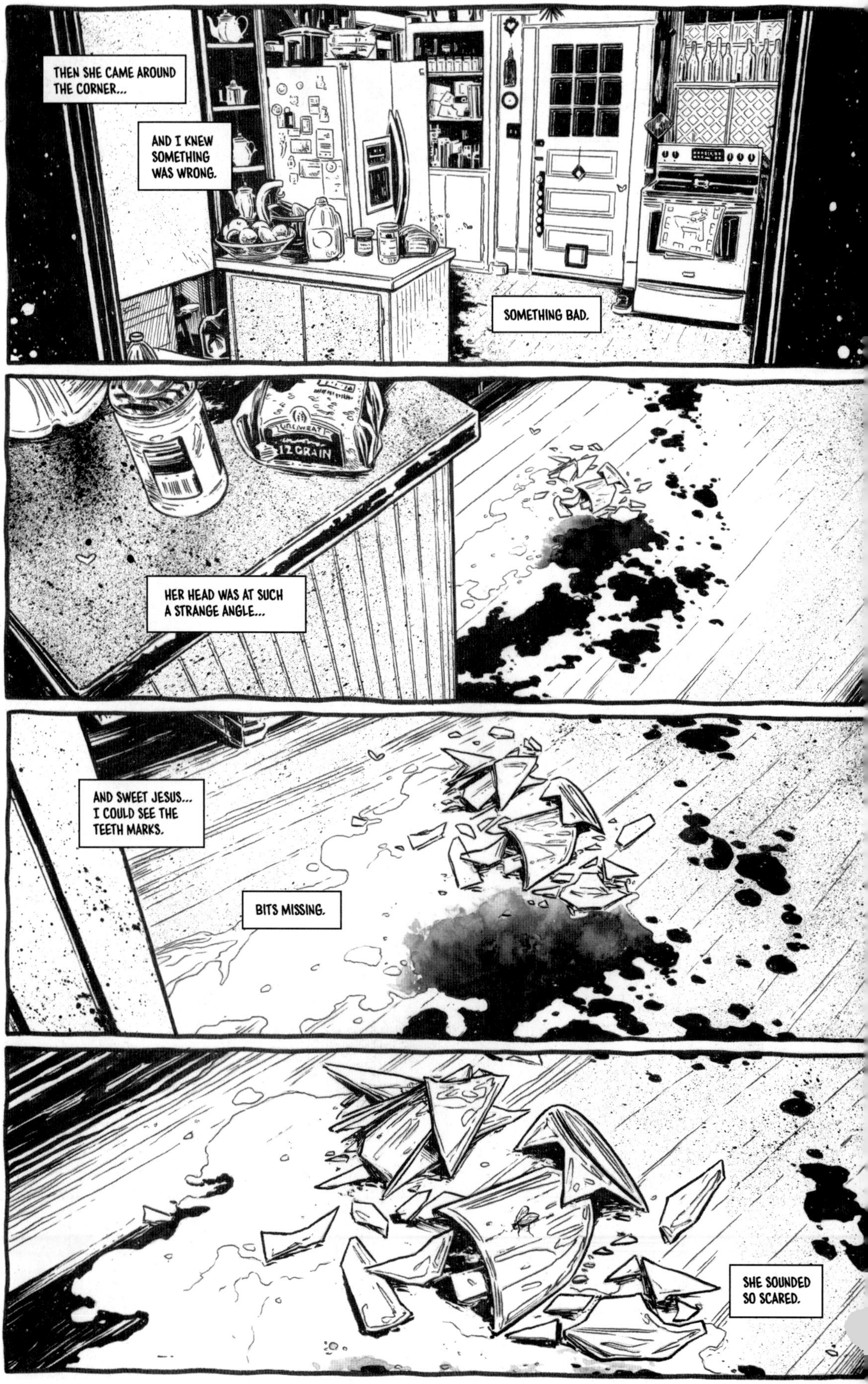
THEN SHE CAME AROUND THE CORNER...
AND I KNEW SOMETHING WAS WRONG.
SOMETHING BAD.
12 GRAIN
HER HEAD WAS AT SUCH A STRANGE ANGLE...
AND SWEET JESUS... I COULD SEE THE TEETH MARKS.
BITS MISSING.
SHE SOUNDED SO SCARED.

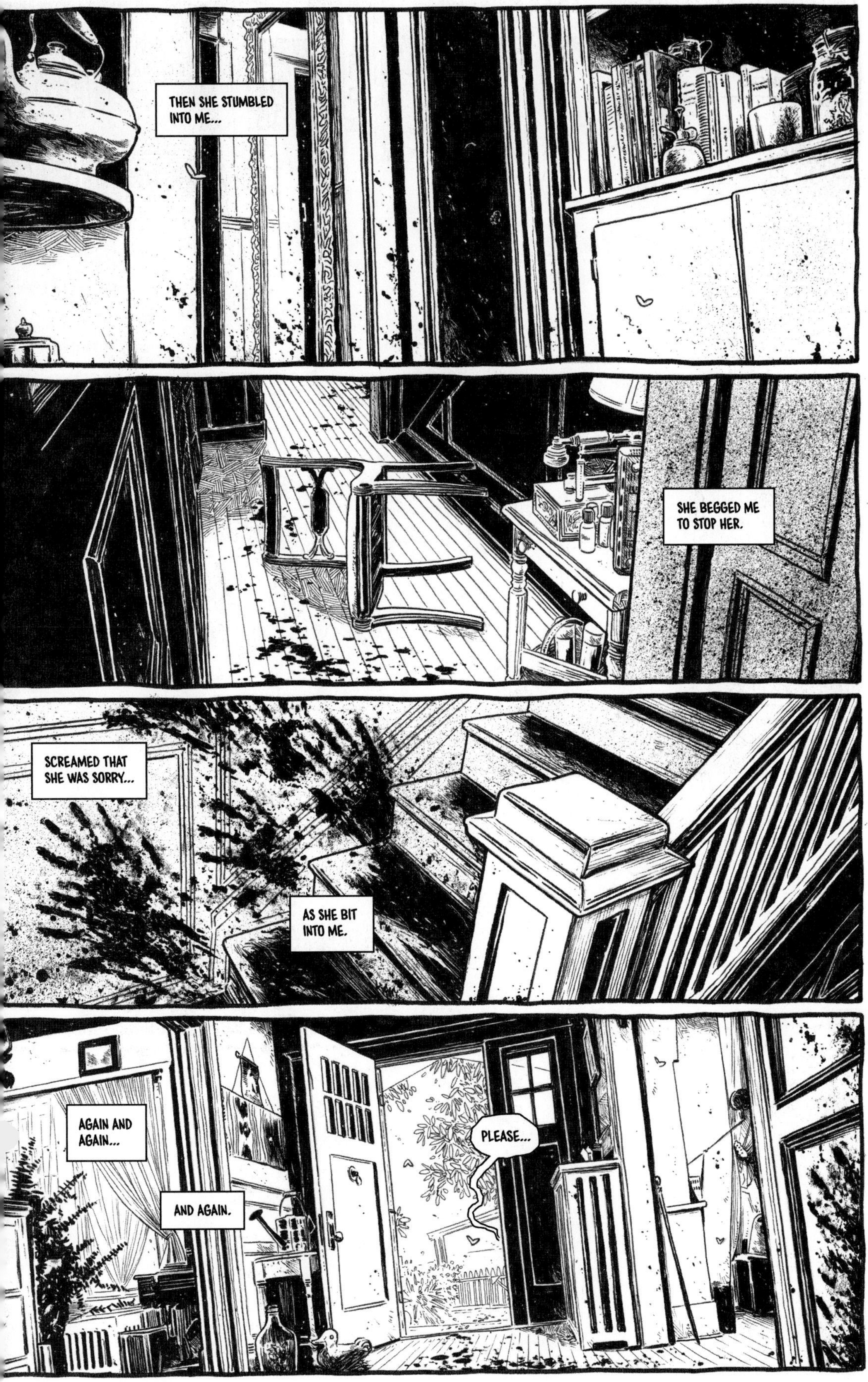
THEN SHE STUMBLED INTO ME...
SHE BEGGED ME TO STOP HER.
SCREAMED THAT SHE WAS SORRY...
AS SHE BIT INTO ME.
AGAIN AND AGAIN...
AND AGAIN.
PLEASE...

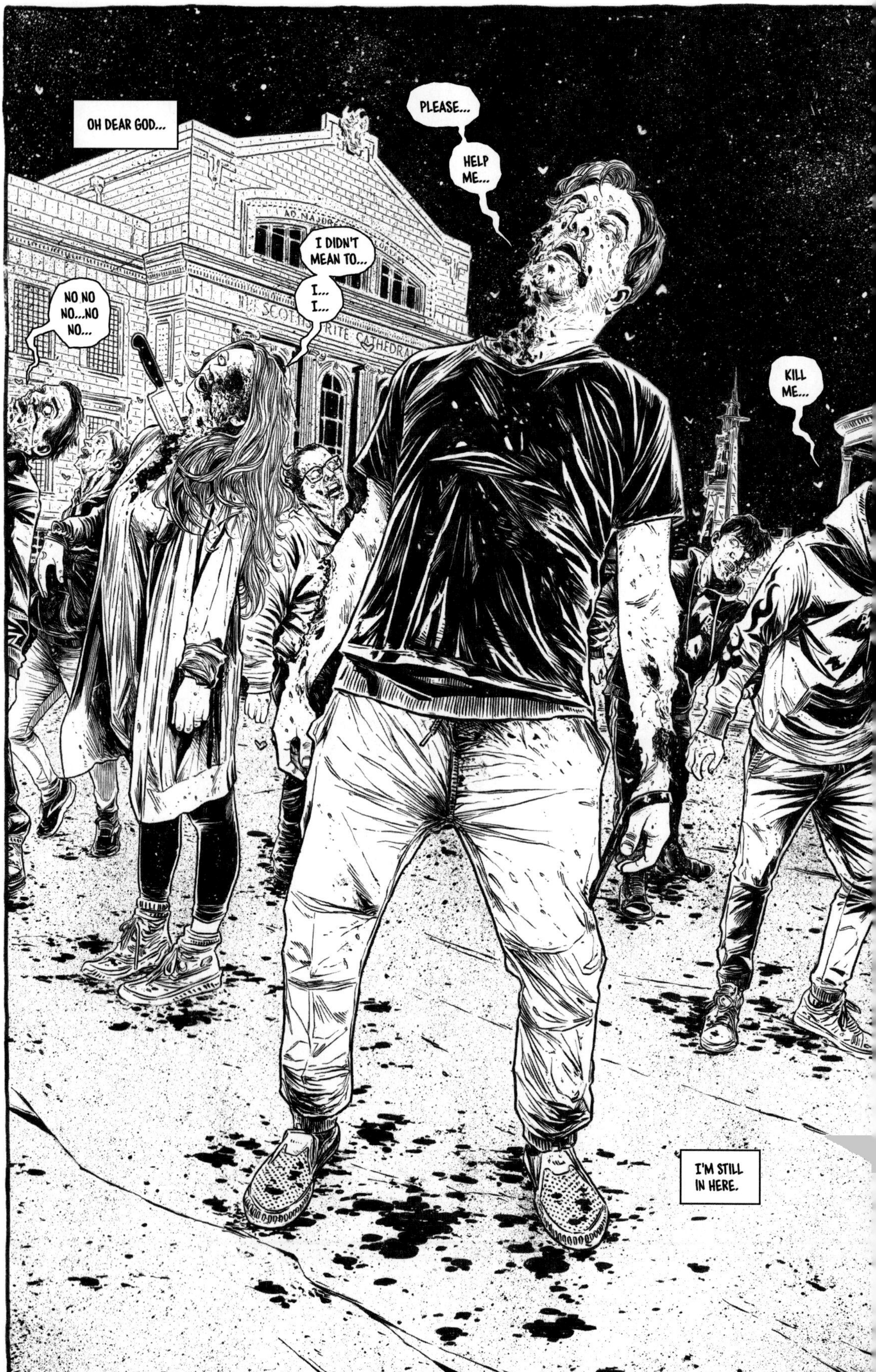
OH DEAR GOD...
PLEASE...
HELP ME...
I DIDN'T MEAN TO...
I... I...
NO NO NO...NO NO...
KILL ME...
I'M STILL IN HERE.

I'LL SLEEP

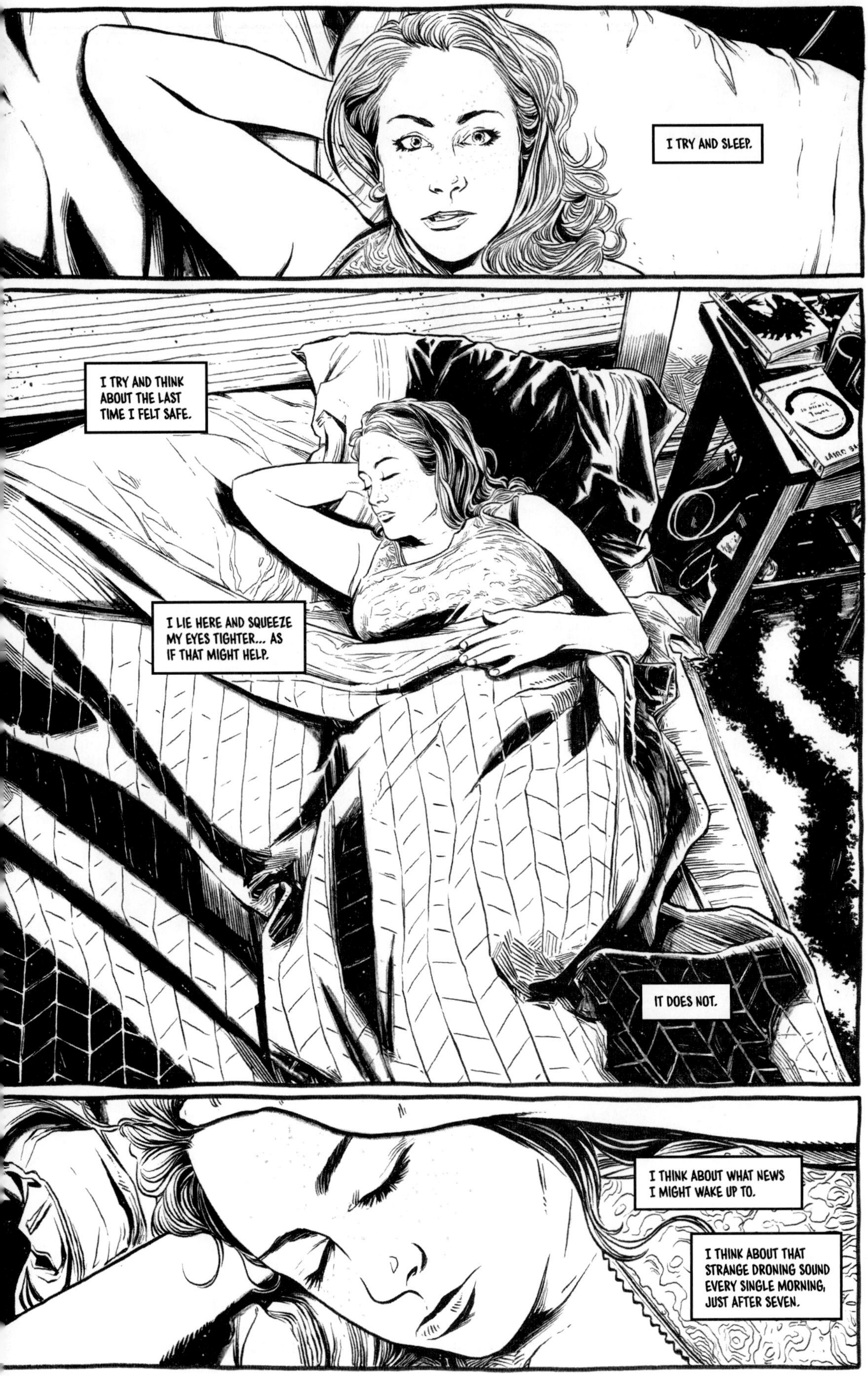
I TRY AND SLEEP.
I TRY AND THINK ABOUT THE LAST TIME I FELT SAFE.
I LIE HERE AND SQUEEZE MY EYES TIGHTER... AS IF THAT MIGHT HELP.
IT DOES NOT.
I THINK ABOUT WHAT NEWS I MIGHT WAKE UP TO.
I THINK ABOUT THAT STRANGE DRONING SOUND EVERY SINGLE MORNING, JUST AFTER SEVEN.

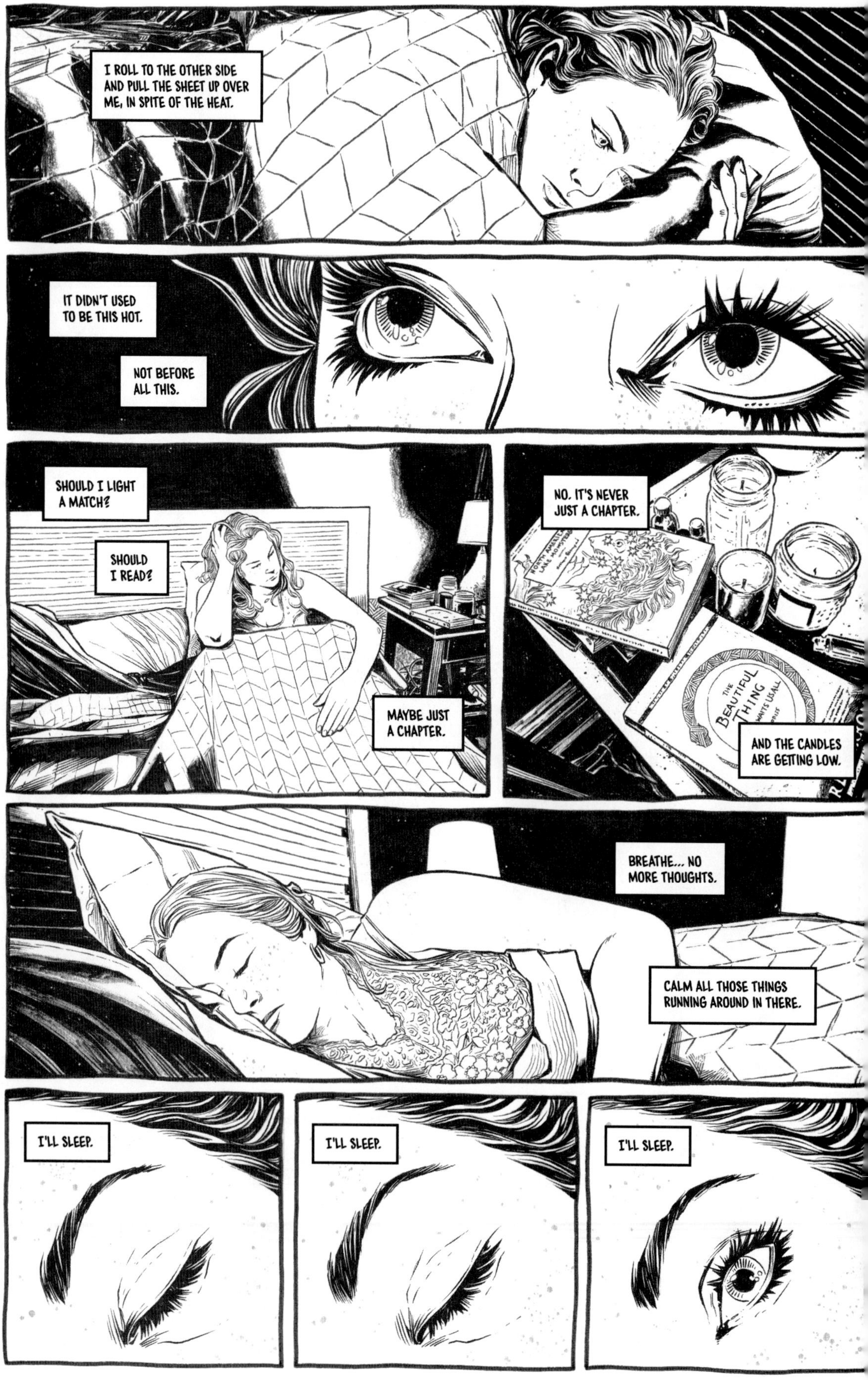
I ROLL TO THE OTHER SIDE AND PULL THE SHEET UP OVER ME, IN SPITE OF THE HEAT.
IT DIDN'T USED TO BE THIS HOT.
NOT BEFORE ALL THIS.
SHOULD I LIGHT A MATCH?
SHOULD I READ?
MAYBE JUST A CHAPTER.
NO. IT'S NEVER JUST A CHAPTER.
THE BEAUTIFUL THING
AND THE CANDLES ARE GETTING LOW.
BREATHE... NO MORE THOUGHTS.
CALM ALL THOSE THINGS RUNNING AROUND IN THERE.
I'LL SLEEP.
I'LL SLEEP.
I'LL SLEEP.

A Haunthology
Silent Night

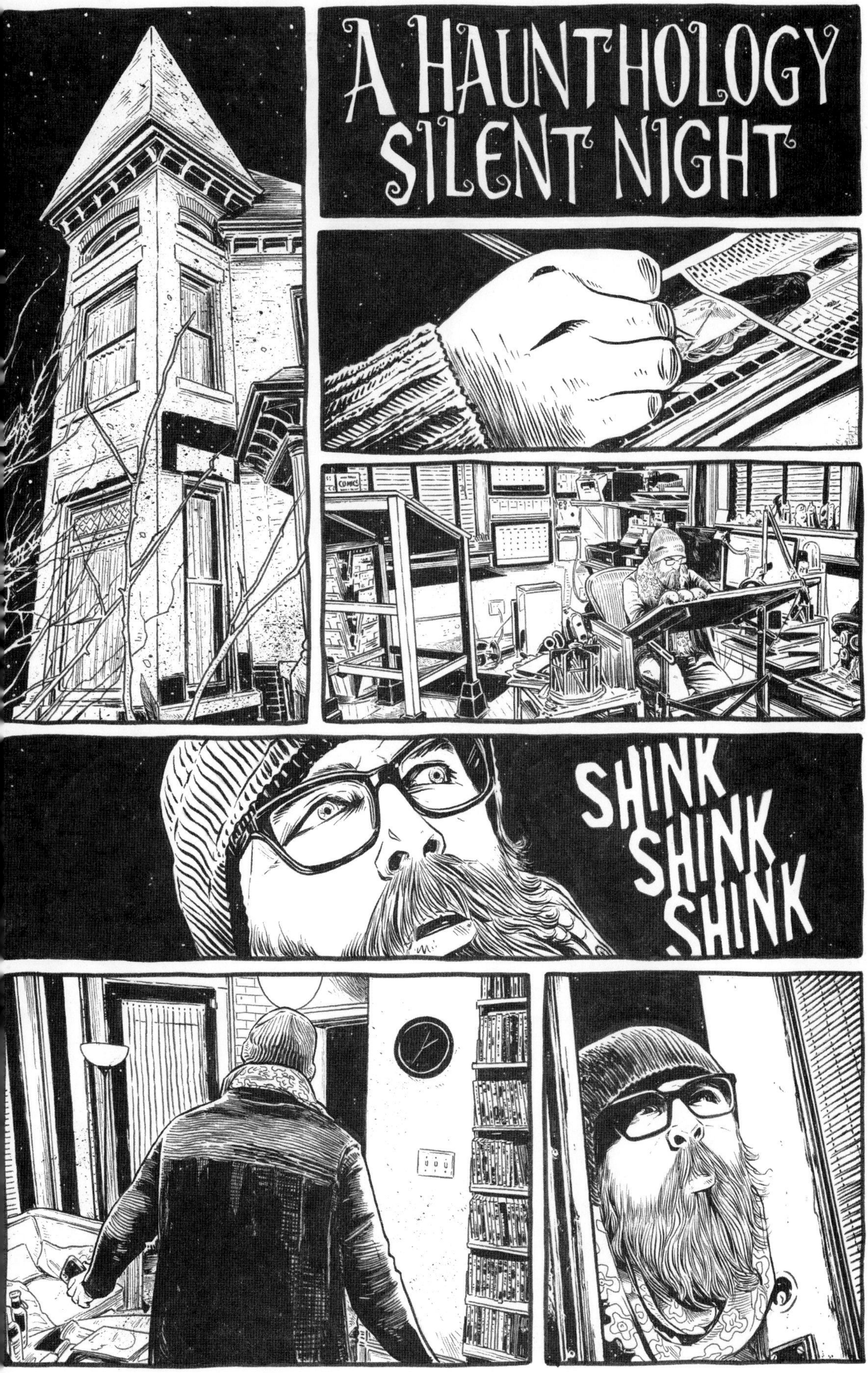
A HAUNTHOLOGY
SILENT NIGHT
COMICS
SHINK
SHINK
SHINK

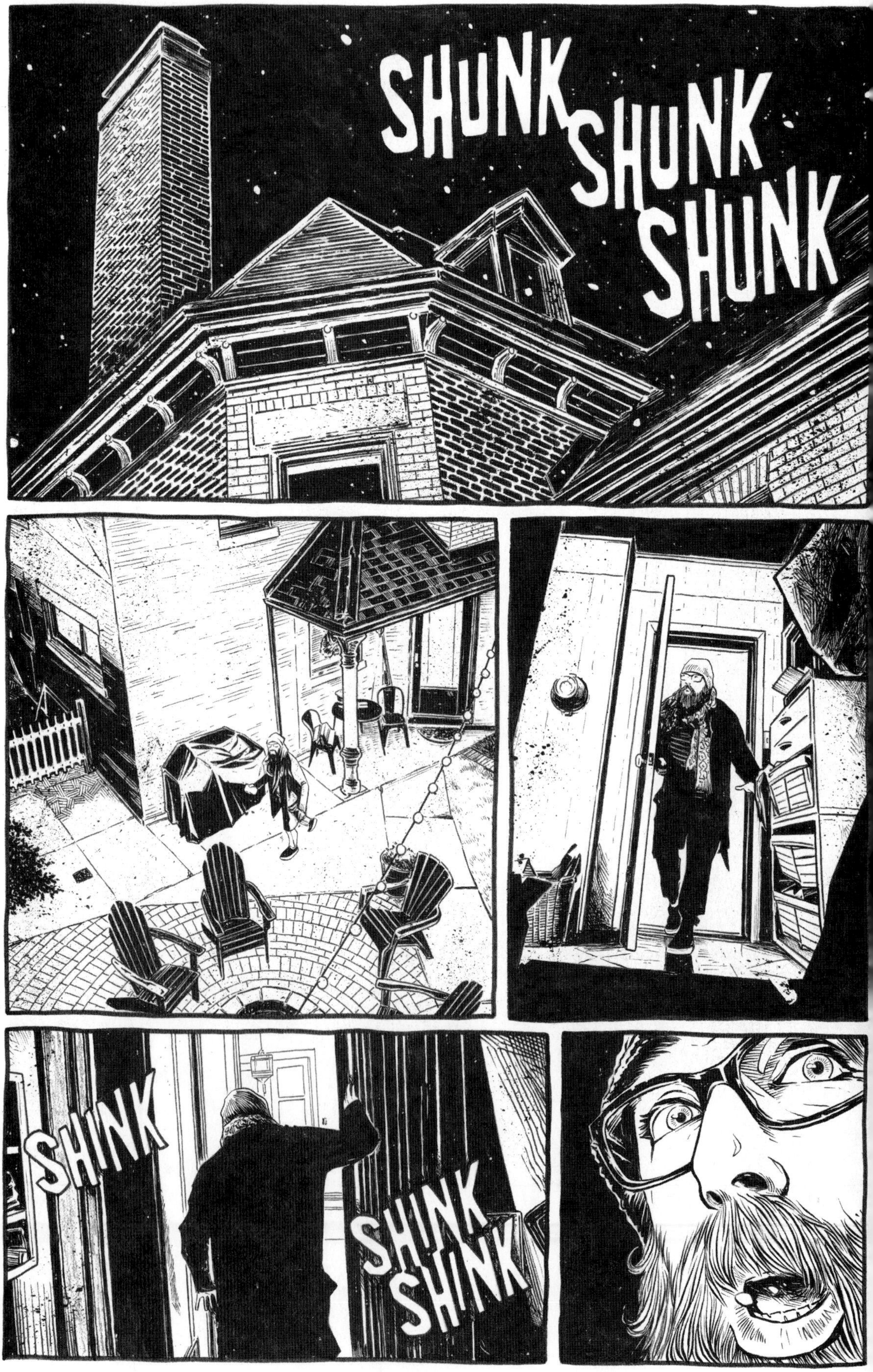
SHUNK SHUNK SHUNK
SHINK
SHINK SHINK

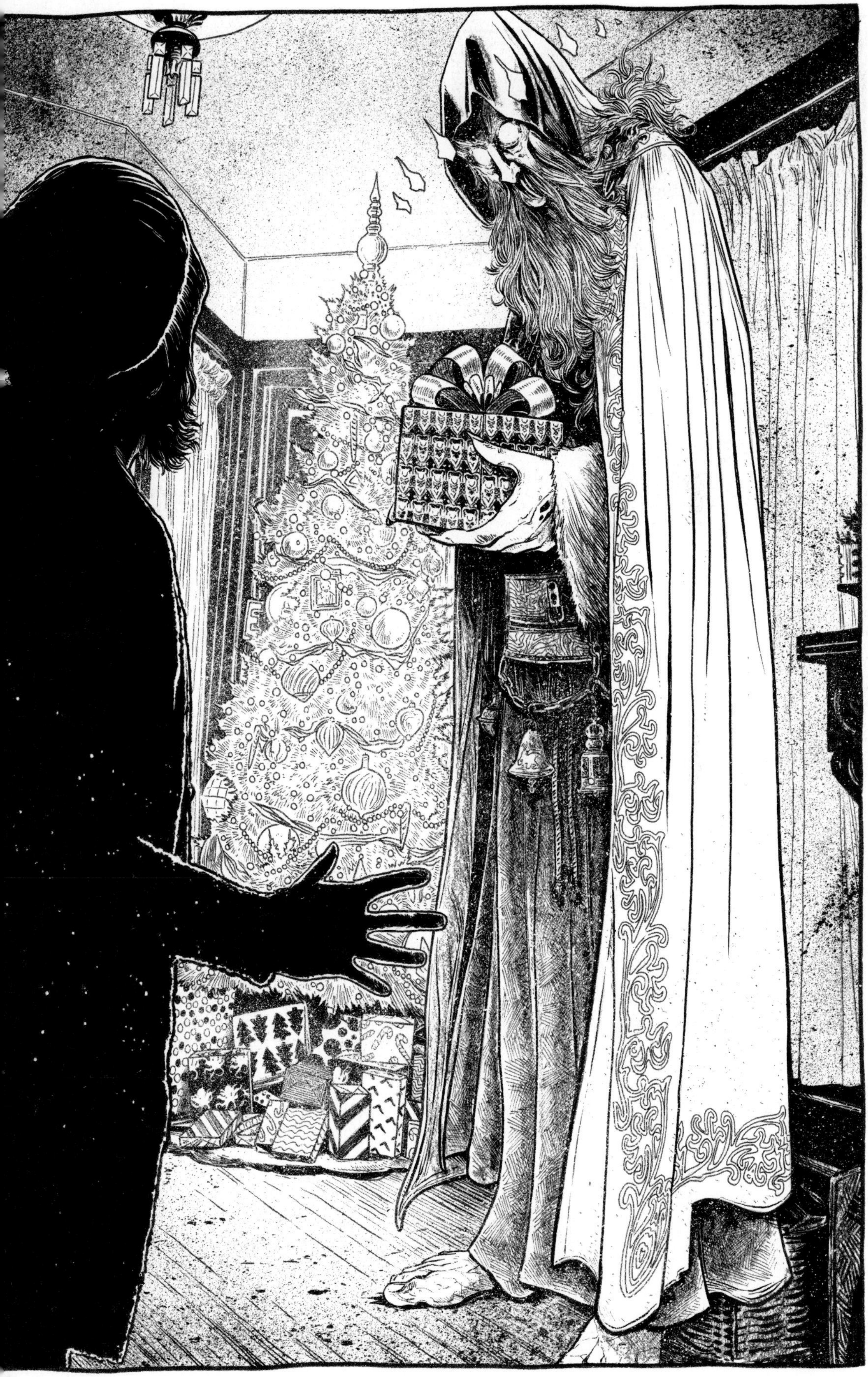

By the Sea.
From the Sea.

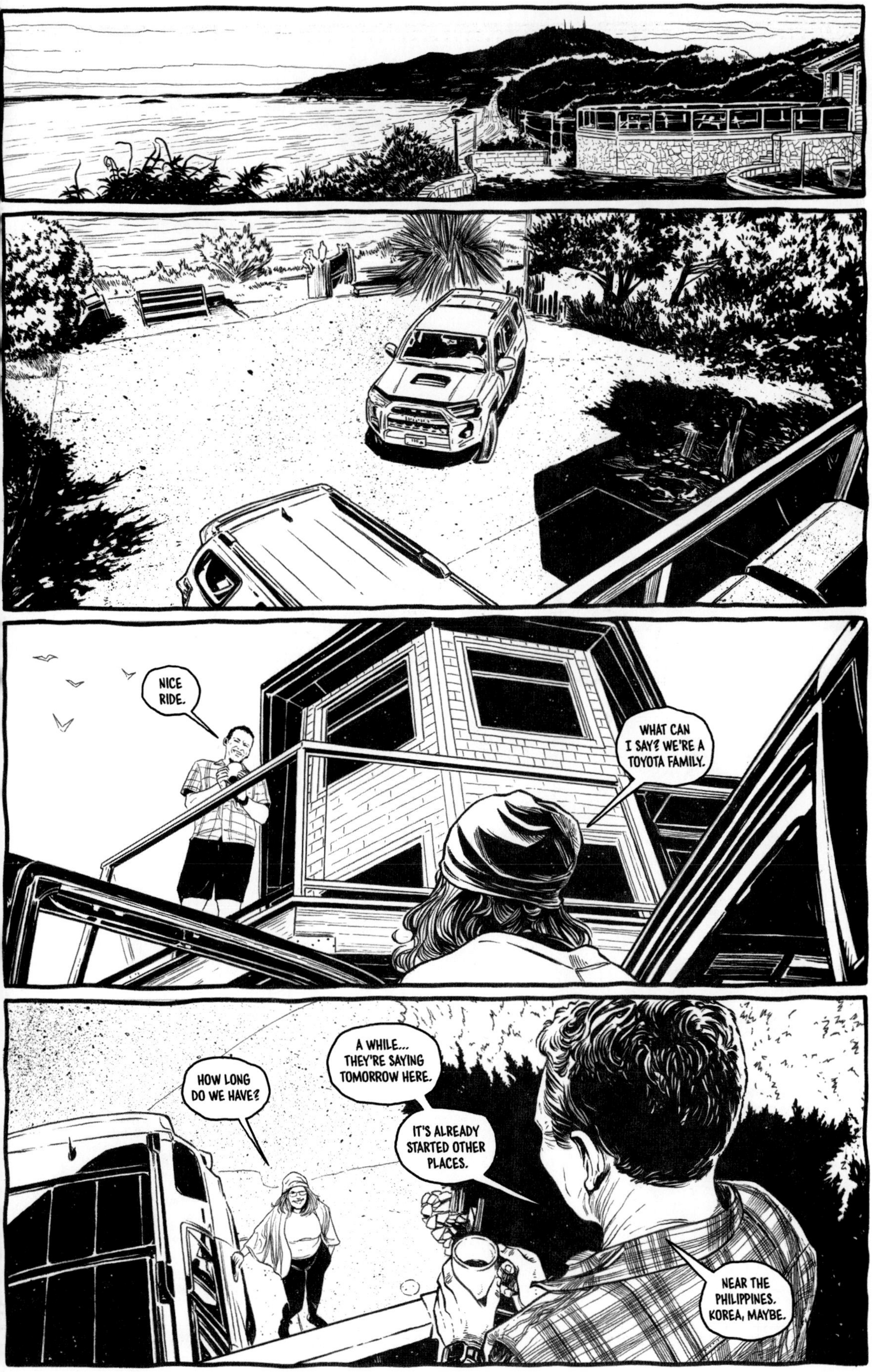
NICE RIDE.
WHAT CAN I SAY? WE'RE A TOYOTA FAMILY.
HOW LONG DO WE HAVE?
A WHILE... THEY'RE SAYING TOMORROW HERE.
IT'S ALREADY STARTED OTHER PLACES.
NEAR THE PHILIPPINES. KOREA, MAYBE.

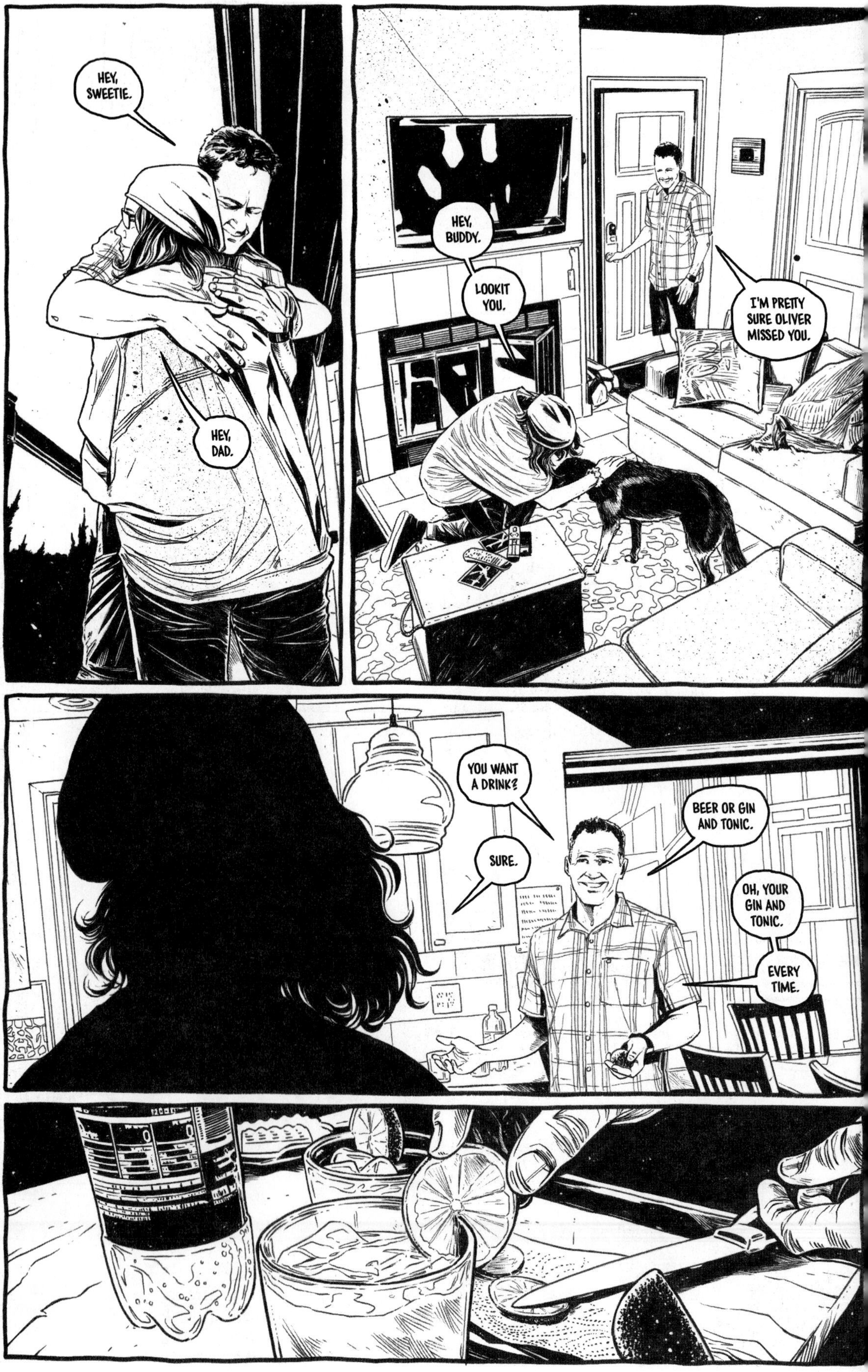
HEY, SWEETIE.
HEY, DAD.
HEY, BUDDY.
LOOKIT YOU.
I'M PRETTY SURE OLIVER MISSED YOU.
YOU WANT A DRINK?
SURE.
BEER OR GIN AND TONIC.
OH, YOUR GIN AND TONIC.
EVERY TIME.

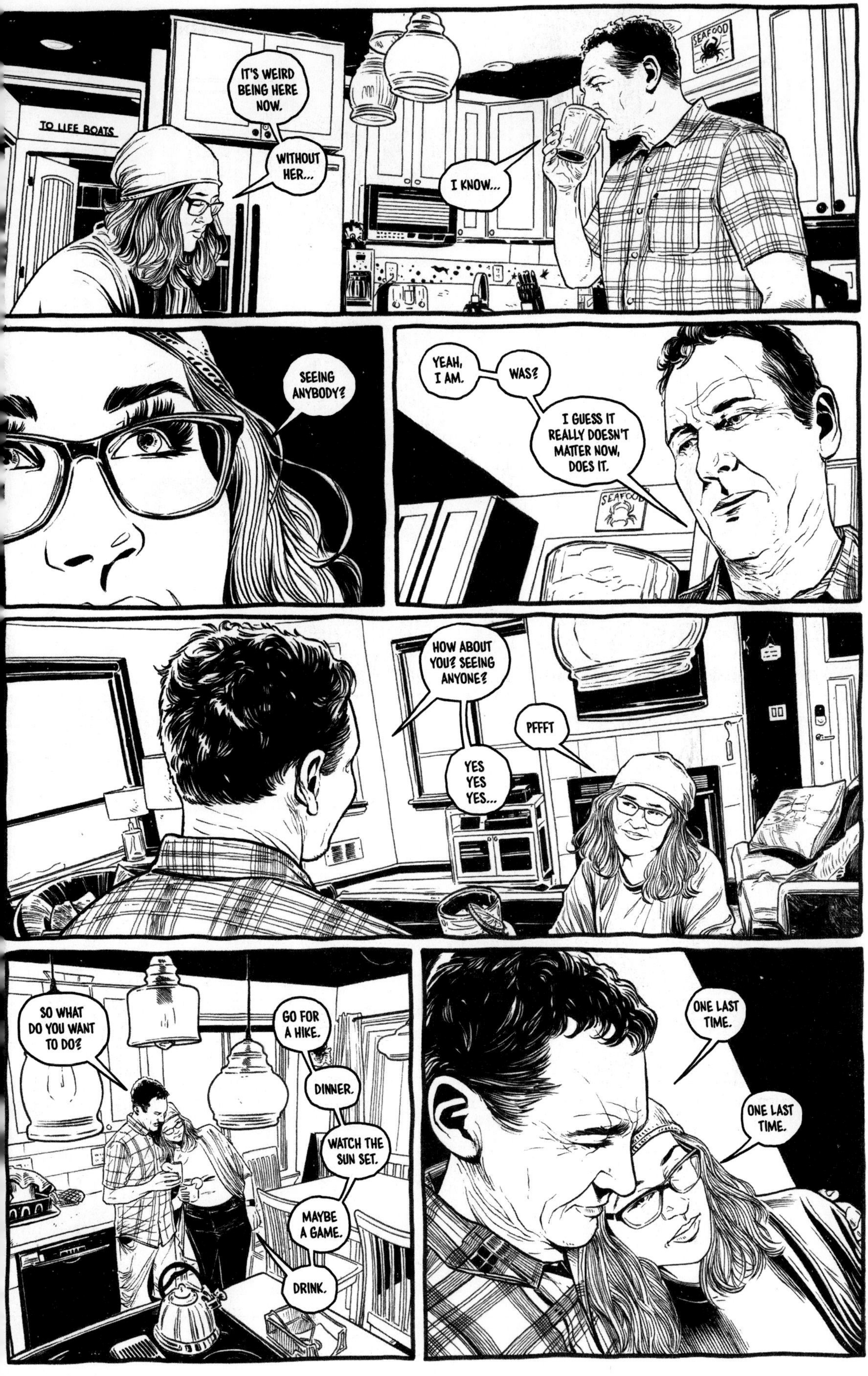
TO LIFE BOATS
IT'S WEIRD BEING HERE NOW.
WITHOUT HER...
I KNOW...
SEAFOOD
SEEING ANYBODY?
YEAH, I AM.
WAS?
I GUESS IT REALLY DOESN'T MATTER NOW, DOES IT.
SEAFOOD
HOW ABOUT YOU? SEEING ANYONE?
YES YES YES...
PFFFT
SO WHAT DO YOU WANT TO DO?
GO FOR A HIKE.
DINNER.
WATCH THE SUN SET.
MAYBE A GAME.
DRINK.
ONE LAST TIME.
ONE LAST TIME.

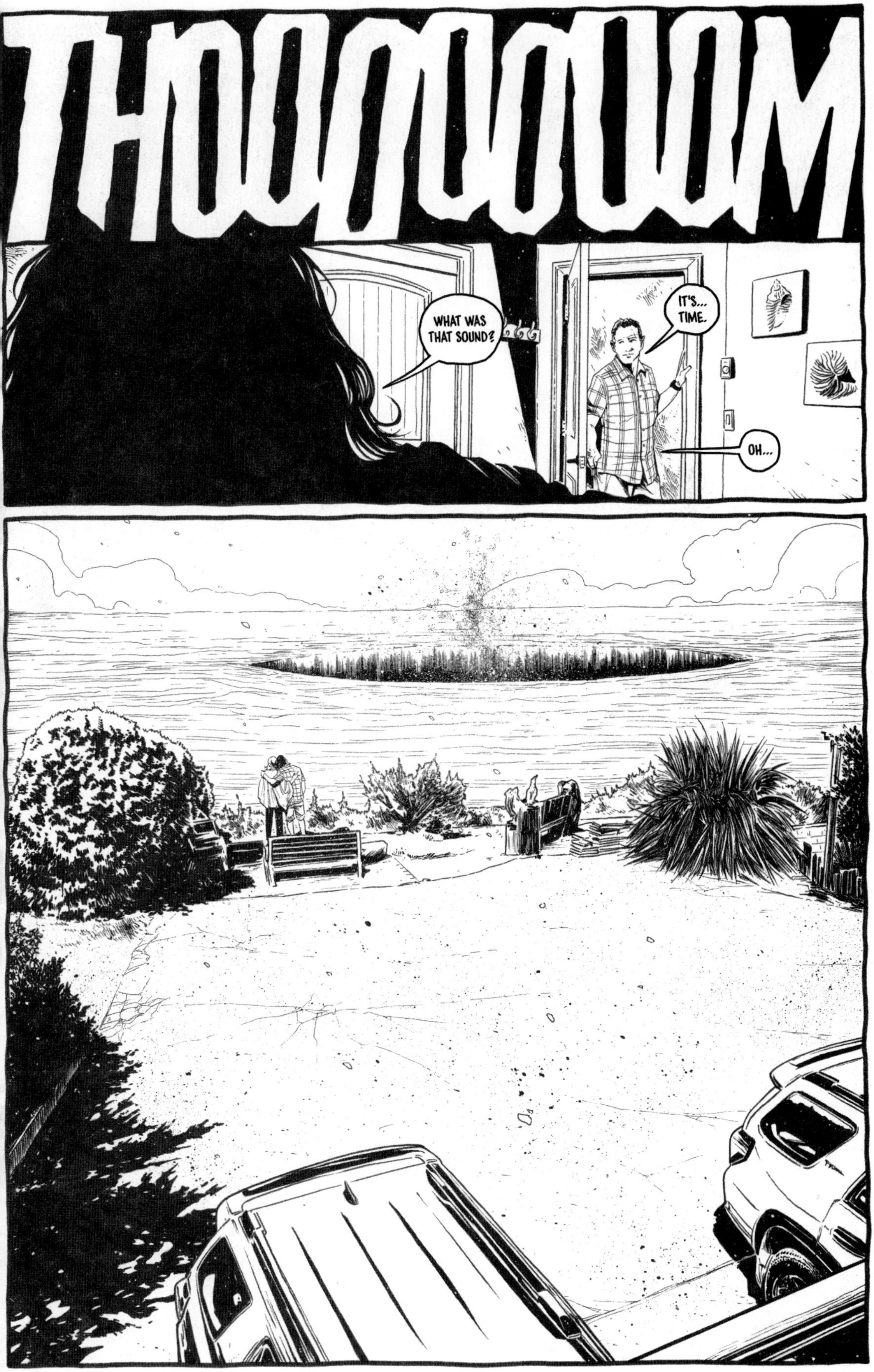
THOOOOOOM
WHAT WAS THAT SOUND?
IT'S... TIME.
OH...

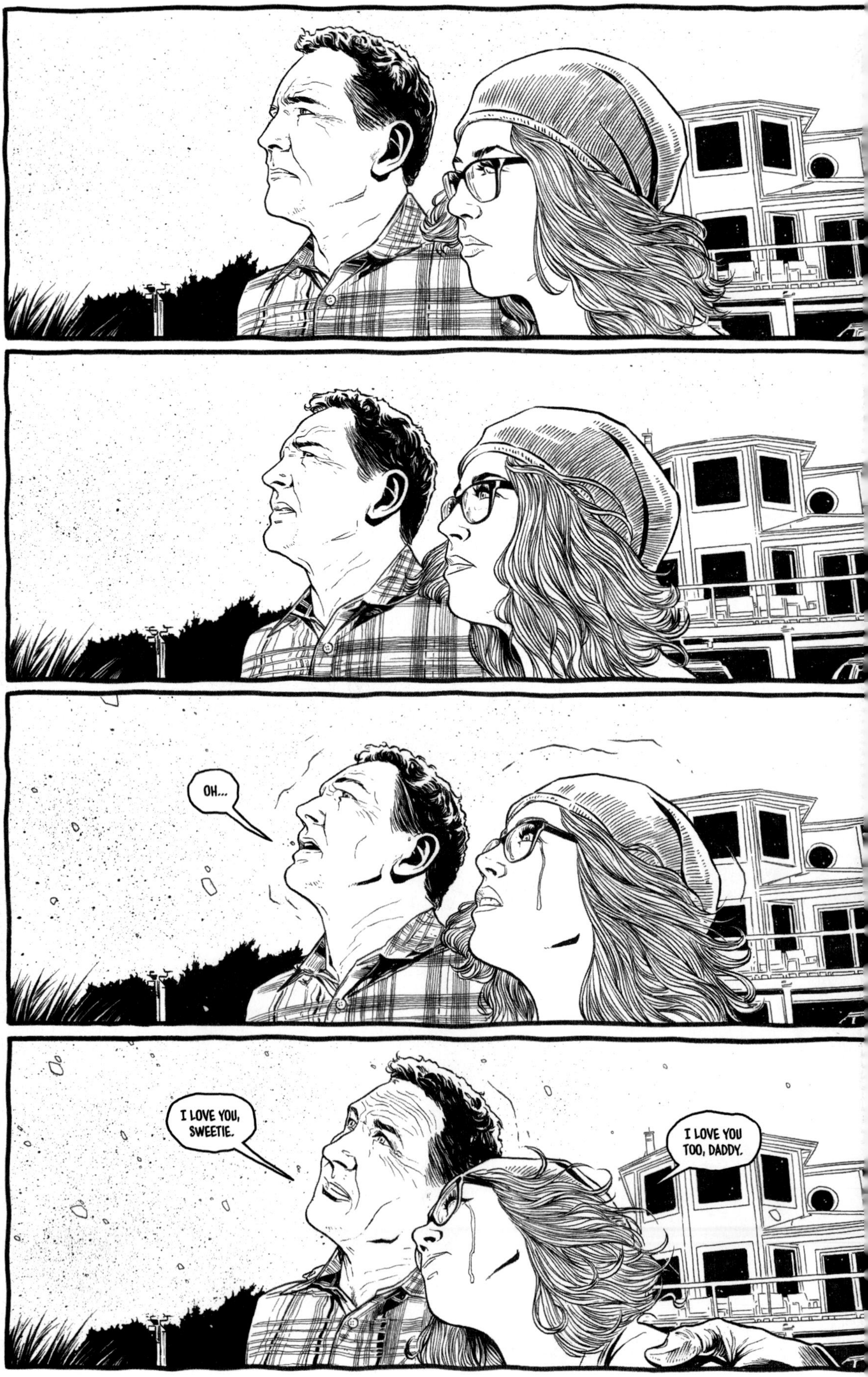
OH...
I LOVE YOU, SWEETIE.
I LOVE YOU TOO, DADDY.

SHOGGOTH IN AN ALLEY BEHIND A BAR IN A SMALL TOWN

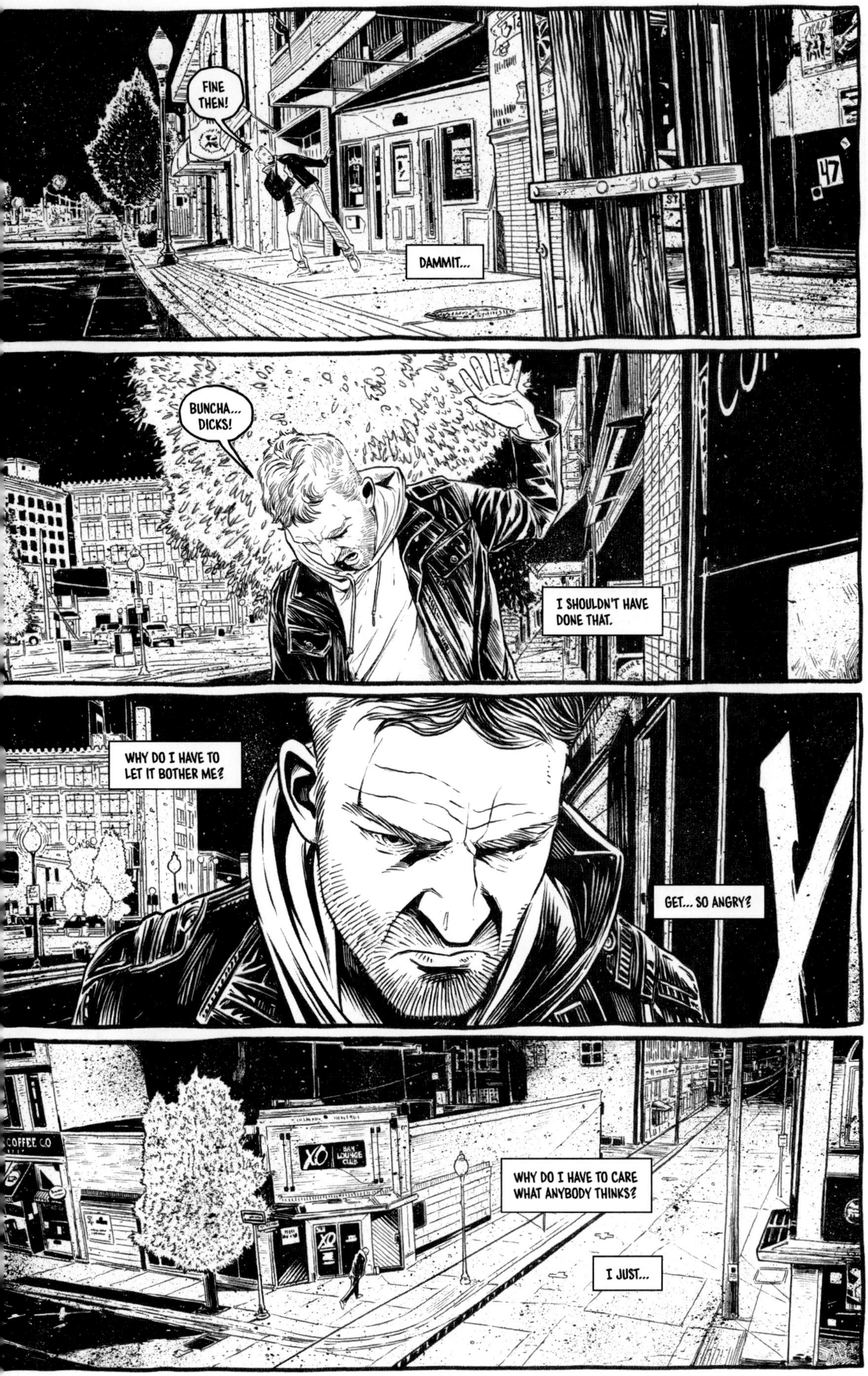
FINE THEN!
DAMMIT...
BUNCHA... DICKS!
I SHOULDN'T HAVE DONE THAT.
WHY DO I HAVE TO LET IT BOTHER ME?
GET... SO ANGRY?
COFFEE CO
XO BAR LOUNGE CLUB
WHY DO I HAVE TO CARE WHAT ANYBODY THINKS?
I JUST...

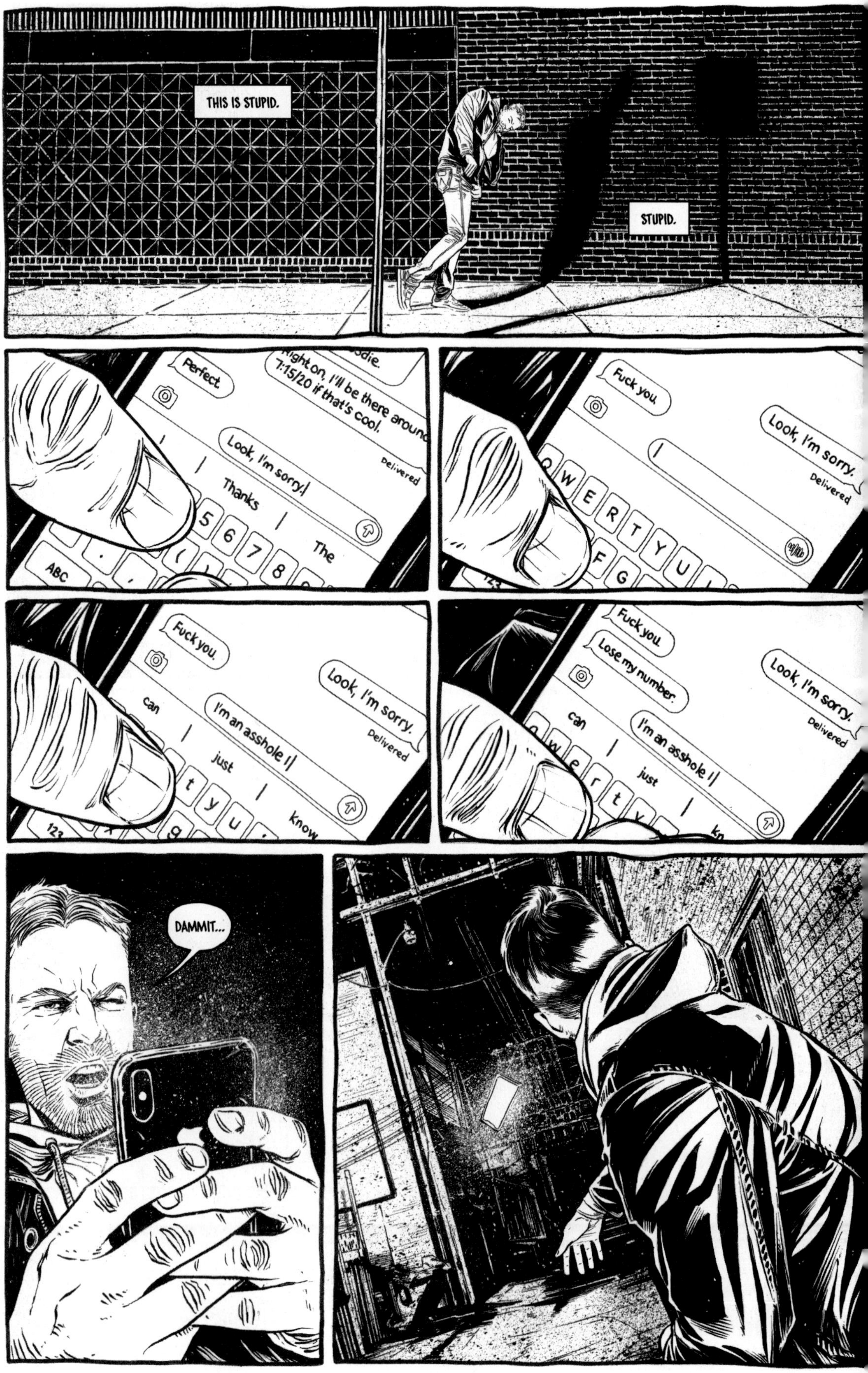
THIS IS STUPID.
STUPID.
Perfect.
Right on, I'll be there around 7:15/20 if that's cool.
Look, I'm sorry.|
Delivered
Fuck you.
Look, I'm sorry.
Delivered
Fuck you.
Look, I'm sorry.
Delivered
I'm an asshole I|
Fuck you.
Lose my number.
Look, I'm sorry.
Delivered
I'm an asshole I|
DAMMIT...

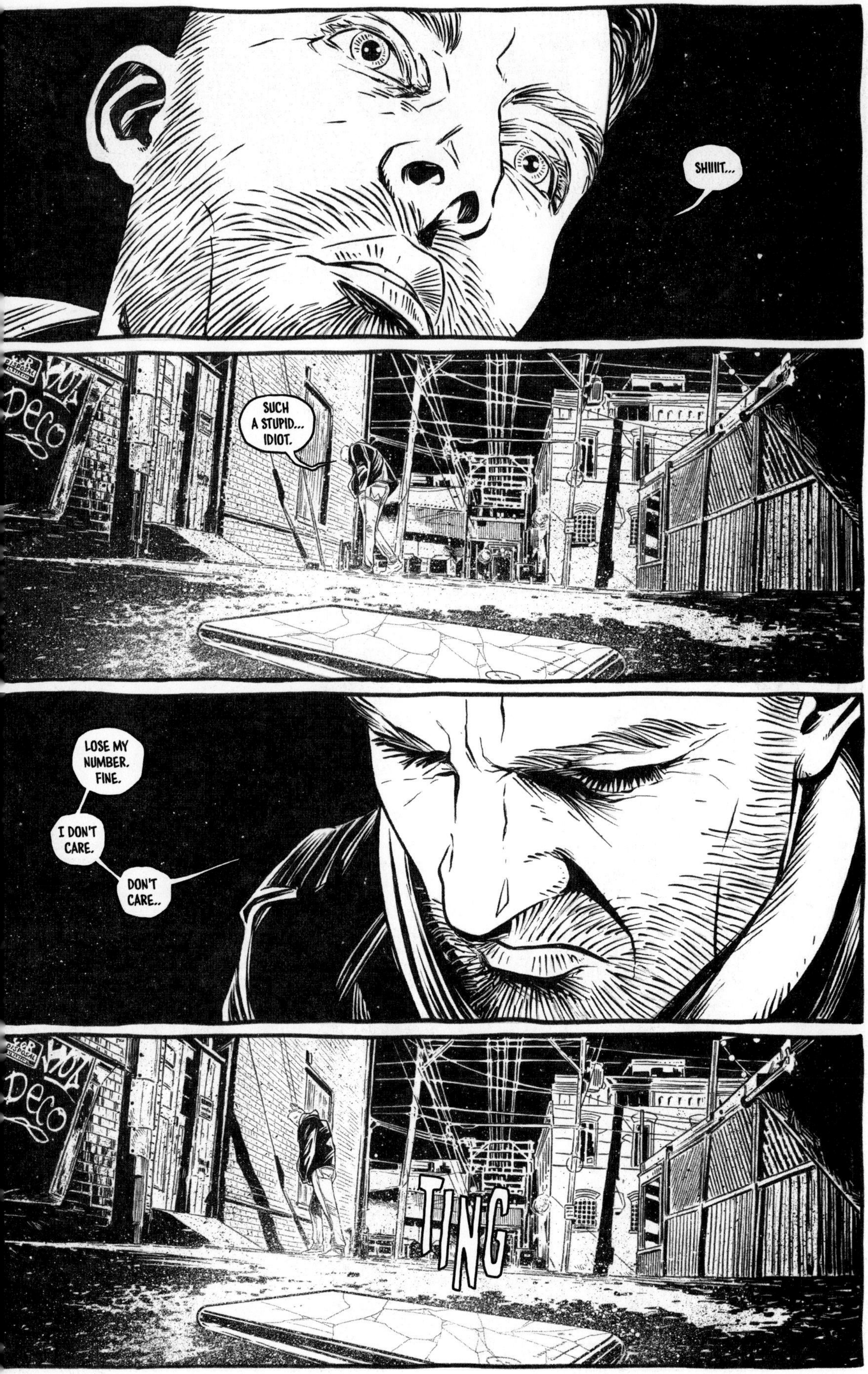
SHIIIT...
SUCH A STUPID... IDIOT.
LOSE MY NUMBER. FINE.
I DON'T CARE.
DON'T CARE..
TING

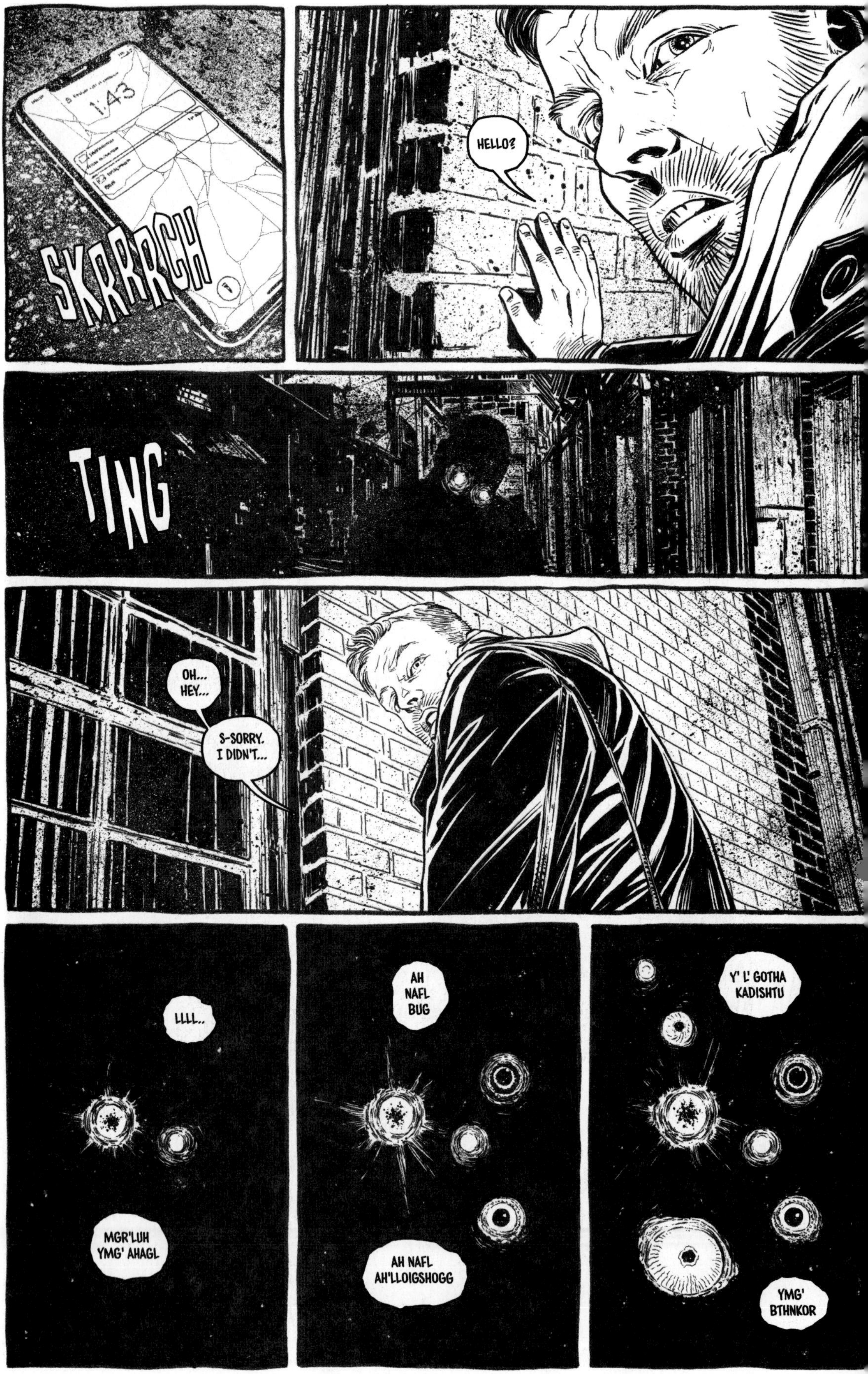

1:43
SKRRRCH
HELLO?
TING
OH... HEY...
S-SORRY. I DIDN'T...
LLLL...
MGR'LUH YMG' AHAGL
AH NAFL BUG
AH NAFL AH'LLOIGSHOGG
Y' L' GOTHA KADISHTU
YMG' BTHNKOR

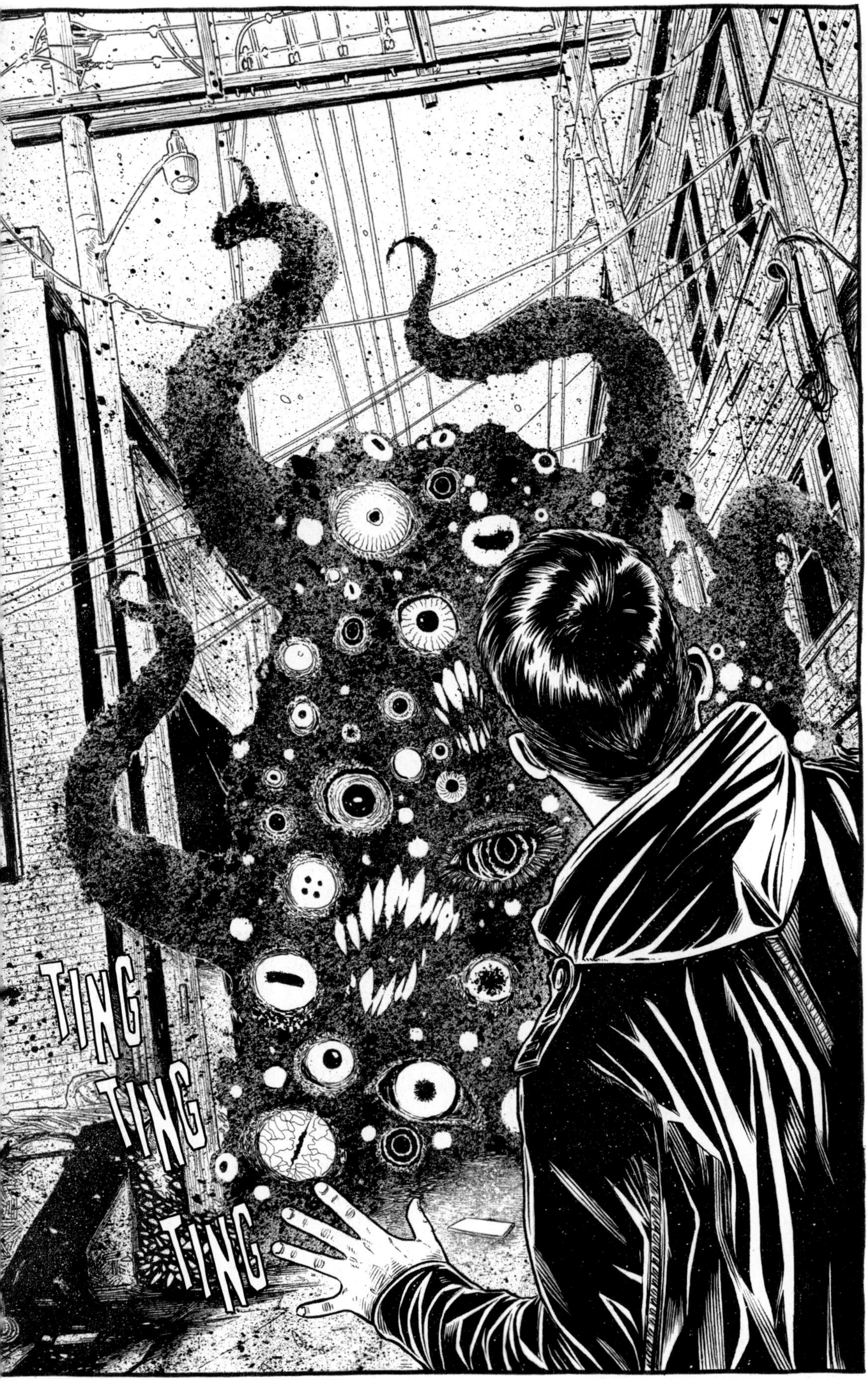
TING
TING
TING

THE DAY THE INTERNET DIED

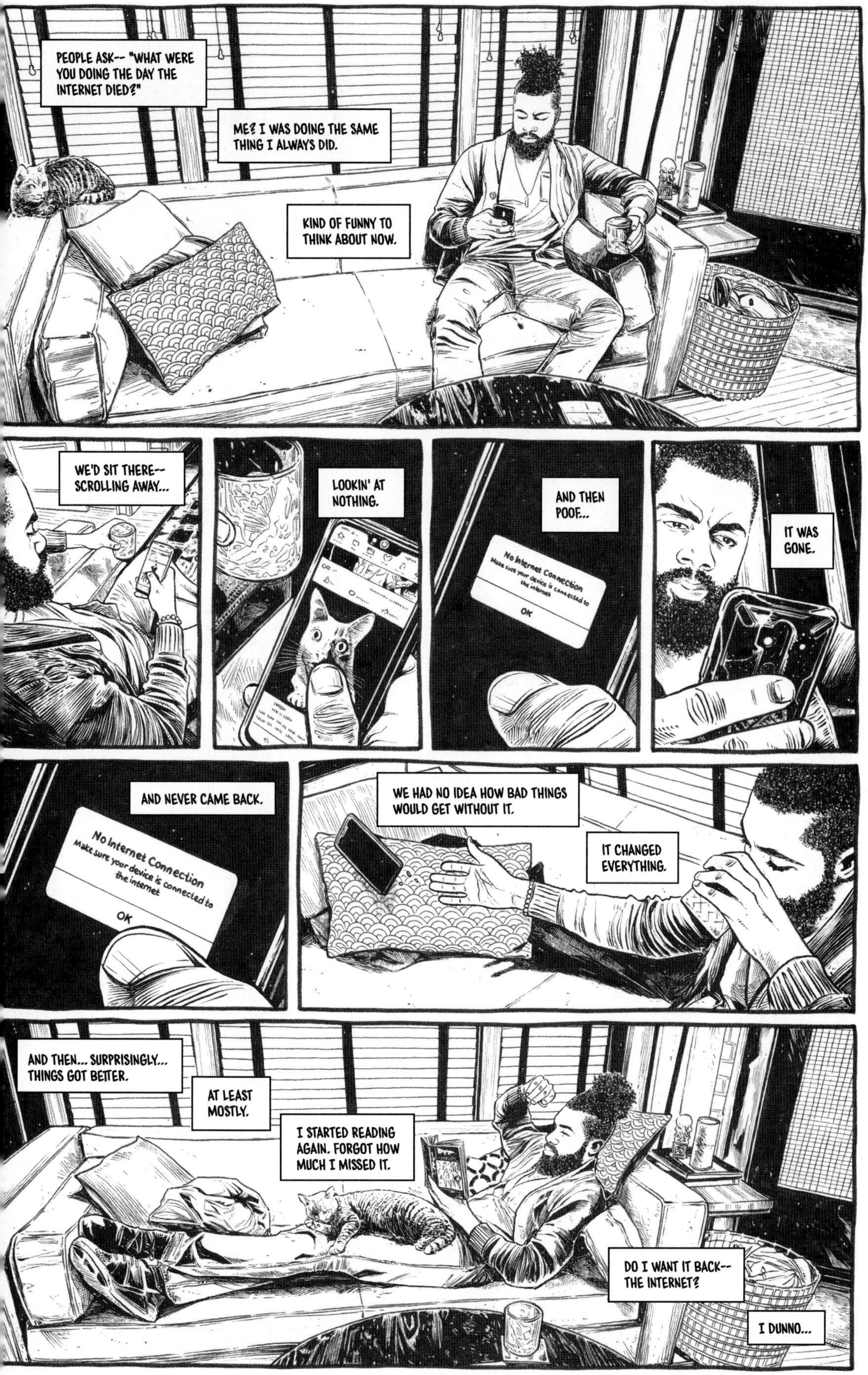
PEOPLE ASK-- "WHAT WERE YOU DOING THE DAY THE INTERNET DIED?"
ME? I WAS DOING THE SAME THING I ALWAYS DID.
KIND OF FUNNY TO THINK ABOUT NOW.
WE'D SIT THERE-- SCROLLING AWAY...
LOOKIN' AT NOTHING.
AND THEN POOF...
No Internet Connection
Make sure your device is connected to the internet
OK
IT WAS GONE.
AND NEVER CAME BACK.
No Internet Connection
Make sure your device is connected to the internet
OK
WE HAD NO IDEA HOW BAD THINGS WOULD GET WITHOUT IT.
IT CHANGED EVERYTHING.
AND THEN... SURPRISINGLY... THINGS GOT BETTER.
AT LEAST MOSTLY.
I STARTED READING AGAIN. FORGOT HOW MUCH I MISSED IT.
DO I WANT IT BACK-- THE INTERNET?
I DUNNO...

ROOMS IN THE FLAT HOUSE

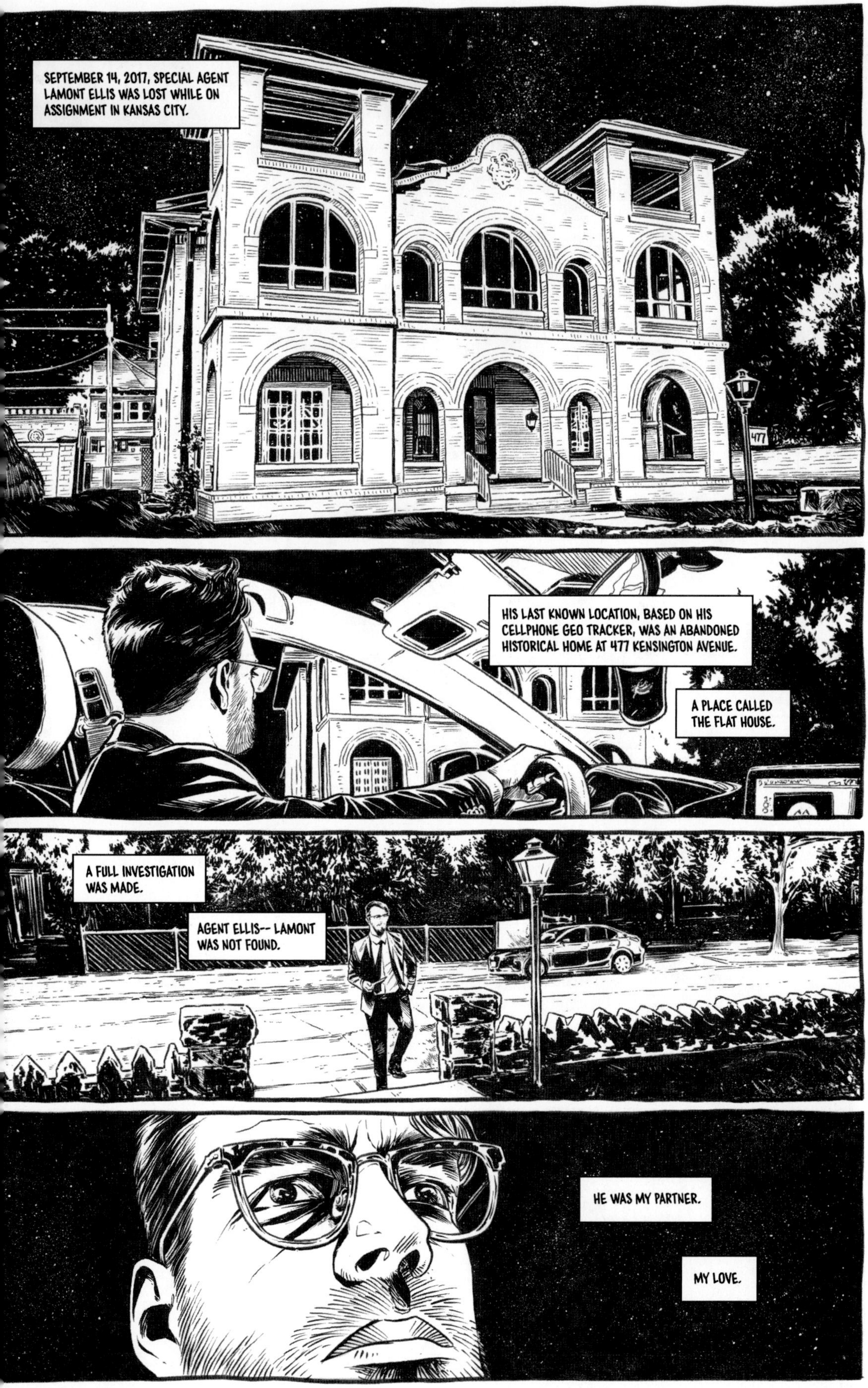
SEPTEMBER 14, 2017, SPECIAL AGENT LAMONT ELLIS WAS LOST WHILE ON ASSIGNMENT IN KANSAS CITY.
477
HIS LAST KNOWN LOCATION, BASED ON HIS CELLPHONE GEO TRACKER, WAS AN ABANDONED HISTORICAL HOME AT 477 KENSINGTON AVENUE.
A PLACE CALLED THE FLAT HOUSE.
A FULL INVESTIGATION WAS MADE.
AGENT ELLIS-- LAMONT WAS NOT FOUND.
HE WAS MY PARTNER.
MY LOVE.

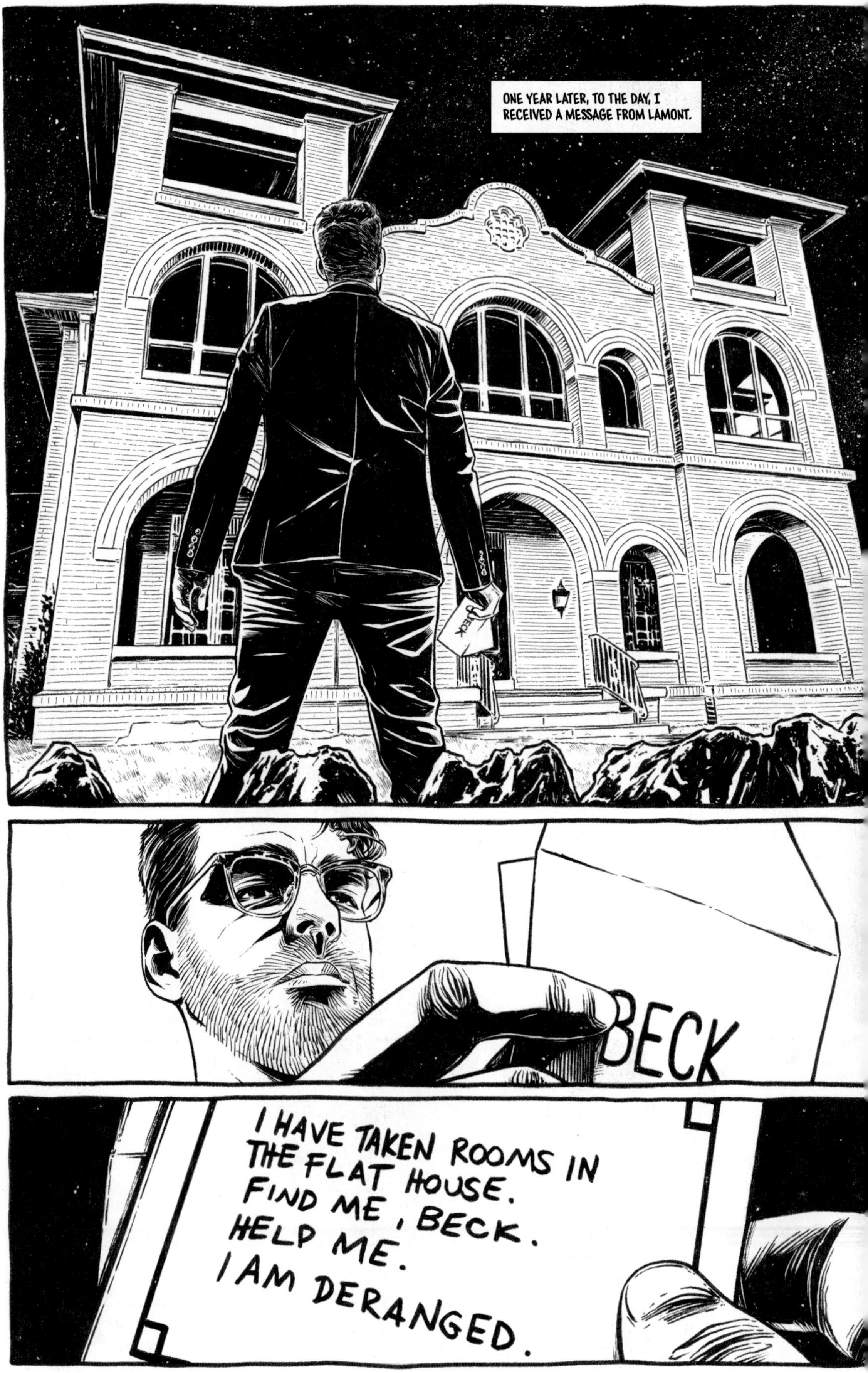
ONE YEAR LATER, TO THE DAY, I RECEIVED A MESSAGE FROM LAMONT.
BECK
BECK
I HAVE TAKEN ROOMS IN THE FLAT HOUSE.
FIND ME, BECK.
HELP ME.
I AM DERANGED.

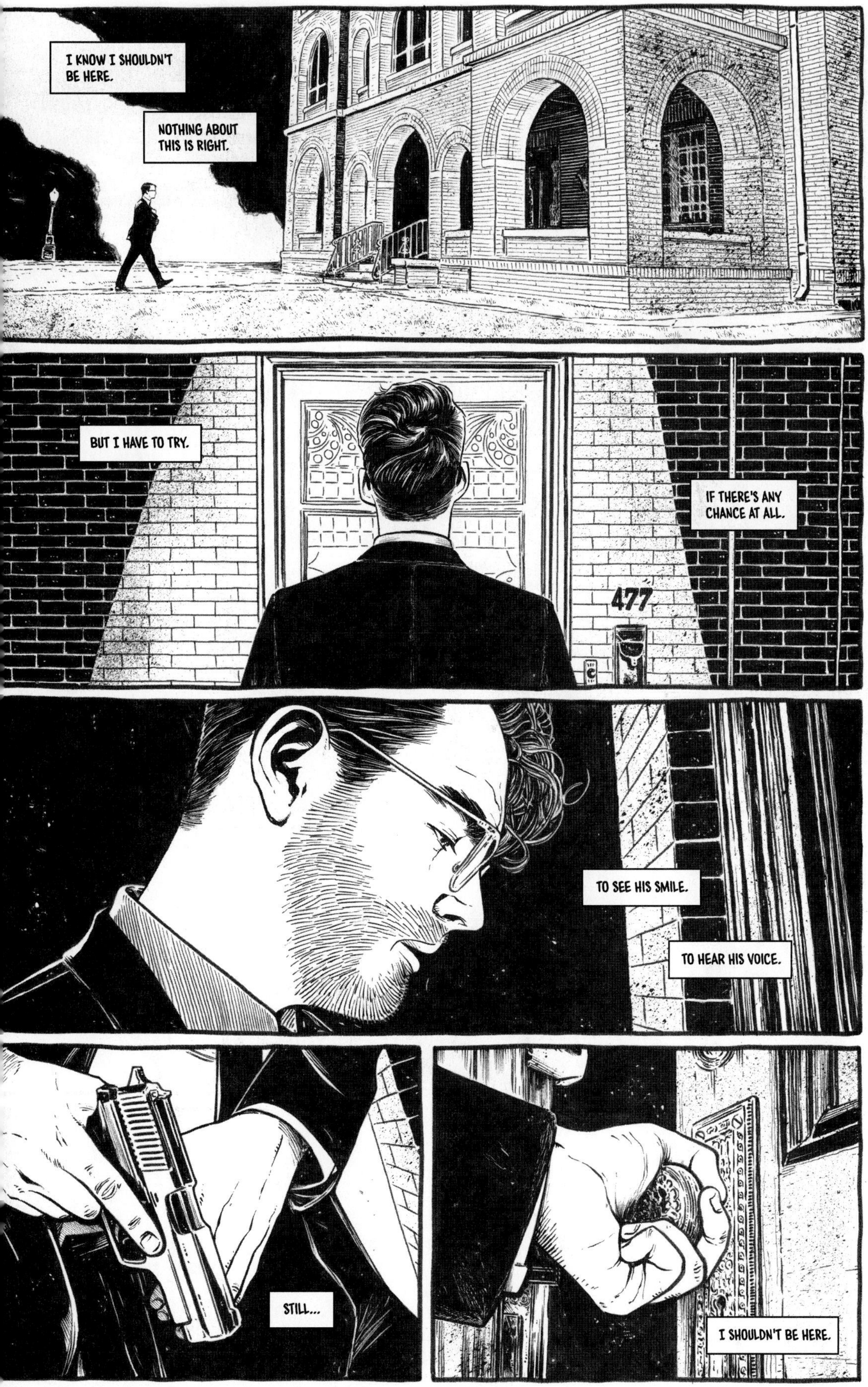
I KNOW I SHOULDN'T BE HERE.
NOTHING ABOUT THIS IS RIGHT.
BUT I HAVE TO TRY.
IF THERE'S ANY CHANCE AT ALL.
477
TO SEE HIS SMILE.
TO HEAR HIS VOICE.
STILL...
I SHOULDN'T BE HERE.

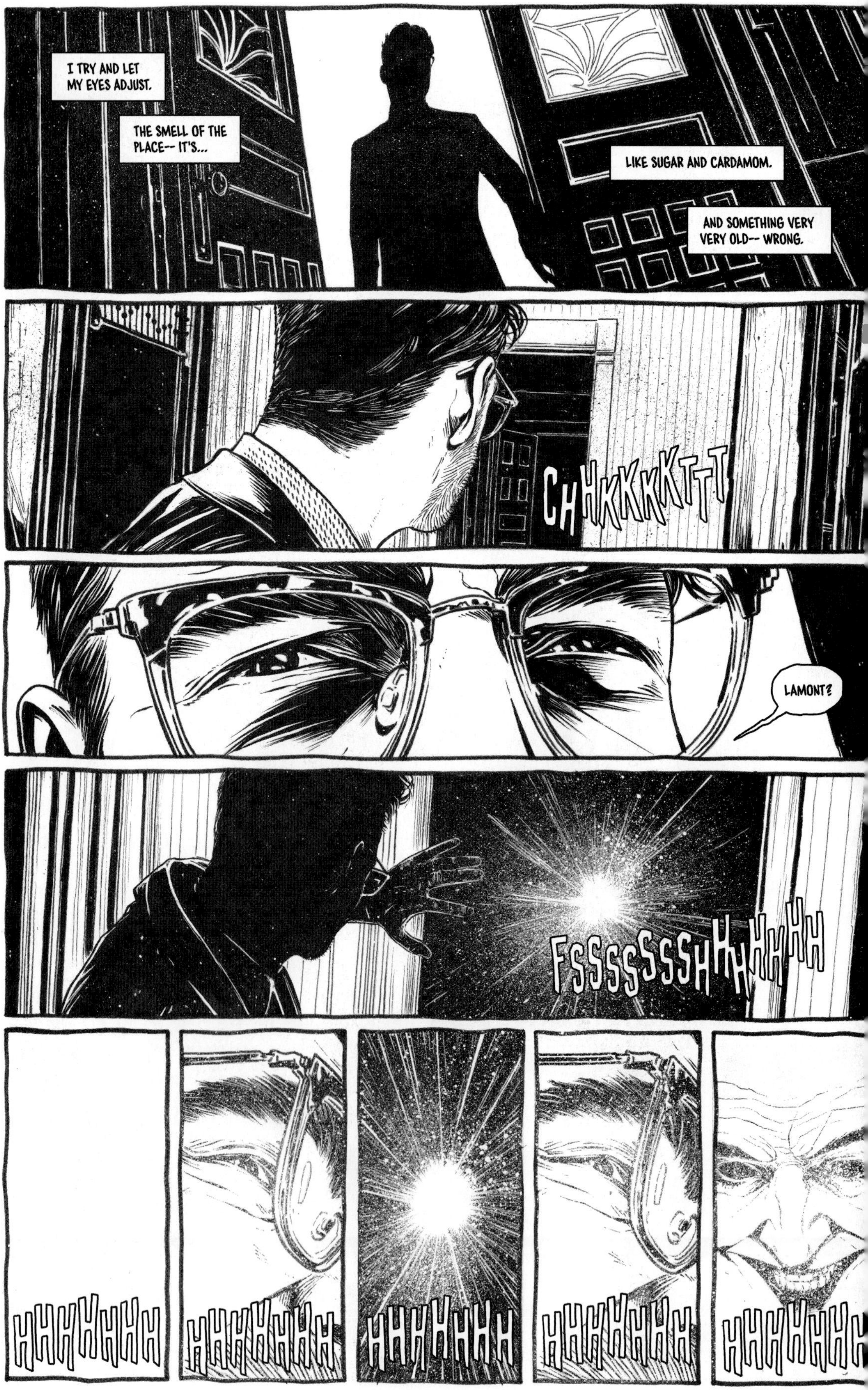
I TRY AND LET MY EYES ADJUST.
THE SMELL OF THE PLACE-- IT'S...
LIKE SUGAR AND CARDAMOM.
AND SOMETHING VERY VERY OLD-- WRONG.
CHHKKKKKTTT
LAMONT?
FSSSSSSSSHHHHHHHH
HHHHHHHH
HHHHHHHHH
HHHHHHHH
HHHHHHHHH
HHHHHHHH

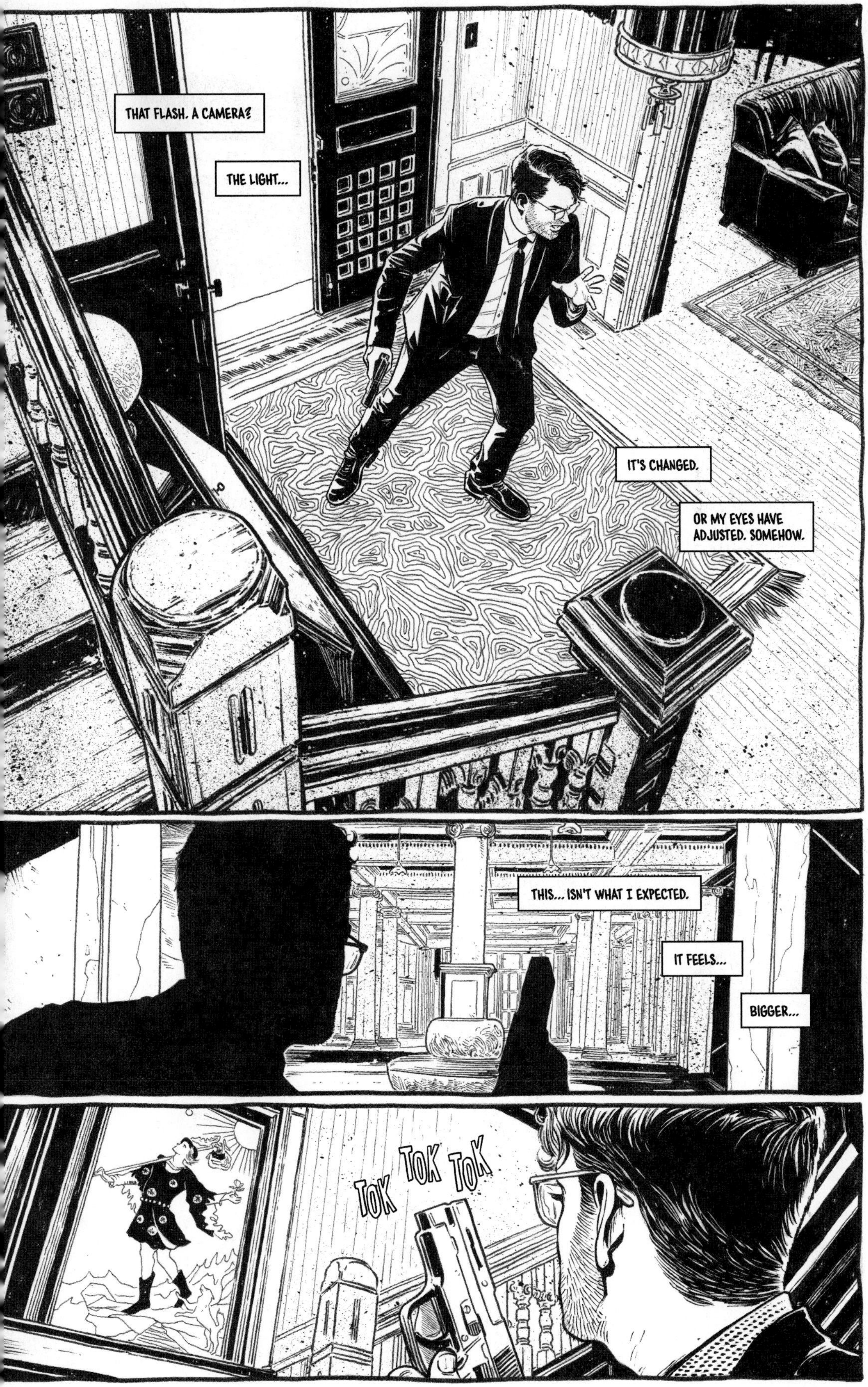
THAT FLASH. A CAMERA?
THE LIGHT...
IT'S CHANGED.
OR MY EYES HAVE ADJUSTED. SOMEHOW.
THIS... ISN'T WHAT I EXPECTED.
IT FEELS...
BIGGER...
TOK TOK TOK

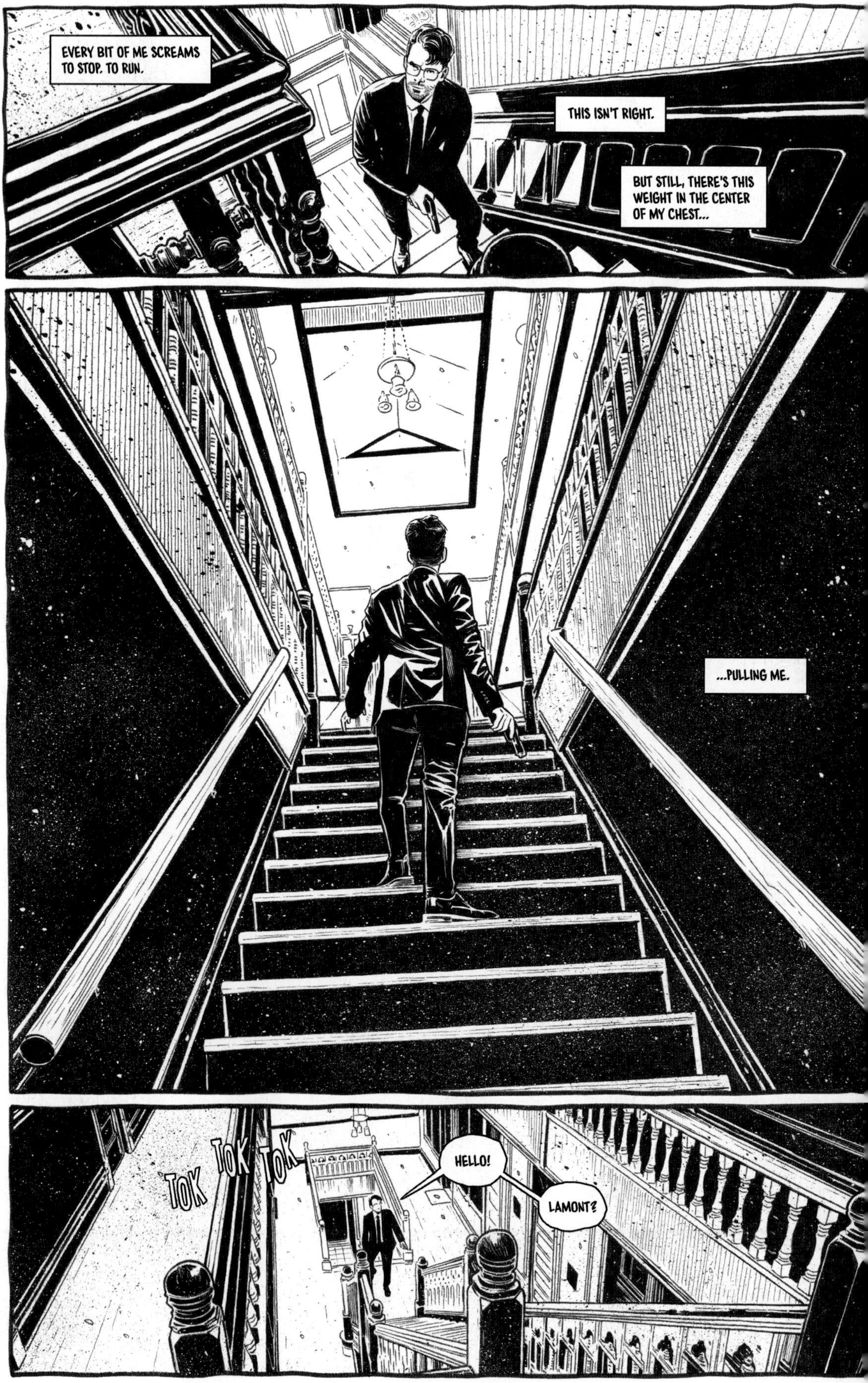
EVERY BIT OF ME SCREAMS TO STOP. TO RUN.
THIS ISN'T RIGHT.
BUT STILL, THERE'S THIS WEIGHT IN THE CENTER OF MY CHEST...
...PULLING ME.
TOK TOK TOK
HELLO!
LAMONT?

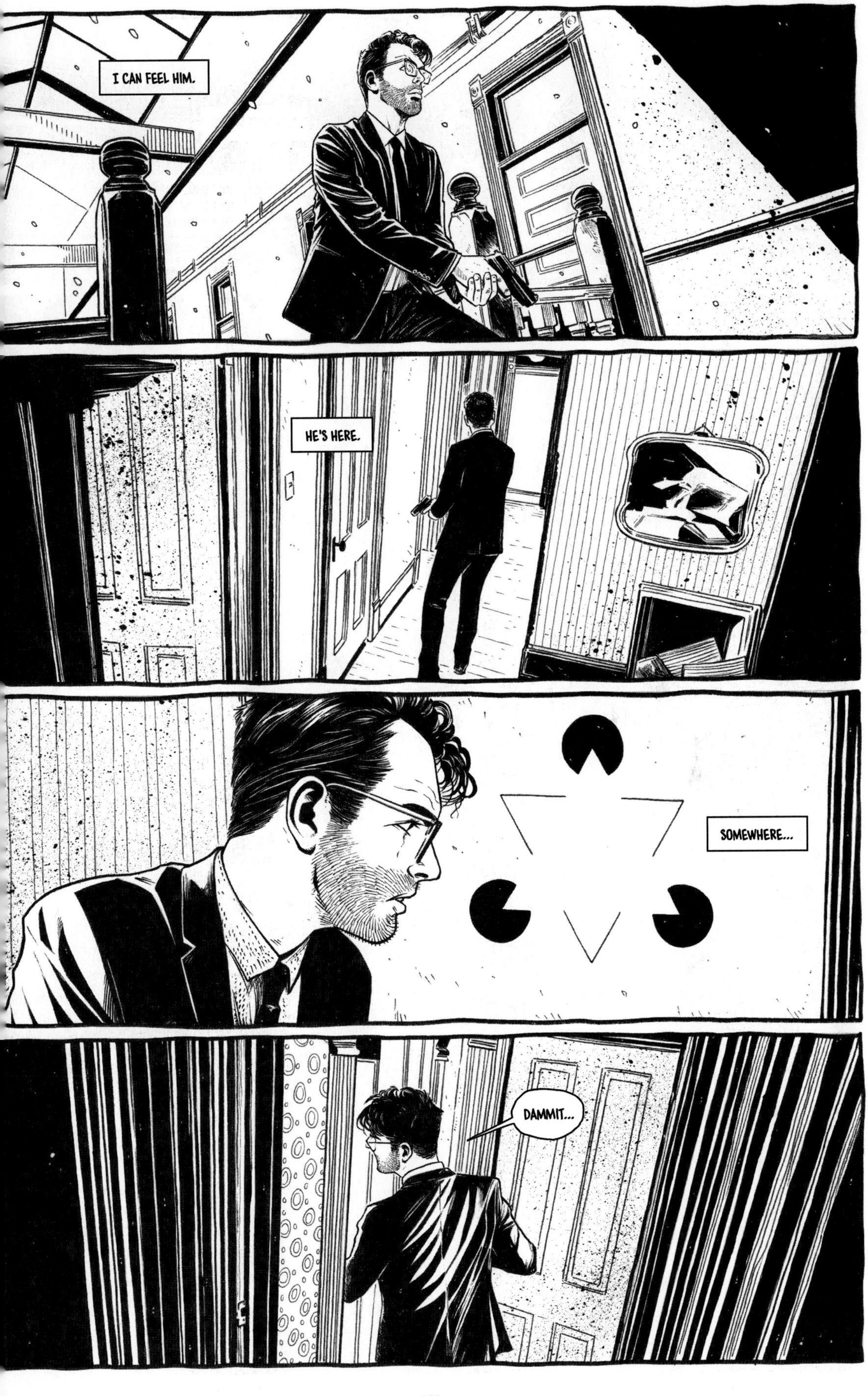
I CAN FEEL HIM.
HE'S HERE.
SOMEWHERE...
DAMMIT...

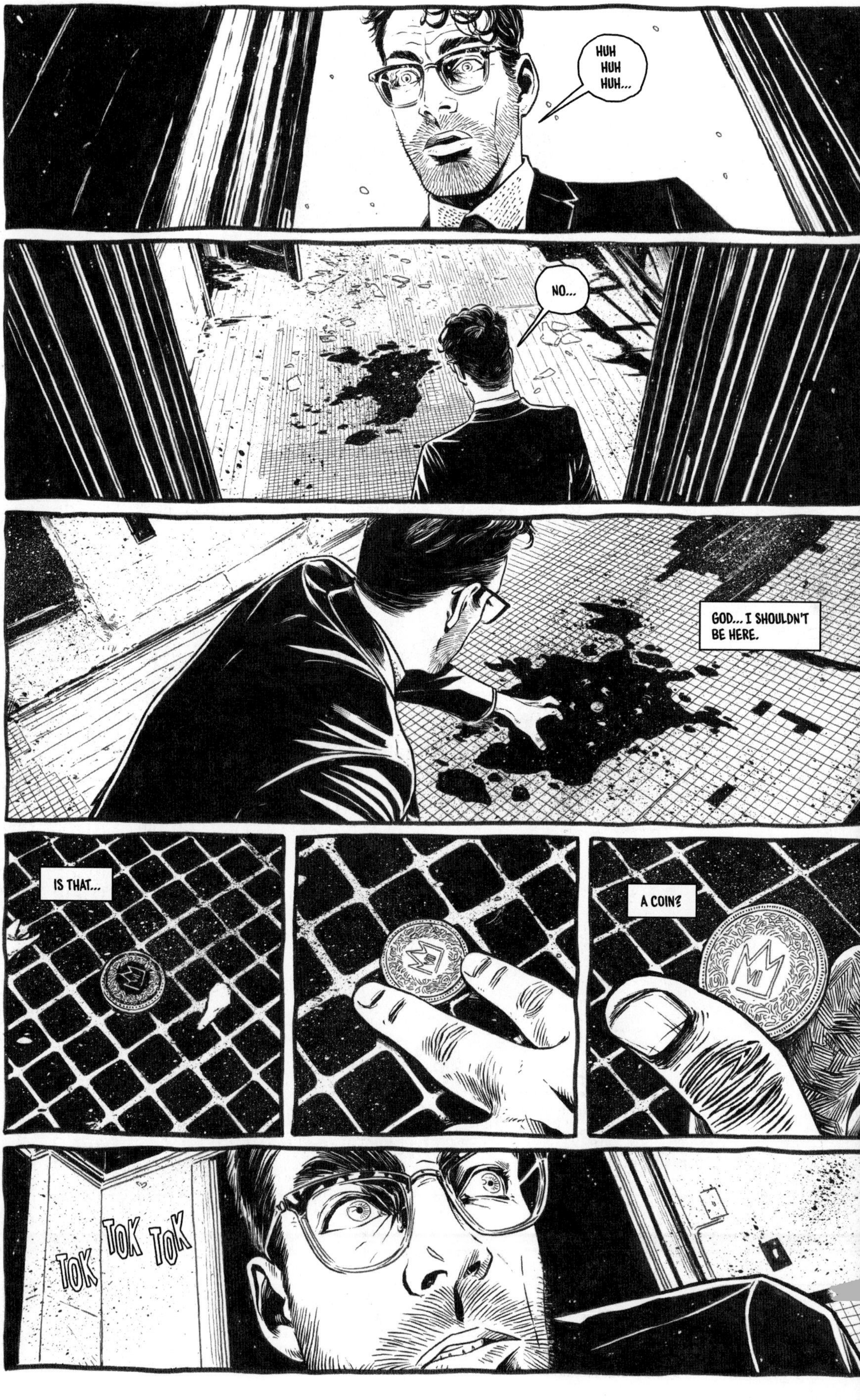
HUH HUH HUH...
NO...
GOD... I SHOULDN'T BE HERE.
IS THAT...
A COIN?
TOK TOK TOK

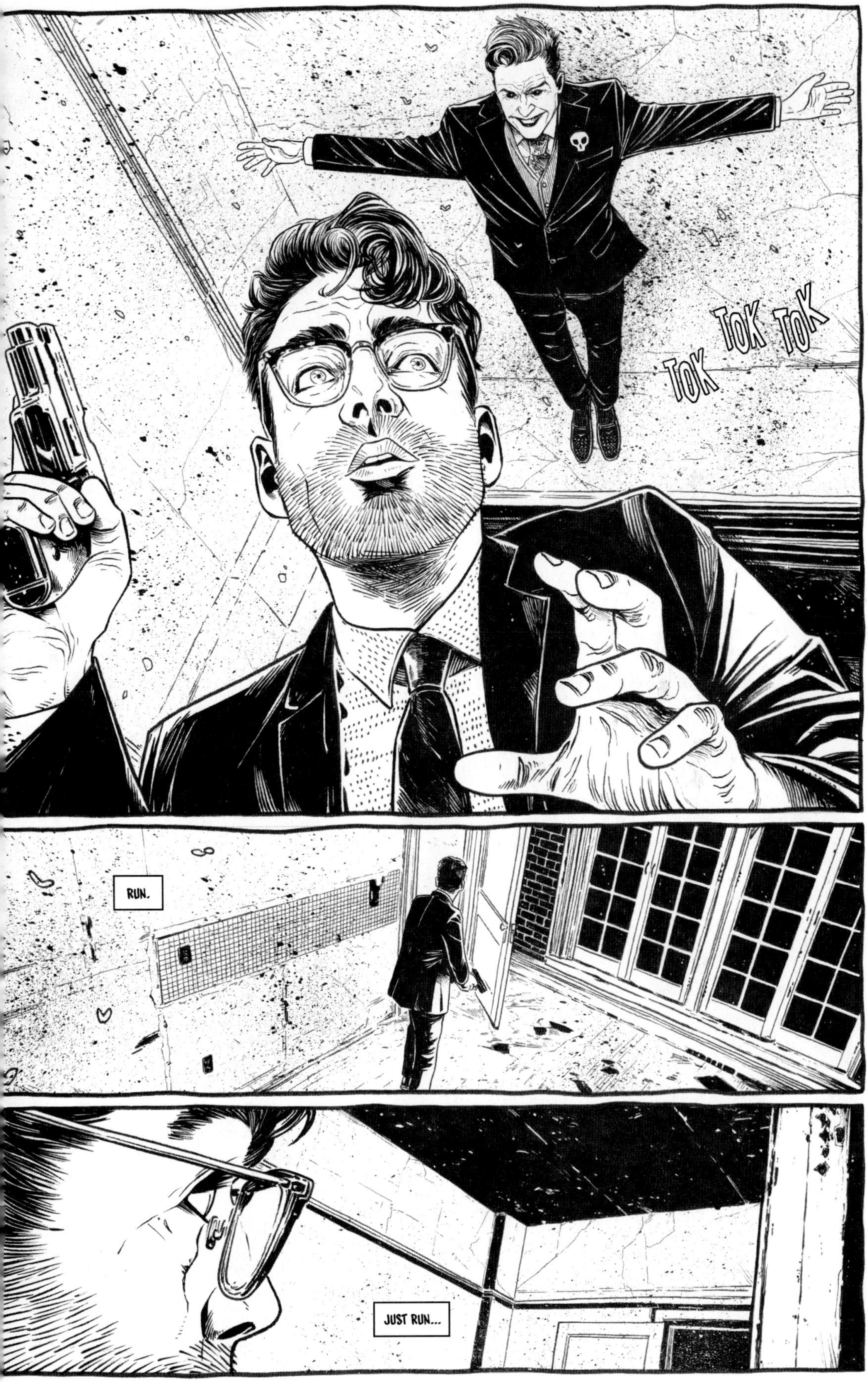
TOK TOK TOK
RUN.
JUST RUN...

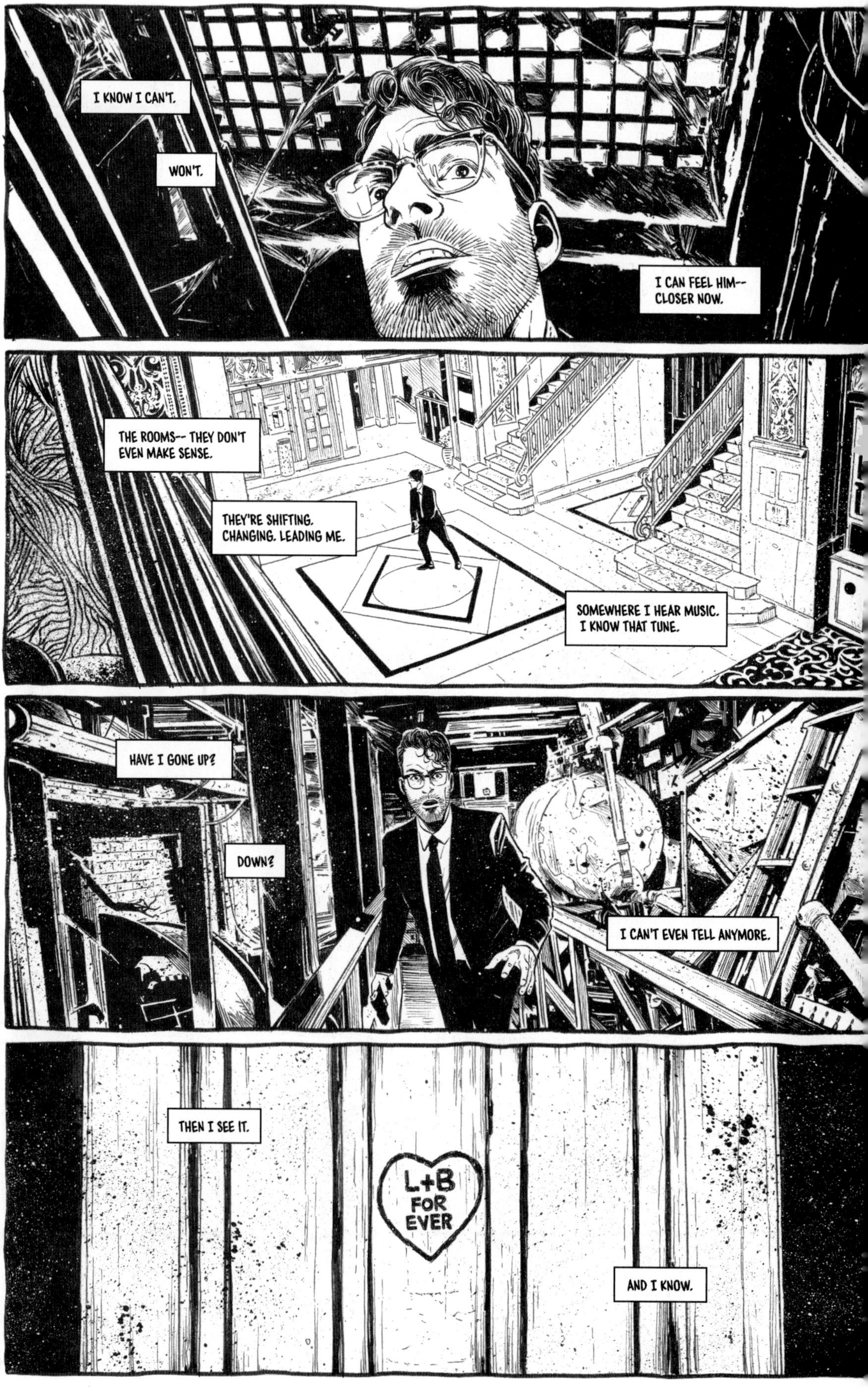
I KNOW I CAN'T.
WON'T.
I CAN FEEL HIM-- CLOSER NOW.
THE ROOMS-- THEY DON'T EVEN MAKE SENSE.
THEY'RE SHIFTING. CHANGING. LEADING ME.
SOMEWHERE I HEAR MUSIC. I KNOW THAT TUNE.
HAVE I GONE UP?
DOWN?
I CAN'T EVEN TELL ANYMORE.
THEN I SEE IT.
L+B FOR EVER
AND I KNOW.

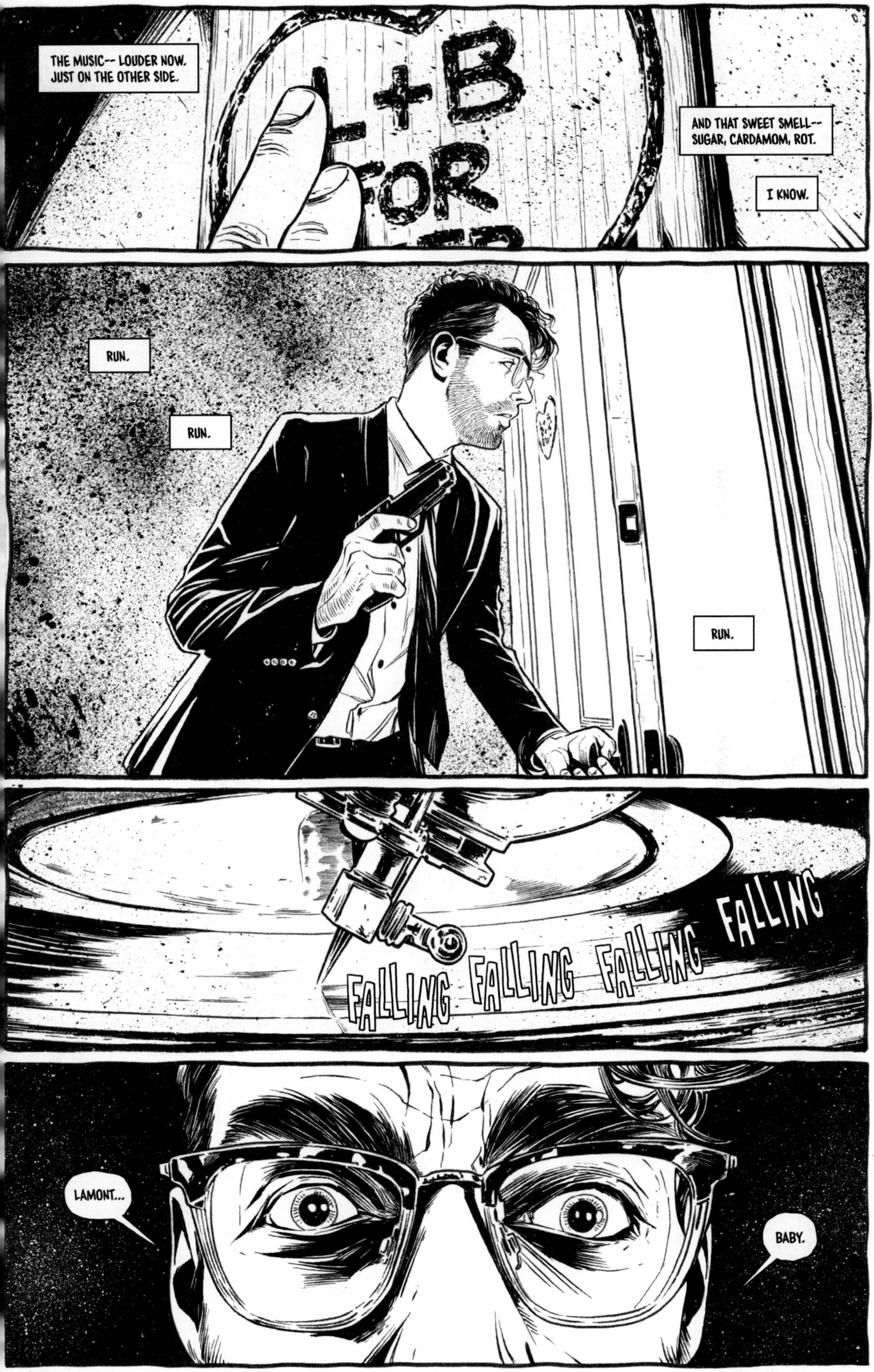
THE MUSIC-- LOUDER NOW. JUST ON THE OTHER SIDE.
L+B FOR
AND THAT SWEET SMELL-- SUGAR, CARDAMOM, ROT.
I KNOW.
RUN.
RUN.
RUN.
FALLING FALLING FALLING FALLING
LAMONT...
BABY.

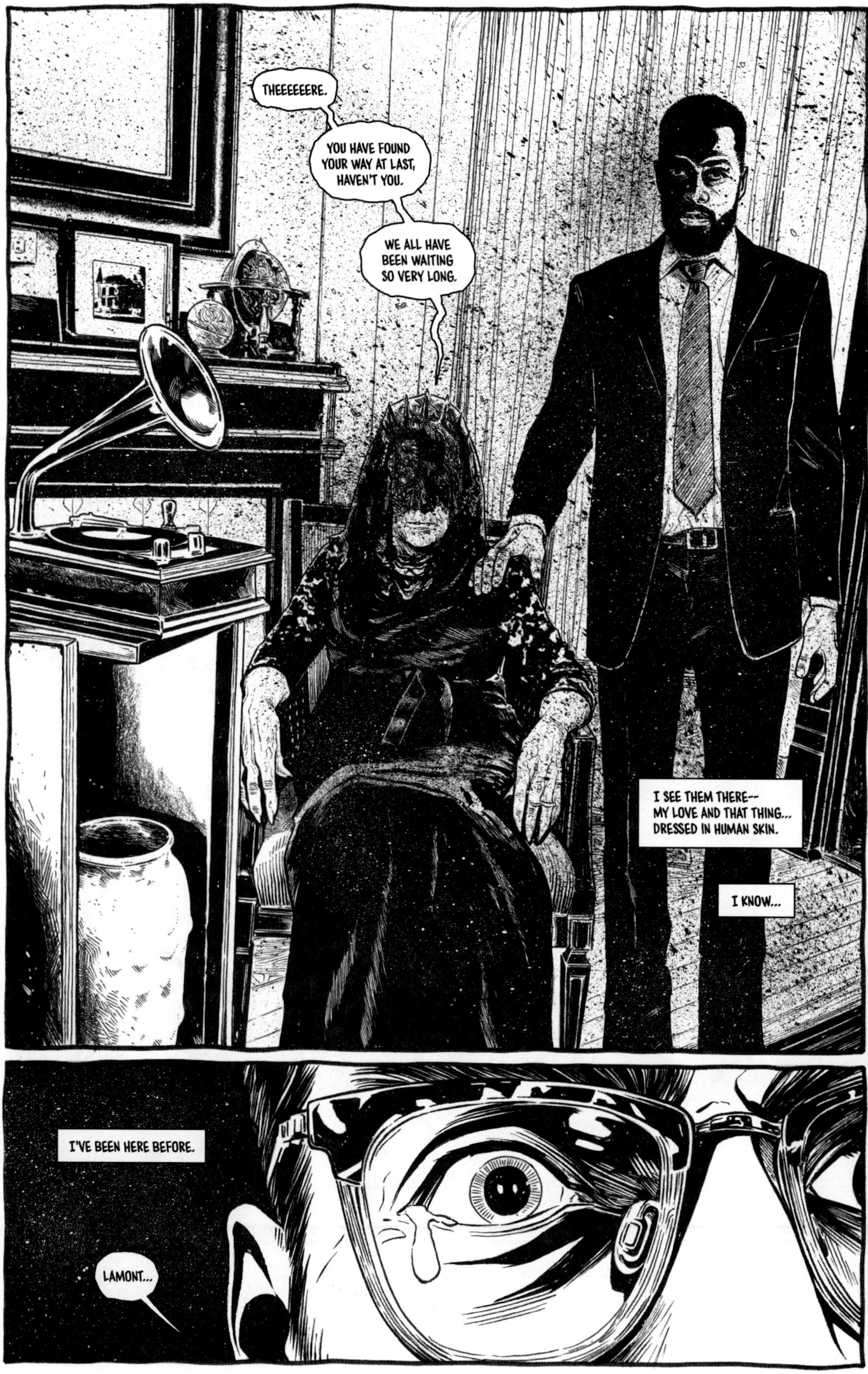
THEEEEEERE.
YOU HAVE FOUND YOUR WAY AT LAST, HAVEN'T YOU.
WE ALL HAVE BEEN WAITING SO VERY LONG.
I SEE THEM THERE-- MY LOVE AND THAT THING... DRESSED IN HUMAN SKIN.
I KNOW...
I'VE BEEN HERE BEFORE.
LAMONT...

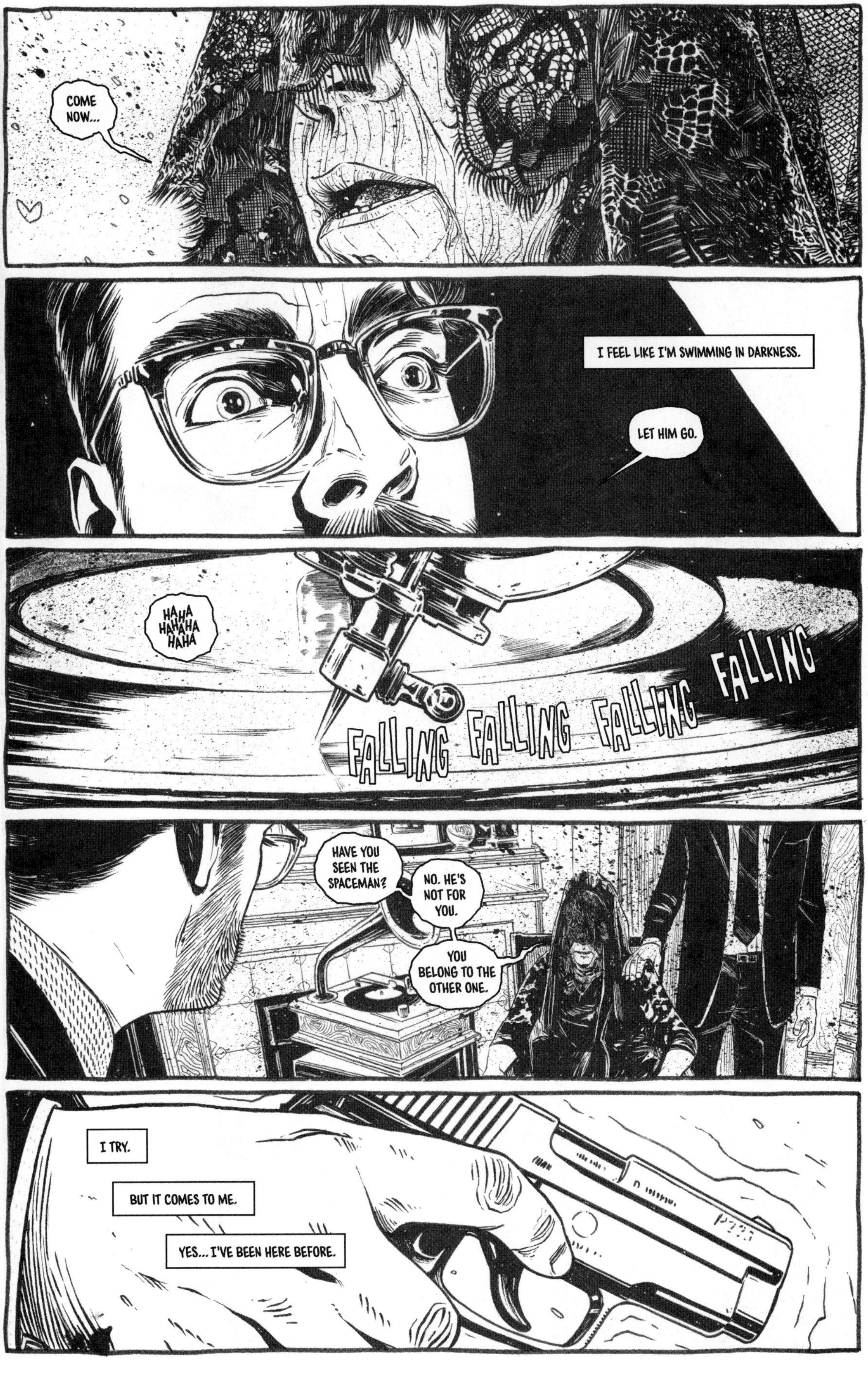
COME NOW...
I FEEL LIKE I'M SWIMMING IN DARKNESS.
LET HIM GO.
HAHA HAHAHA HAHA
FALLING FALLING FALLING FALLING
HAVE YOU SEEN THE SPACEMAN?
NO. HE'S NOT FOR YOU.
YOU BELONG TO THE OTHER ONE.
I TRY.
BUT IT COMES TO ME.
YES... I'VE BEEN HERE BEFORE.

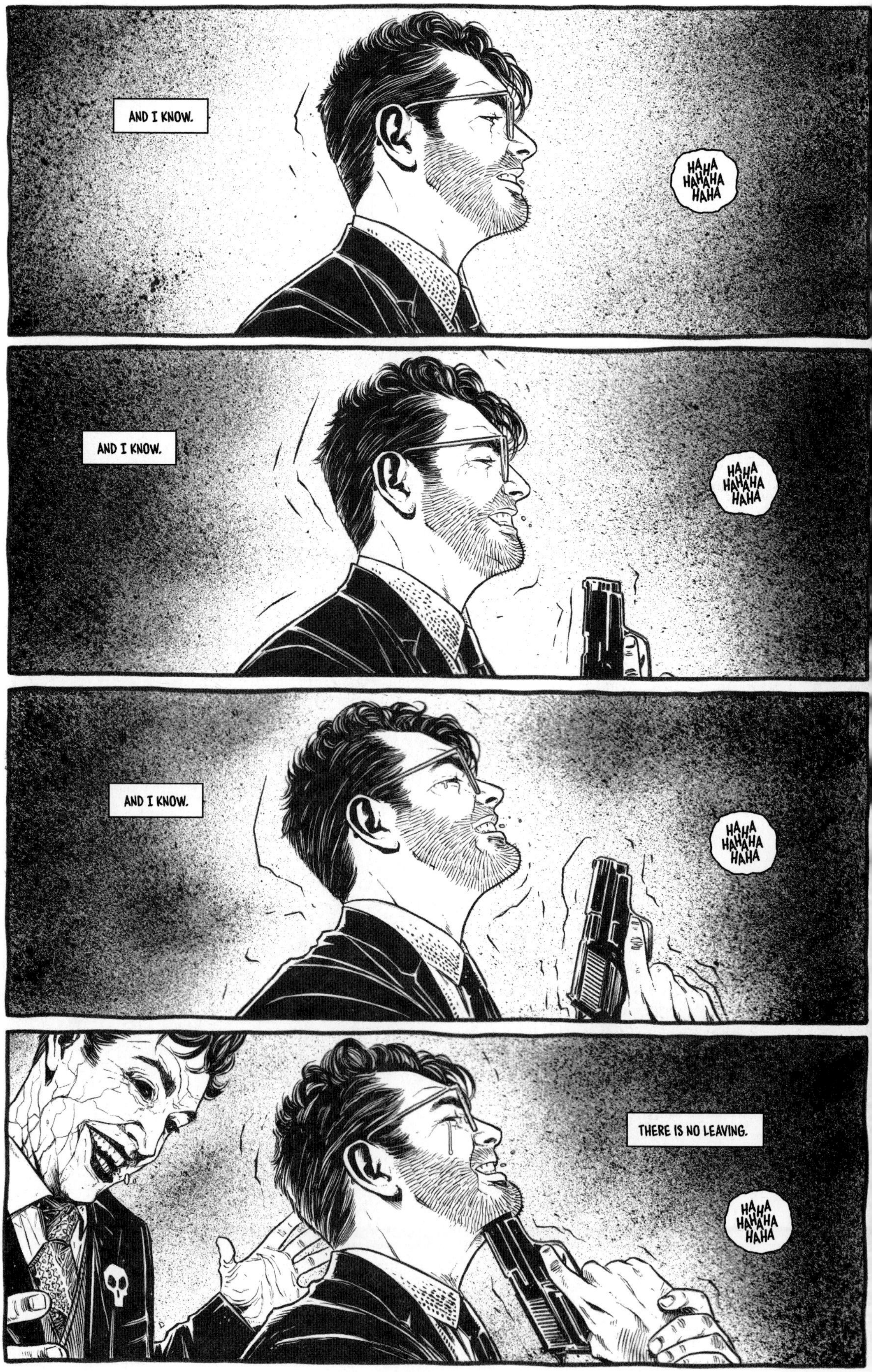
AND I KNOW.
HAHA HAHAHA HAHA
AND I KNOW.
HAHA HAHAHA HAHA
AND I KNOW.
HAHA HAHAHA HAHA
THERE IS NO LEAVING.
HAHA HAHAHA HAHA

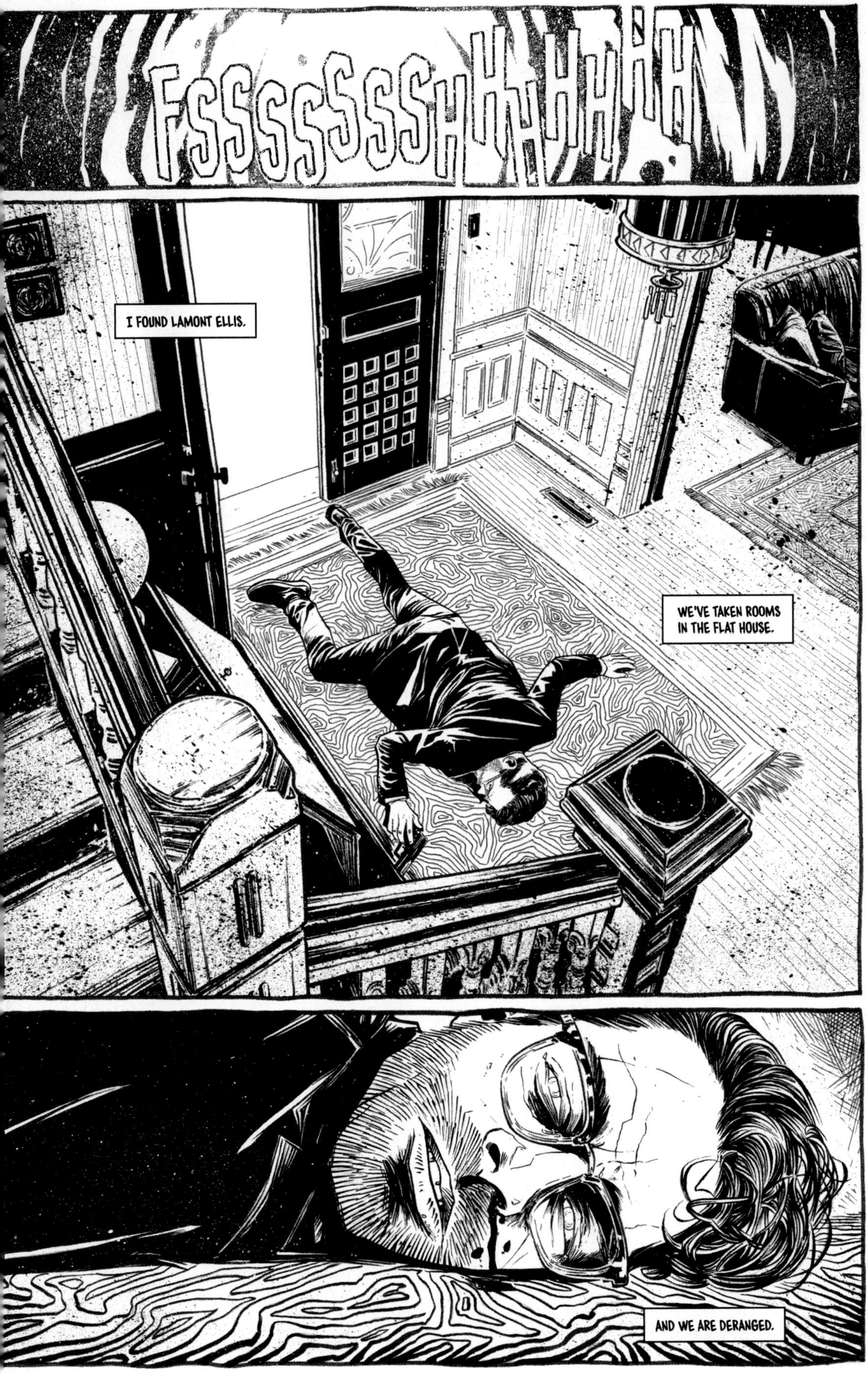
FSSSSSSSSHHHHHHH
I FOUND LAMONT ELLIS.
WE'VE TAKEN ROOMS IN THE FLAT HOUSE.
AND WE ARE DERANGED.

PROBABLE MOMENTS

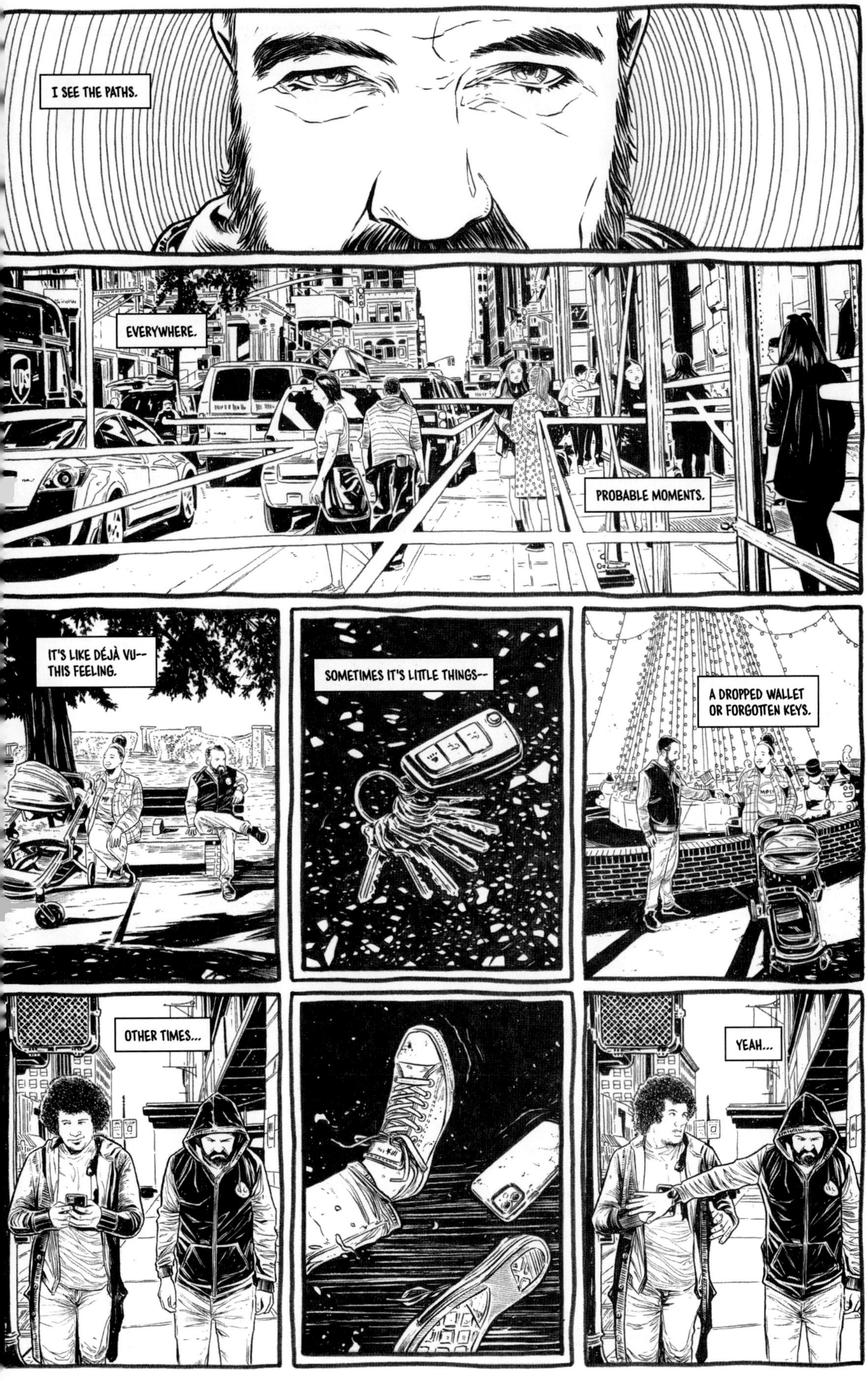
I SEE THE PATHS.
EVERYWHERE.
PROBABLE MOMENTS.
IT'S LIKE DÉJÀ VU--
THIS FEELING.
SOMETIMES IT'S LITTLE THINGS--
A DROPPED WALLET
OR FORGOTTEN KEYS.
OTHER TIMES...
YEAH...

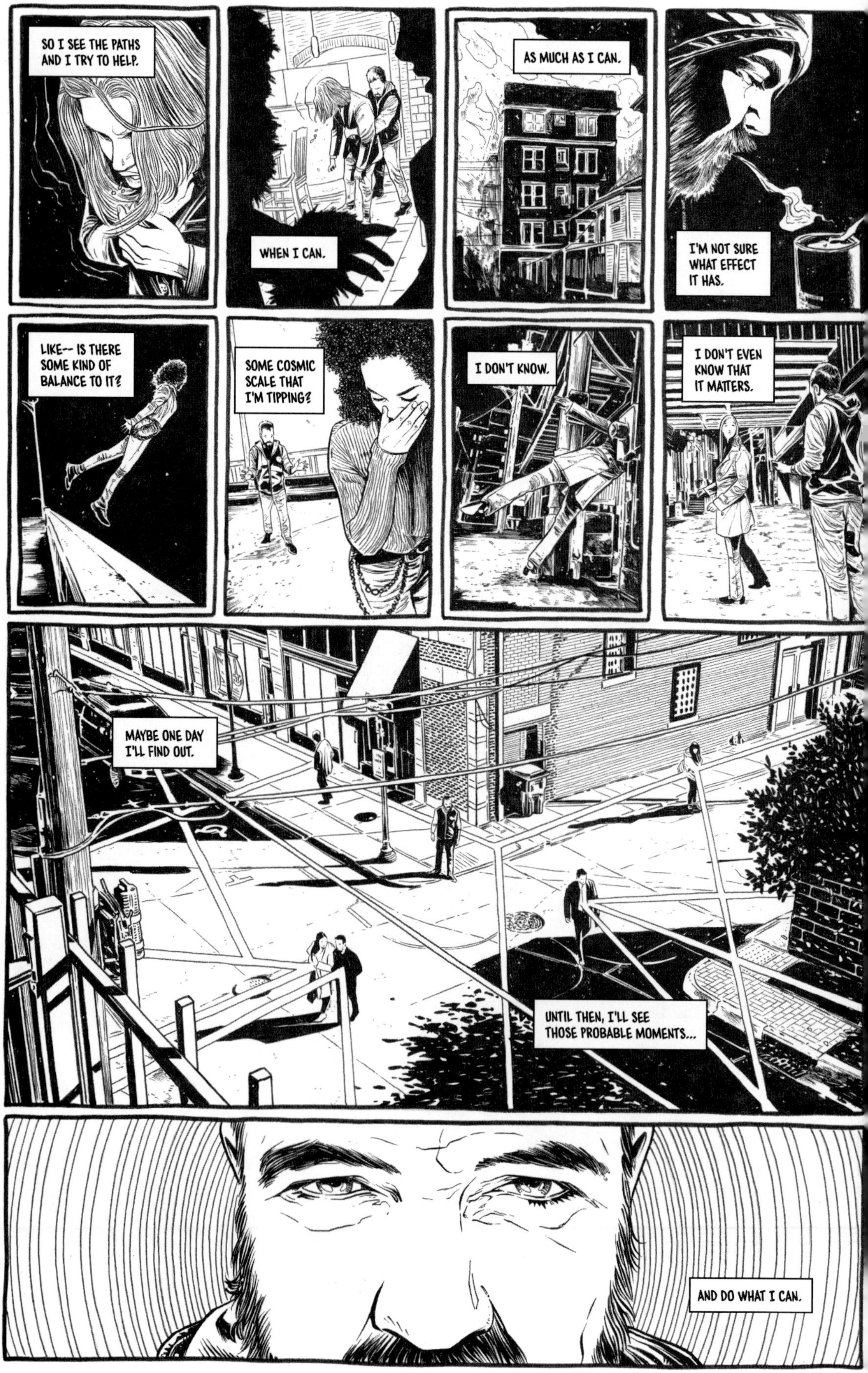
SO I SEE THE PATHS AND I TRY TO HELP.
WHEN I CAN.
AS MUCH AS I CAN.
I'M NOT SURE WHAT EFFECT IT HAS.
LIKE-- IS THERE SOME KIND OF BALANCE TO IT?
SOME COSMIC SCALE THAT I'M TIPPING?
I DON'T KNOW.
I DON'T EVEN KNOW THAT IT MATTERS.
MAYBE ONE DAY I'LL FIND OUT.
UNTIL THEN, I'LL SEE THOSE PROBABLE MOMENTS...
AND DO WHAT I CAN.

FEVER DREAM

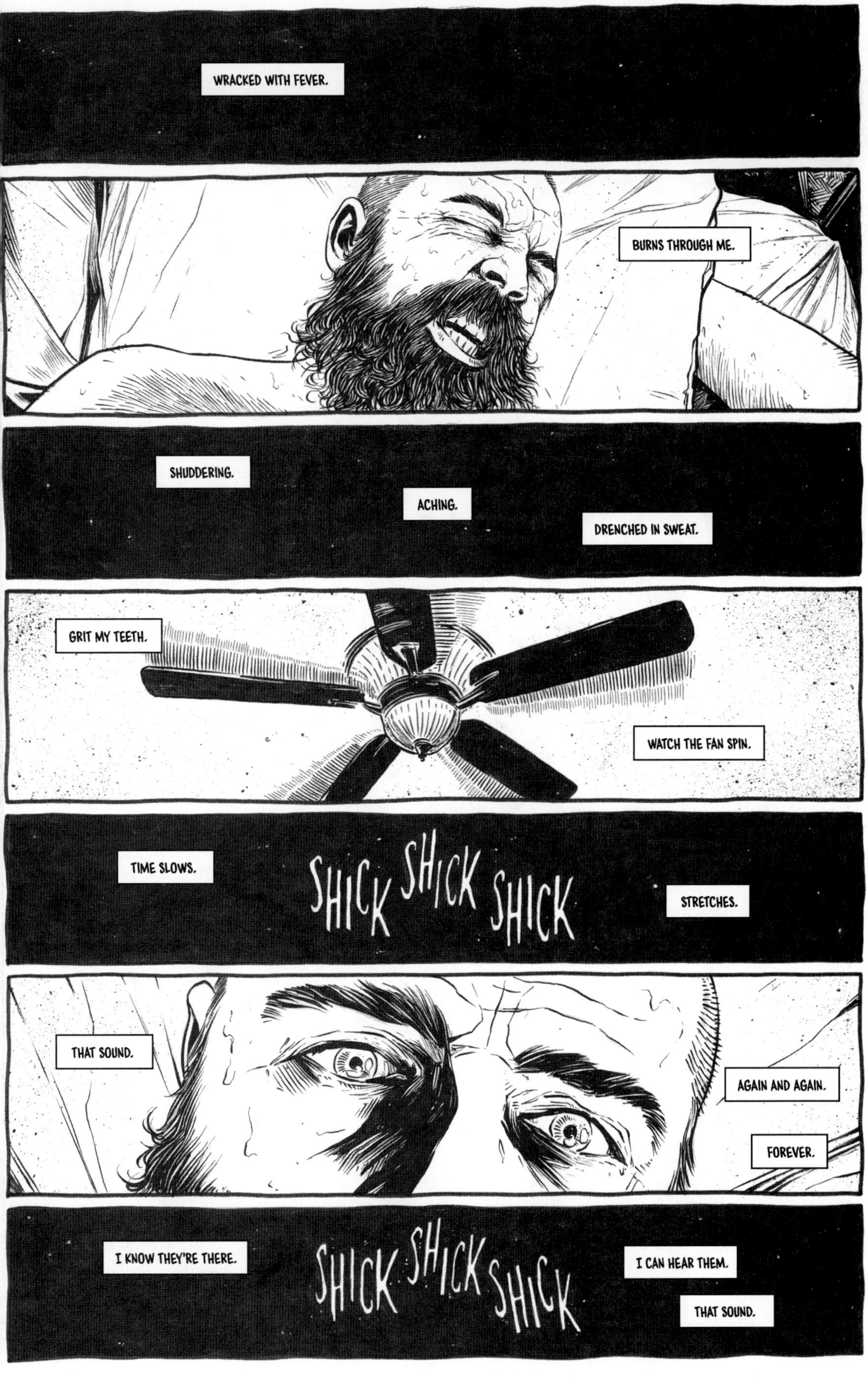
WRACKED WITH FEVER.
BURNS THROUGH ME.
SHUDDERING.
ACHING.
DRENCHED IN SWEAT.
GRIT MY TEETH.
WATCH THE FAN SPIN.
TIME SLOWS.
SHICK SHICK SHICK
STRETCHES.
THAT SOUND.
AGAIN AND AGAIN.
FOREVER.
I KNOW THEY'RE THERE.
SHICK SHICK SHICK
I CAN HEAR THEM.
THAT SOUND.

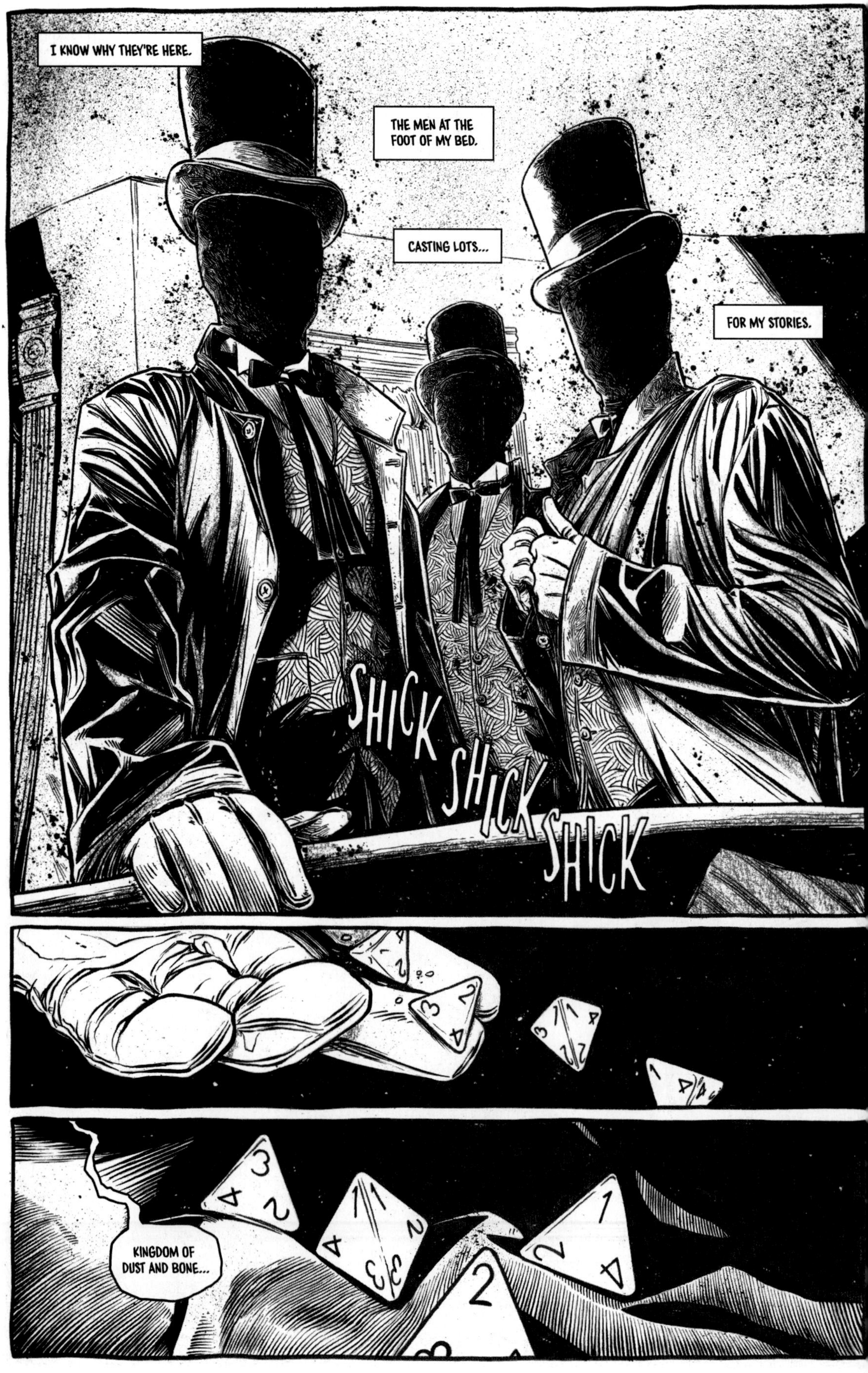
I KNOW WHY THEY'RE HERE.
THE MEN AT THE FOOT OF MY BED.
CASTING LOTS...
FOR MY STORIES.
SHICK
SHICK
SHICK
KINGDOM OF DUST AND BONE...

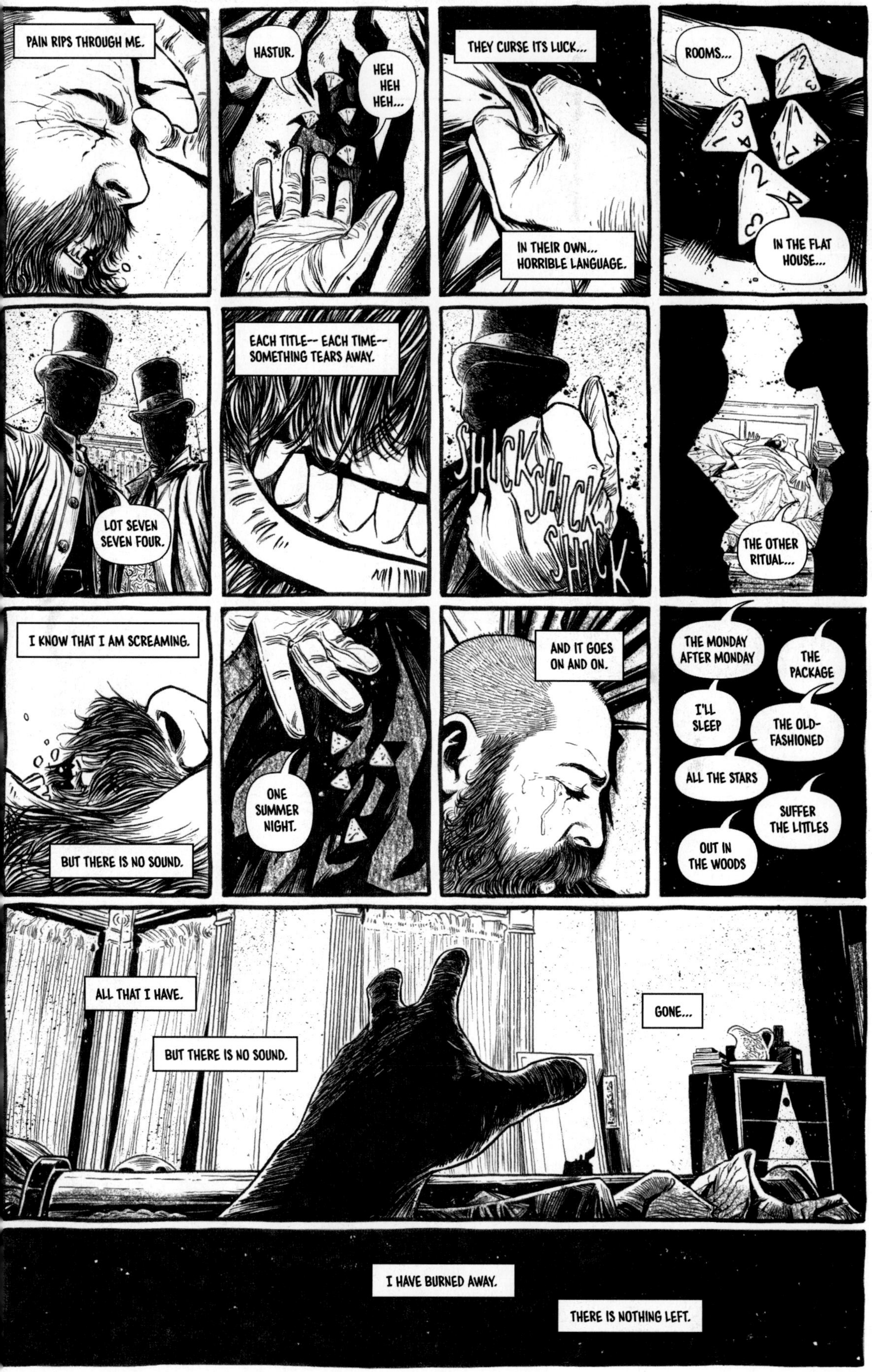
PAIN RIPS THROUGH ME.
HASTUR.
HEH HEH HEH...
THEY CURSE ITS LUCK...
IN THEIR OWN... HORRIBLE LANGUAGE.
ROOMS...
IN THE FLAT HOUSE...
LOT SEVEN SEVEN FOUR.
EACH TITLE-- EACH TIME-- SOMETHING TEARS AWAY.
SHICK SHICK SHICK
THE OTHER RITUAL...
I KNOW THAT I AM SCREAMING.
BUT THERE IS NO SOUND.
ONE SUMMER NIGHT.
AND IT GOES ON AND ON.
THE MONDAY AFTER MONDAY
THE PACKAGE
I'LL SLEEP
THE OLD-FASHIONED
ALL THE STARS
SUFFER THE LITTLES
OUT IN THE WOODS
ALL THAT I HAVE.
BUT THERE IS NO SOUND.
GONE...
I HAVE BURNED AWAY.
THERE IS NOTHING LEFT.

The Love of Old Things

HERE'S TO THE LOVE OF OLD THINGS.

TO HOURS SPENT TOGETHER...

DRINKS IN HAND.

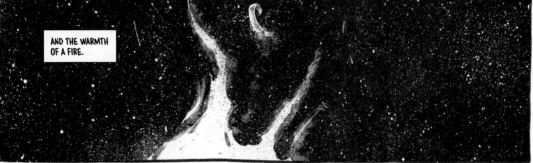

AND THE WARMTH OF A FIRE.

HERE'S TO BELIEVING THAT THINGS ARE WORTH SAVING.

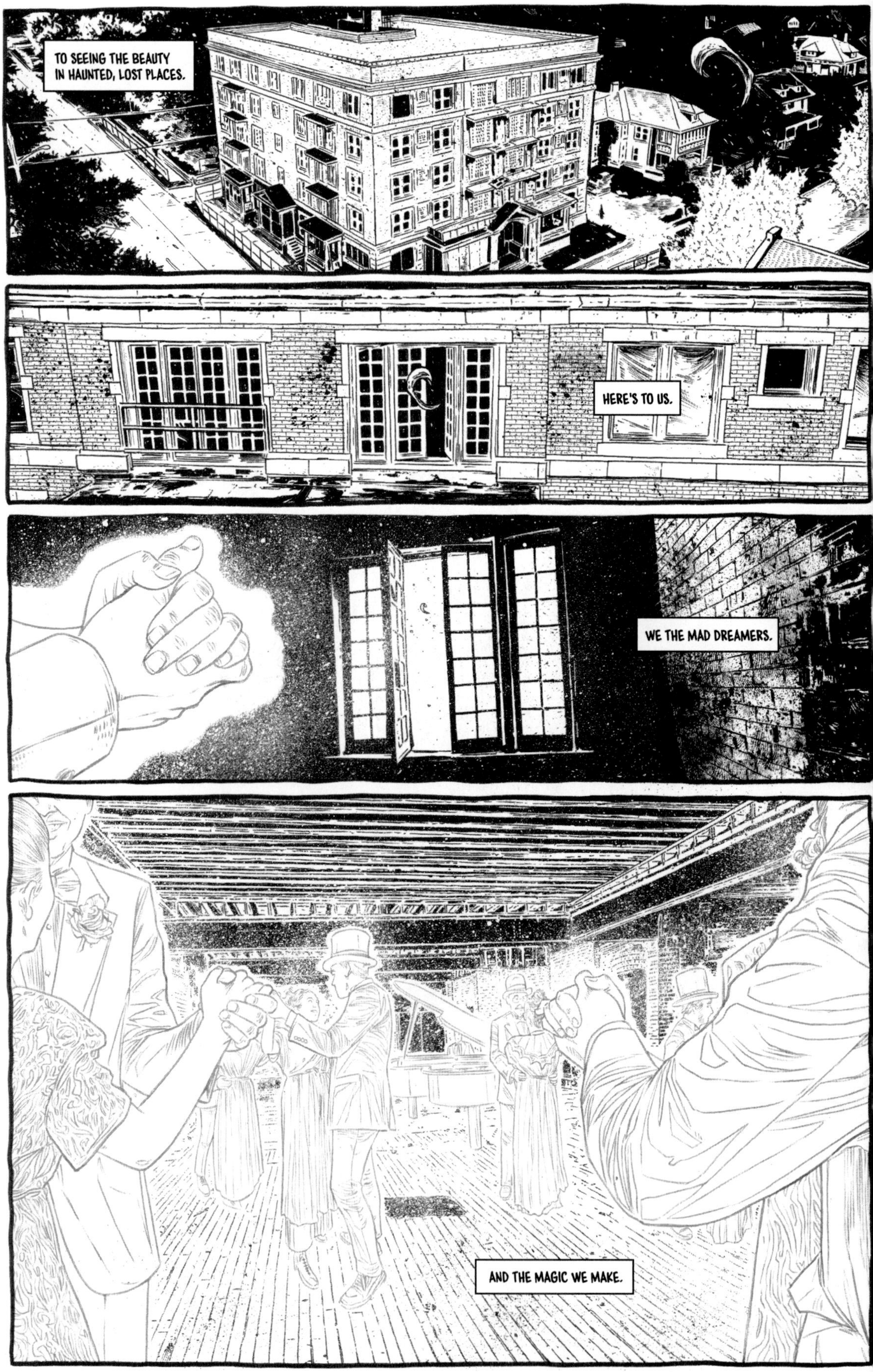
TO SEEING THE BEAUTY IN HAUNTED, LOST PLACES.
HERE'S TO US.
WE THE MAD DREAMERS.
AND THE MAGIC WE MAKE.

To Finish

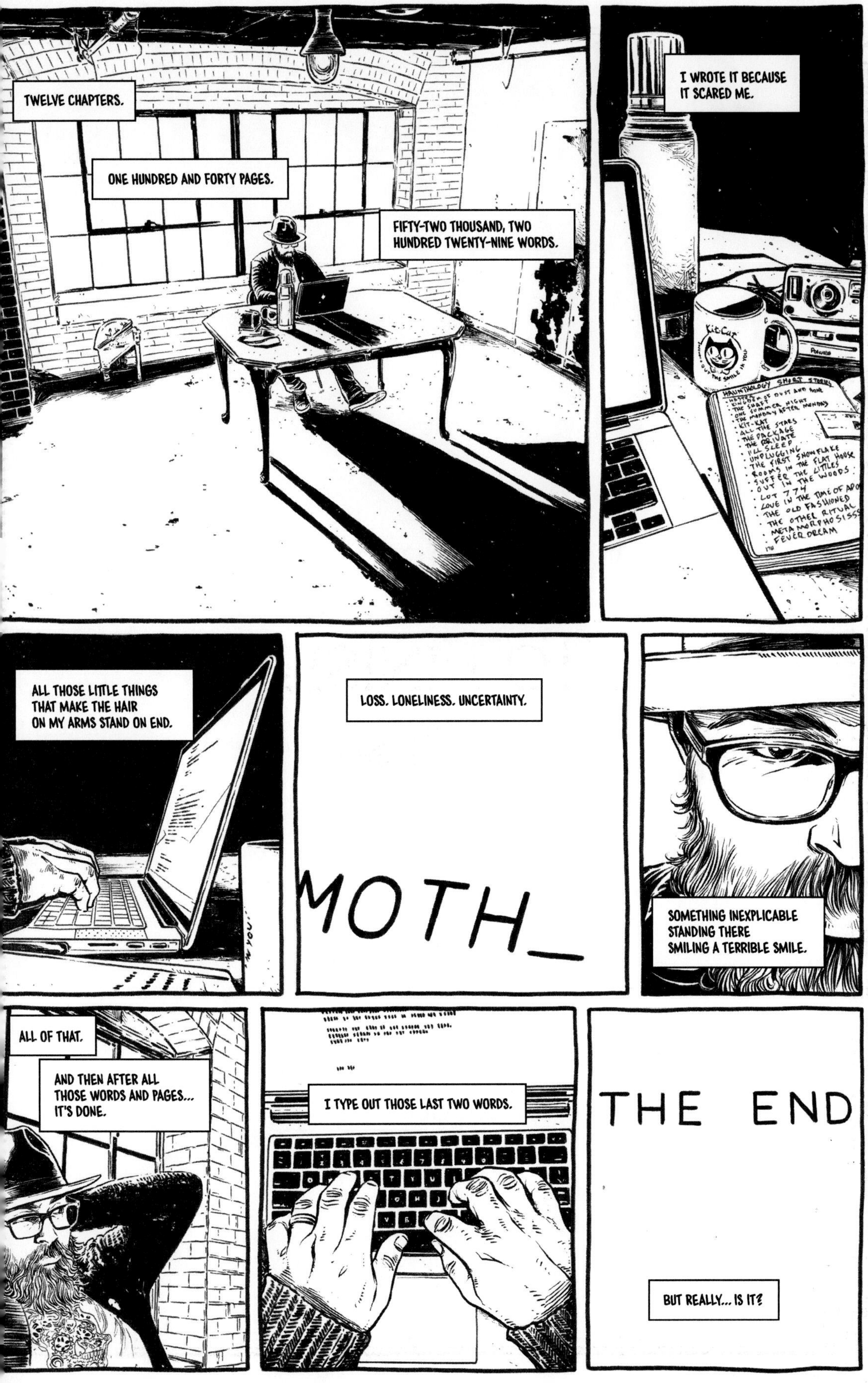
TWELVE CHAPTERS.
ONE HUNDRED AND FORTY PAGES.
FIFTY-TWO THOUSAND, TWO HUNDRED TWENTY-NINE WORDS.
I WROTE IT BECAUSE IT SCARED ME.
ALL THE STARS
THE PACKAGE
UNPLUGGING
THE FIRST SNOWFLAKE
OUT IN THE WOODS
LOT 774
FEVER DREAM
ALL THOSE LITTLE THINGS THAT MAKE THE HAIR ON MY ARMS STAND ON END.
LOSS. LONELINESS. UNCERTAINTY.
MOTH_
SOMETHING INEXPLICABLE STANDING THERE SMILING A TERRIBLE SMILE.
ALL OF THAT.
AND THEN AFTER ALL THOSE WORDS AND PAGES... IT'S DONE.
I TYPE OUT THOSE LAST TWO WORDS.
THE END
BUT REALLY... IS IT?

ABOUT THE AUTHOR

JEREMY HAUN is a comic book writer and artist and the creator of *The Beauty* and *The Realm*, from Image Comics, as well as *The Red Mother* for Boom! Studios, and *40 Seconds* for Comixology. Over his twenty years in comics, he has worked for nearly every publisher in the industry.

Jeremy resides in a crumbling mansion in Joplin, Missouri with his wife, two sons, and an orange cat. Jeremy has created two successful Kickstarter campaigns: *Bad Karma* (as part of the Bad Karma collective) and *Dino Day*.